THE GOLD COAST TRANSFORMED

From Wilderness to Urban Ecosystem

Editors: Tor Hundloe, Bridgette McDougall and Craig Page

PUBLISHING

National Library of Australia Cataloguing-in-Publication entry

The Gold Coast transformed : from wilderness to urban ecosystem /
Tor Hundloe, Bridgette McDougall, Craig Page, editors.

9781486303298 (paperback)
9781486303304 (epdf)
9781486303311 (epub)

Includes bibliographical references and index.

Environmental impact analysis – Queensland – Gold Coast.
Urban ecology (Sociology) – Queensland – Gold Coast.
Gold Coast (Qld.) – Environmental conditions.

Hundloe, T. J. (Torstein John), editor.
McDougall, Bridgette, editor.
Page, Craig, editor.

363.7009943

Published by

CSIRO Publishing
36 Gardiner Road, Clayton VIC 3168
Private Bag 10, Clayton South VIC 3169
Australia

Telephone: [+613] 9545 8555
Email: csiropublishing@csiro.au
Website: www.publishing.csiro.au

Front cover (from top left): Rainbow lorikeets, © worldswildlifewonders; Rainforest at Tamborine Mountain, Queensland, © Pawel Papis; Australian common brushtailed possum, © worldswildlifewonders; View from Q1 tower, Gold Coast, © Paul Burdett.
Back cover: photo © Pawel Papis

Set in 10.5/12 Minion & Stone Sans
Edited by Adrienne de Kretser, Righting Writing
Cover design by James Kelly
Typeset by Thomson Digital
Index by Bruce Gillespie
Printed by Ingram Lightning Source

Feb26_RP_ILS

Contents

About the editors

The editors of this book bring significantly different generational perspectives to their task. This is deliberate on our part. We seek to have our readers, of whatever age, come to understand the when, why and how of the building of the city of the Gold Coast. The how and its consequences are at the centre of the story: from wilderness to an urban ecosystem.

The senior editor, Tor Hundloe, was born on the Gold Coast in the 'baby boomer' era. His early childhood was spent on a dairy farm in the Gold Coast hinterland. He attended primary school at both Numinbah Valley State School, a one-teacher school with only a handful of students, and Burleigh Heads State School. He was witness to the sand mining of Gold Coast beaches, the construction of the first high-rise and the dredging of the first canal estates.

A generation-plus younger is Craig Page. Craig was also born on the Gold Coast. He attended school at Elanora State High School and then studied at the Gold Coast's Bond University. Between Tor's birth and Craig's, much happened in terms of city building and environmental change. The Gold Coast developed from a scattering of small coastal villages and tiny hinterland towns into a linear city with dominating groupings of high-rise apartments, extensive canal estates and sea-walls doing their best to protect the property of those who unwisely built on sand. Craig understands the Gold Coast of Tor's youth via photos.

Neither Tor nor Craig can view the Gold Coast through the eyes of a newcomer to the city. This brings us to our third editor, Bridgette McDougall. Bridgette brings to the editorial team both youth and an 'outsider's' perspective. Growing up in country Victoria, she left Bendigo and moved to the Gold Coast to study at Bond University. She views the city as it is today, without the nostalgia that would come from personal experiences of an earlier Gold Coast. That the Gold Coast includes a western borderline of pristine rainforest was an initial surprise for Bridgette.

We came to the idea for the book after taking field trips to degraded beaches and into forested catchments (taking water samples), making boat trips along the Nerang River and canal estates, visiting koala habitat and spending time interviewing residents. When we found little published literature that might have helped us with the knowledge we sought from forays into the field, we decided to gather a group of experts who would assist in documenting the Gold Coast story.

We did not have to look far. All of the contributors to this book are, or have been, associated with environmental science, environmental management or town planning in Australia's first school of sustainable development.

On 11 August 2008, the then Education Minister, and future Prime Minister, Julia Gillard opened the environmentally friendly, multiple-award winning building that is home to the staff and provides the lecture theatres for Bond University's Institution of Sustainable Development. It attracts students from far and wide. It is from Bond University's academic staff and past students that we drew our contributors. We introduce them next, in alphabetical order.

List of contributors

Lynne Armitage is an Associate Professor of Urban Development at Bond University. She came to this position from a background in chartered surveying, urban studies and environmental planning. One of her major research interests is in determining the value of heritage properties.

Bhishna Bajracharya is an Associate Professor of Urban Planning at Bond University. He received his PhD and Masters degree in Urban and Regional Planning from the University of Hawaii and his Bachelor in Architecture degree from the School of Planning and Architecture, Delhi University. Bhishna has conducted research on master-planned communities, smart cities and knowledge-based urban development, disaster management, sustainable campus, transit-oriented development and urbanisation in Asian countries.

Shelley Burgin was one of the first new-age, mature-aged females to enter university life in the mid 1970s. Her undergraduate degree was gained in the first environmental science program in Australia, at Griffith University. Her Master's degree was undertaken in Papua New Guinea, on crocodiles. Her PhD was on evolutionary genetics. Today Shelley is an Emeritus Professor, University of Western Sydney and Professor of Environmental Science and Management, Bond University.

Simon Grigalius is a celebrity chef and a graduate of the new discipline of sustainability science. In his spare time he is undertaking research for a higher degree at Bond University. His goal is to ascertain how better links can be made between his two passions, food and sustainable food production.

Tor Hundloe is a pioneer of environmental education and an author of several books in the field of sustainable development, economics and natural resources. In 2003, he was made a Member of the Order of Australia for his contribution to coastal zone management, eco-tourism, protected area management, environmental economics, and fisheries. In the same year he was awarded a Centenary Medal for education. In 2010, he received the United Nations Association of Australia Individual Award for outstanding service to the environment. Tor is presently a Professor at Bond University, an Emeritus Professor, University of Queensland and an Adjunct Professor, Griffith University.

Isara Khanjanasthiti is a Teaching Fellow in town planning at Bond University. His research interests include smart cities and planning at the airport and community interface. He is currently undertaking a doctoral study on the economic contributions of airports in non-capital cities.

Bridgette McDougall is a graduate from Bond University and is a Tutor in the field of sustainability science while she pursues a higher degree in environmental education. Her key focus is on education for conservation, particularly as delivered by 'hands-on' experience in field settings, such as David Fleay's Wildlife Park on the Gold Coast.

Daryl McPhee is a leading researcher in the field of fisheries and coastal environments. His book *Fisheries Management in Australia* is the only one of its kind. Daryl is an Associate Professor in Environmental Science and Management and Associate Dean of Research in the Faculty of Society and Design, Bond University.

Daniel O'Hare is Associate Professor of Urban Planning at Bond University. He holds a PhD and MA in Urban Design from Oxford Brookes University, UK, and a Bachelor of Town Planning (Hons, Medal) from the University of NSW. Danny's main research interests are the transformation of coastal cultural landscapes of tourism into sustainable urban regions, urban design for walkable cities, and planning for knowledge-based city regions.

Craig Page is an Adjunct Tutor and research scholar attached to the Faculty of Society and Design, Bond University. He spends considerable time in South-east Asia, particularly Vietnam (he speaks Vietnamese), assisting in the promotion and development of sustainability projects.

Sophie Telfer is a logistics officer with BHP Billiton in her home town of Roxby Downs, having recently graduated with a Bachelor of Environmental Management.

Linda Too has been an academic for more than two decades. Her research interests include promoting healthy and active living through urban planning as well as developing a sustainable campus. Linda was an Associate Professor of Urban Development at Bond University from 2006 to 2013.

Madelaine (Maddy) Waters works for Griffith University in the simulated patient practice unit. She also tutors high school students and is otherwise engaged in environmental auditing. Maddy is a graduate in Environmental Management (Sustainable Development) from Bond University.

Acknowledgements

The publication of various books by Gold Coast historian Robert Longhurst proved invaluable in developing our knowledge of the Gold Coast from its earliest days of European settlement through to the 1950s. Rather than acknowledge every fact gathered from Longhurst's work, which would clutter parts of the text, we take this opportunity to express our gratitude for the work he put into his books (namely *Nerang Shire: A History to 1949* and *Southport: Images of Yesteryear 1880–1955*). Other local historians also provided information that we have drawn on but this is very much limited in contrast and we make specific reference to their works.

It is said that 'a picture is worth a thousand words'. In our task of documenting the environmental impact of building the city of the Gold Coast, this we do not doubt. While Bridgette McDougall was able to scour the city as it is today to capture images that help tell the story of the modern Gold Coast, she couldn't enter a time machine and photograph Cobb &Co. coaches traversing the beaches, rounding rocky headlands and crossing rivers, carrying tourists from Southport to Coolangatta. For photos of this earlier era, stretching back into the last years of the 19th century, we were fortunate to have the assistance of librarian Kyla Stephan and the photographic collection she commands in the Gold Coast Local Library. Thank you, Kyla. For maps of the ever-changing administrative boundaries of the city, we thank Sandra Smith of the Gold Coast City Council for locating these in the archives. And yet another person who assisted us to locate old photographs was Karen Wright. Karen is the creator of 'Have you Seen the Old Gold Coast' Facebook page.

This is the second time that Tor Hundloe has been fortunate to be guided by the wisdom of Ted Hamilton of CSIRO Publishing. At various stages in the crafting of the book we benefited from Ted's advice, and for that we are thankful. It was Ted who suggested the title, one that clearly captures our focus. Since Ted's retirement from CSIRO Publishing in mid 2014, we have had the much welcomed advice of Lauren Webb, and Julia Stuthe came to our assistance on an important matter. Editorial Manager Tracey Millen once again came to the rescue at the stage where the t's had to be crossed and i's dotted and photos placed appropriately, the little but big things writers need help with. We thank these CSIRO Publishing staff. Our editor was Adrienne de Kretser. We thank her for her extremely thorough work.

We must acknowledge the efforts of those who reviewed the book in draft form. Reviewers go unrecognised by name. That is the nature of their work. Yet their contribution to scientific advancement is of great importance.

We spoke to many people, including some old-timers, in researching the book. Particular thanks go to Rosemary Fleay-Thompson, daughter of David Fleay, the pioneer of Australian wildlife preservation. A small group of descendants of the early settlers of the Numinbah Valley provided valuable background material. Scott (Scottie) Cooper provided helpful assistance when it came to our queries about land development. A cheerful chat with Scottie would brighten the occasional dull day.

Several experts from various fields influenced avenues of our investigation and provided useful advice. One particular expert deserves special mention. He is Don Young, civil engineer and, during his period as Deputy Co-ordinator General of Queensland, a strong proponent of protecting the foreshore and mangroves. Don's approach to conservation was well before his time and the very significant changes in attitude to coastal development are his legacy.

Chapter 1

Introduction: the structure of the book

T. Hundloe and C. Page

This is the story of a unique city, Australia's premier tourist city, a city cut out of coastal vegetation, including paperbark swamps, mangroves and rainforests of worldwide significance. The city has a relatively short history as until half a century ago (two human generations) it was but several relatively small villages, each with its own natural and social features. Two generations is a very short time for a city to grow to be the sixth-largest in population in Australia and to have global recognition as the country's beach playground. The Gold Coast ranks with Honolulu in Hawaii, with Palm Beach in Florida and with the French Riviera in tourist promotions and is a high-priority destination in the minds of beach-lovers worldwide.

Australia will never see another city like the Gold Coast. We have learned so much about the value and the function of natural systems in the past 50 years, particularly from the spectacular mistake of building on frontal sand dunes. Spectacular, because when viewed after a severe storm or cyclone the normal undulating vegetated sand hills are but a 4 m cliff, the beach no more.

Plates 1 and 2 illustrate the extent of foreshore erosion – and threat to property – at two points in time. The first photograph (Plate 1) was taken in 1967 after the cyclones of that year. The photograph in Plate 2 was taken in 2013 after a series of storms, not cyclones, battered the Gold Coast.

Foredunes have a propensity to shift around as nature dictates, unlike a jelly poked by an inquisitive child. The jelly will resettle rather quickly and it won't look much different when it does. A beach poked, pushed and pulled by cyclonic waves, high and low tides, and fierce off-shore winds will move as the jelly but – and here is the difference – when it reforms many months will have passed and there will be noticeable differences. Beach creeks will have carved completely new routes from the dunes to the ocean, the reconfigured dunes in their now different shape recolonised by ghost crabs and the plant we call pig face. In scientific terms this process is described as dynamic disequilibrium: in lay language, expect change at the interface of the ocean and the land, but be comforted that the landforms and vegetation that exist inland from the foredunes are protected by the buffering withstood by the ever-changing beachfront ecosystem. Only over an extended period of time will a bare sand dune encroach upon vegetated territory, and this is likely to occur very rarely and in only a few locations.

Picture, if you will, the Gold Coast before the first settlers and first holiday-makers came. This is an extremely difficult task unless you are familiar with similar environments that have been protected from development. Without knowledge of such places, where would you look for clues? Certainly not the beachfront, walled and sandbagged in anticipation of the next storm. Certainly not along the estuaries and lower reaches of the city's rivers, where nature has been forced to give way to residential canal estates dug into river floodplains. And not in the paspalum and kikuyu-grassed farms in the city's hinterland where once giant cedars, hoop pines, black beans and beech trees reached above the rainforest canopy. Later in the book we will explain where to find the few remaining clues to the city's past.

Having seen the Gold Coast's beachfront covered with every type of building from massive high-rise apartments to conventional beach houses, local government officials, town planners and engineers have been forced to treat the symptoms of our environmental ignorance and thoughtless attitude to nature. Given the dramatic changes made to the natural ecosystems, we have no option but to continue seeking 'solutions'. We use inverted commas because it is not obvious that, having built on sand, a sustainable solution is available, except at the very significant cost of replenishing the sand after every extreme weather event. That has its own environmental problems. The sand has to come from somewhere; another ecosystem is altered and possibly harmed in an attempt to make amends for our own lack of environmental knowledge and short-sightedness.

It is not only what we did at the interface of the shore and the ocean that will not be repeated. Today, if one were to fell a mangrove tree – in fact, even do harm to one – the court-imposed fine is likely to be hundreds of thousands of dollars. The canal estates which were cut into the Nerang River floodplains destroyed many mangrove trees. Again, this occurred in the past 50 years.

If we go back to the initial European thrusts into the Gold Coast area, ~150 years ago, we discover the ecological damage that was done in the hinterland rainforests. Red cedar trees, some ancient (hundreds of years old, if not older), were to the timber-getters a drawcard pulling all, from emancipated convicts to free-settler timber merchants, to the rainforests as gold pulled miners to Ballarat and Bendigo. Cedar was known as 'red gold'. Take a red cedar tree out of a national park today and imprisonment awaits.

The timber-getters made bullock tracks which opened up the Gold Coast river valleys to farmers. No longer was there selective logging but wholesale tree clearing, reaching high up the rainforested mountains. Natural grasses were displaced by exotic ones, all the better for exotic animals – dairy cattle that had originated in the Channel Isles and were named after these islands, Guernsey and Jersey.

With the degree of habitat destruction that occurred from the mid 1800s to the present, the Gold Coast's native fauna took a serious hit. The koala population has been near-decimated on the coastal strip. Two generations ago koalas in their favourite gum trees could be viewed in the back streets of Burleigh Heads. Today, best save your time and energy and visit a theme park to see a handful of koalas in captivity.

The dramatic changes in natural systems are evidenced, first along the foreshore, then the coastal floodplains and finally into the hinterland catchments. From this perspective, the Gold Coast has lost most of its natural attributes. But matters become somewhat confused once we consider the Gold Coast by reference to its formal political boundaries. Today the city is much larger than it once was. This we will illustrate below with maps. And then there is the public perception of what the Gold Coast is. A Melbournite heading to the Gold Coast for a holiday envisages visiting beaches and theme parks, not the new northern, north-western and north-eastern suburbs which are as close to Brisbane as to Surfers Paradise.

Today the city of the Gold Coast as a defined political and administrative area is more than beaches, floodplains turned into canal estates and hinterland ecosystems. In the present era, several South Moreton Bay Islands, including the relatively large South Stradbroke Island, are included in the city's boundaries. The inclusion of these islands adds a considerable area of protected ecosystems to the city. The smaller islands are national parks and, in the case of South Stradbroke Island, a large area is a conservation park. Furthermore, the inclusion of the hinterland World Heritage area (the Gondwana Rainforests of Springbrook and Numinbah) adds a very considerable area of natural forests to the area of the city. It is important to be mindful of these relatively new city boundaries when considering the data on the proportion of natural land remaining in the city. Because of the expansion of the city, it appears that we have done far less environmental damage than we have actually done. The map in Plate 3 illustrates the change in the official boundaries of the Gold Coast. What we refer to as the 'old' Gold Coast – the coastal area traditionally and conventionally thought of as the Gold Coast – is shown.

Plate 3 shows the boundary of the Gold Coast in 2014 plus the areas conventionally thought of as the 'old' Gold Coast. This is circled in red, as are the hinterland towns and locations associated with the Gold Coast.

The area most would recognise as the Gold Coast is the coastal strip from Southport to Coolangatta. It has been close to denuded of its original vegetation, which would have been banksia, heath, casuarina, melaleuca, eucalyptus, littoral vine forest, open forest and woodlands. The beach was a typical foredune complex, moving into open forest and woodlands, with small pockets of rainforest. In clearing this land we re-contoured the landform from coastal dunes and meandering creeks and rivers into flat beachfront land for high-rise apartments, millionaires' mansions and canal estates intermixed with impervious surfaces of tar and cement. The extent of land clearing that has occurred can be seen in Plate 4. The white area represents land that has been cleared of its original vegetation, for urban development in the coastal area and farming in the Jacobs Well area, plus smaller areas in the hinterland.

At this very early stage, it will help if the Gold Coast land uses are identified; for this purpose we present Plate 5. It shows the present land use strategy as endorsed by the Gold Coast City Council. The location of 'urban residential' (red) land and 'residential/tourism-pacific coast' (purple) land tells a story of building as close to the ocean as possible. The stretch of coastal land between Southport and Coolangatta represents the 'old' Gold Coast before expansions north and north-west. The 'old' Gold Coast has lost virtually all of its natural vegetation. The areas designated as 'rural/nature conservation' (orange), 'open space/nature conservation' (green circles) and 'agricultural' (green) show the amount of land that is natural, near-natural or partially forested.

In the public perception of the 'old' Gold Coast, parts of the hinterland were included and considerable natural and near-natural land was part of the Gold Coast. The narrow river valleys running up the Nerang River and Tallebudgera Creek and Currumbin Creek catchments, where dairy and banana farming occurred, were thought of by farmers (who would visit relatives in the coastal villages) and coastal residents (who had farmers as relatives or friends) as part of the Gold Coast. For example, the Currumbin Creek rockpools were a favourite fresh water swimming area for local residents and holiday visitors, as was the Natural Bridge (Arch) at the top of Numinbah Valley.

The farmers with their holdings in three major catchments (Tallebudgera, Currumbin and Nerang) thought of themselves as part of the Gold Coast. The village settlements on Springbrook and Beechmont were also deemed to be part of the Gold Coast, as were the more distant Lamington Plateau eco-tourism businesses. However, these areas were not officially part of the Gold Coast as virtually all of the land west of the coastal strip was in another jurisdiction, the rural Albert Shire. Today, most of Lamington Plateau is in another shire (the Scenic Rim Shire).

Obviously, the Gold Coast biography is one fashioned by significant environmental impact, increasing over time as more and more tourists came and more and more permanent residents built houses stretching ever westward from the beaches. Much of the impact is irreversible in time-frames humans comprehend. The city's economic success – and it has been successful – has come at a very high cost. We now realise that the city could have been a tourist mecca without the destruction of the foreshore. Habitat for koalas and other native animals could have been preserved. How pleasing would that have been? Imagine foreign tourists being able to sit in small footpath cafes and view koalas in the gum trees next door! This is not far-fetched. In a similar environment to that of the Gold Coast, on North Stradbroke, we can sip coffee and contemplate the life of a koala, promoted by the sight of one perched in the footpath gum tree.

Evidence of what could have been on the Gold Coast can be found in parts of the Sunshine Coast and North Stradbroke Island, where dwellings and road infrastructure have been deliberately situated way beyond the ever-changing coastal dunes, and much natural vegetation remains. The Sunshine Coast tourists still come and they are far from disappointed with the environmental setting. This is a tale of two cities.

On the Gold Coast, the clearing of land for the construction of residences, shopping complexes, golf courses and industry destroyed the habitat of the natural fauna. It would have been possible to have protected more, although not all, of the coastal koala population by prohibiting residential development in forested corridors stretching from the ocean to the hinterland; a prime example would have been corridors from Burleigh Head National Park westward to Springbrook. Only recently has the Gold Coast City Council commenced to use an environmental levy on rate-payers to purchase bushland which managed to escape the developers' bulldozers. This land, when rehabilitated, will form corridors and should assist in connecting the few remaining coastal koala populations to the larger inland populations.

There is a high degree of conjecture involved in writing about what might have been. Later in the book we will point to the difficulty of estimating native animal populations in an era when few people cared and records were scanty, if kept at all. Of course, the koalas are not the only animals fighting for survival. However, the koala's attractiveness to tourists cannot be overlooked. The analysis is dated now, but nevertheless indicative of this animal's economic importance: in 1997, a study of foreign tourists to Australia ranked koalas as the number one animal they wanted to view, just ahead of kangaroos. It was estimated that the koala-viewing industry generated over $1 billion per annum for the Australian economy (Hundloe and Hamilton 1997). Given increased tourist numbers and inflation, that figure would be much higher today.

In addition to the koala, on the Gold Coast a range of other animals have lost habitat or are otherwise under threat by the large-scale land-use changes and ever-increasing human population numbers. There is the platypus, there are various frogs and birds which were once numerous but are rarely seen today. On the other hand, we will illustrate the resilience of Mother Nature when modified, near-natural habits remain or new ones are created, as in the extensive canal estates. Native animals reappear and establish viable populations.

The Gold Coast is an enigma. Most tourists come to appreciate and experience the natural environment. They come to swim or simply cavort in the surf. If all they sought was a swim, fresh-water pools abound in Australian cities and towns. The beach is special.

The salt air is invigorating. While the Surfers Paradise beach is far from the empty wilderness of a Fraser Island beach in mid-winter, its appeal is still to nature. To make a valiant, if unsuccessful, attempt to catch a wave is to become one with nature.

Clearly, the beach is by far the most visited of the many different environments on offer. When extreme weather events destroy the beaches, tourists don't come in the same numbers until the media ceases to publicise the erosion.

Japanese, and increasingly Chinese, visitors come for many reasons, but ask them why and a common reason is that they would love to see a koala in the wild. The entrepreneurs who have played a major role in fashioning the city of the Gold Coast have compensated in part for the loss of natural attributes by constructing theme parks where koalas can be nursed while the obligatory photos are taken. It is difficult to overlook the irony. Accredited eco-tourism establishments provide an authentic introduction to the area's natural attributes. There are three in the hinterland. Then there are the native animals that have colonised Gold Coast suburbia, thanks to the planting of native gardens. It is not all negative on today's Gold Coast. Even the once ecologically dead canals have developed local ecosystems that support a range of marine life, including dangerous bull sharks. Lives have been lost in the canals as a consequence of shark attacks.

The biography of the Gold Coast, in particular the environmental destruction that was performed in its development, only makes sense if we understand what drove the development. History is a key discipline here. So are geography and economics. We have to cover broad territory if we are to fulfil our task of analysing the environmental impacts that went hand-in-glove with the creation of one of the world's premier tourist cities.

With these few paragraphs setting the scene, the remainder of this introductory chapter sketches the interrelated themes of the chapters that follow. We have brought to the task of compiling this book an extraordinary group of individuals from Bond University, including ecologists, economists, a real-estate valuer, town planners, a chef-cum-environmental scientist and four graduates in sustainability science, the emerging discipline of the 21st century.

The early chapters set the scene for an assessment of the environmental impact of the construction of the city of the Gold Coast. Following that we turn to the environmental impacts associated with the city today. We commence with the overwhelming land-use changes that commenced when the first red cedar tree was felled in the rainforest and, some decades later, the first 'iconic' residence was built on the foreshore at Southport. We trace the impacts, as they accumulate through to the present, noting the irreversible losses. The logical progression of our analysis is to the city today and the day-to-day environmental matters we have to deal with in the 21st century, followed by consideration of the future. The principle of sustainability requires us to do that.

We expect that it is not going to be an easy job to draw a line in the sand and announce that we have reached it, that no more interfering with nature will be permitted on the Gold Coast. It is not in the DNA of Australian-style city-building to say 'enough is enough' whether that applies to population growth, cutting more housing lots out of near-natural bushland, investing in more industry or expanding the already extremely well catered for entertainment and nightlife opportunities. This is not to argue that the city of the Gold Coast, its residents and tourists, would not appreciate and benefit from some degree of rejuvenation. A long established and still valid principle in the economics of tourism is the Butler Cycle, commencing with take-off, followed by development and consolidation and then a plateau, with the prospect of rejuvenation or decline. It can be postulated that the Gold Coast plateau as a tourist resort city has been reached. What next? This question and its answers form part of our narrative.

The Butler Cycle illustrates significant changes in tourist experiences, the facilities available to them, the growth of local businesses and of residential population. The lack of reliable data on tourist numbers in the early years prevents the construction of a Butler Cycle for the Gold Coast. However, it is possible to graph the relationship between particular events such as 'discovery' of the area by a 'celebrity,' improved transport, the construction of the first high-rise building and the growth of the city's residential population (see Fig. 1.1).

In delving into the functioning of the city as it is today, we take up the issue of environmental impact in the city's 'operational phase'. We assess the environmental impacts that are ongoing. This is what we mean by the operational phase. Dealing with these continuous impacts is not simply about 'holding the fort' so that further environmental impacts are avoided. It is about reversing, where possible, the negative impacts we caused in building the city in the manner we did. In other words, we can do some remedial work if only thought of as little, although the little we do could amount to significant benefits in terms of long-term sustainability. Restoring degraded land for wildlife corridors and replanting rainforests on former farmland are examples. In considering the present we will identify a small number of surprisingly positive impacts from an environmental perspective. All is not bad when the possibility of balancing the pleasure of living in or visiting the Gold Coast can be made consistent with preserving its increasingly valuable natural attributes. However, the challenges will be great if the city's population is forced to grow (particularly in the coastal region) as is proposed by the Queensland government.

A chapter-by-chapter synopsis

Chapter 2 is a snapshot of the Gold Coast, a lead-in to the detailed discussion in following chapters. As noted above, the Gold Coast is a city carved out of sand dunes, river floodplains, mangrove swamps and subtropical rainforests. Very little of the original natural

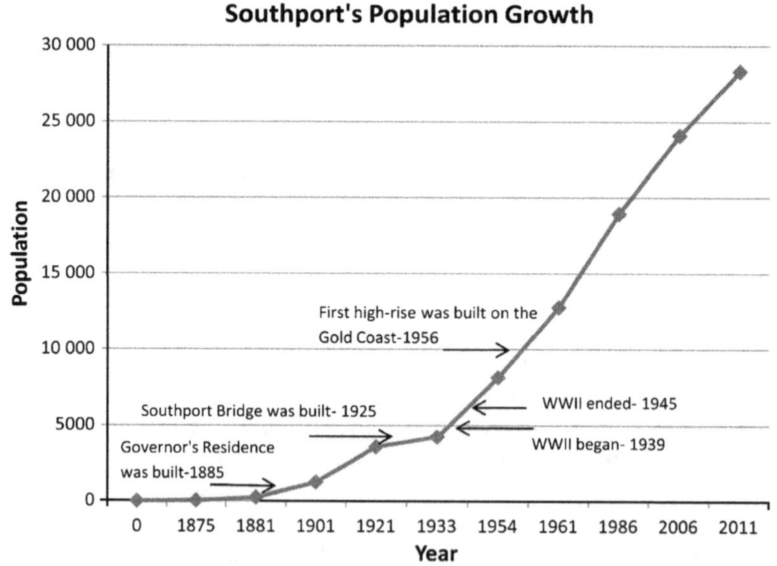

Fig. 1.1 Southport population, 1875–2011.

environment remains in a pristine state. There are small patches of magnificent beech forests which form a part of the UNESCO World Heritage-listed Gondwana Rainforests; there is Australia's smallest national park protecting Big Burleigh headlands and its littoral rainforest; there are small areas of koala habitat that could, with imagination and money, be linked into corridors to permit the animals to range as far as they did only half a century ago.

In place of the natural environment there are great clusters of high-rise apartments, including the highest yet built in Queensland, beachfront millionaires' mansions (the greatest concentration dubbed 'Millionaires' Row'), more housing canal estates than in Venice, and suburb after suburb spreading westwards and northwards into the foothills of the hinterland as the city continues to expand in the only directions (except up) that it can.

In terms of population, the Gold Coast is Australia's sixth-largest city. Its population of over half a million is greater than that of 30+ countries and that number of countries is about one-sixth of the planet's total. The Gold Coast demands to be noticed on population size alone. However, it is not all tourist accommodation and beach-loving residents. A few hobby farms and a scattering of old-style farm properties along the rivers that flow from the hinterland complete the picture. All this in an area of 1453 km^2, stretching ~60 km in length and 29 km in width at its broadest point.

The Gold Coast was home to 526 173 people in 2012. Of those, 241 128 were in some form of local employment (converting to 202 893 full-time equivalent jobs), most in retail trade which is mainly in small businesses (there were 60 015 local businesses). A sizeable percentage of residents from the Gold Coast make the commute to Brisbane for work. A lesser number commute down from Brisbane to work on the Gold Coast. We cannot discount the notion of the Gold Coast becoming part of a mega-city (from Noosa to NSW) and dormitory suburbs of this mega-city. That would result if the residential population continued to grow strongly and tourism stagnated. In that case, significant numbers of Gold Coast residents would be forced to travel to Brisbane for work.

The residents and tourists of the Gold Coast on occasion appreciate the impact their predecessors have had on the environment, and recognise nature's fury now that the inbuilt protection of the foredunes has been destroyed. Storms, the occasional cyclone plus high tides and massive swells batter the flat, stone-walled land on which the high-rise apartments and residents' dwellings precariously sit. Once there were high, undulating, ever-changing dunes which allowed Mother Nature to do her thing with no threat to humans and their structures. Today rock and sandbag walls do their best to keep the Pacific Ocean from claiming the vast investment in properties that are all the more valuable because they front the beach.

We announce the historical start to the foundation of the Gold Coast – John Oxley landing on Mermaid Beach (his boat was named *Mermaid*) at the time the first European settlement was being established in Moreton Bay, Queensland. It was much later that the first exploitation of the natural resources of the Gold Coast commenced, in the second half of the 19th century, when the red cedar timber-getters came. Farming followed soon after. By the end of that century there was an embryonic tourism industry. When the 20th century came it was to be one of continuous change.

History rarely turns on one event. But we believe we have discovered an exception. In 1885 the Governor of Queensland, Sir Anthony Musgrave, decided that he would build his summer residence in Southport. We take you back to that time (Box 1.1).

Box 1.1: The cumulative impacts of a celebrity discovering the Gold Coast

The Governor sought permission from his superior in the UK, Queen Victoria, to build a palatial residence at Southport. She had recently read the works of Ernst Haeckel who in 1866 introduced the new discipline 'ecology'. Queen Victoria instructed the Governor to prepare an Environmental Impact Statement (EIS) before turning a sod of soil (actually sand). She referred the Governor to the newly enacted law that required environmental assessment before major projects could be approved. This statute had a conventional legalistic title, the *Environment Protection (Impact of Proposals) Act 1884*. There was also a subsidiary law, the *Administrative Procedures Pursuant to the Environment Protection (Impact of Proposals) Act*. The latter listed a range of matters that required attention in the EIS the Governor was required to send to the Queen.

What was the direct impact on the environment of constructing the dwelling? Rather straightforward to answer. A certain amount of land would be cleared and flattened, but not on a scale that would concern anyone.

Next were directions to analyse the indirect, induced and cumulative impacts.

Here matters become tricky: the Governor needed to think about these. First, what did these terms mean? Collectively they referred to the flow-on consequences of building a grand summer residence in a beautiful natural environment. This is how the Governor responded in his EIS.

> *Your Majesty, I am following your command and postulating the induced and cumulative environmental impacts if you permit me to build my summer retreat at Southport.*
>
> *The fact that I have chosen the Gold Coast will lead to the well-off citizens of Brisbane following suit. It seems to be human nature to take the lead from those who can afford conspicuous consumption. [Thorstein Veblen had yet to write his book on this subject.]*
>
> *They will complain about the arduous and uncomfortable Cobb & Co. transport and the difficulties of fording rivers. A road will need to be built. A train line would be better. [It was built in 1889.] Soon the average Brisbane-ite will be able to holiday on the Gold Coast, even if it is to be camping in tents.*
>
> *I know that the first modern oil-well started producing in 1859. I also know of Carl Benz messing around to build a motorised vehicle. [Success came in 1886.] I expect it won't be long before the richer Brisbane-ites own cars. A proper road to Southport will be needed, and next a bridge across the Nerang River. [That had to wait until 1925.]*
>
> *I expect word will spread about the beautiful beaches, the fish, crabs and oysters. I predict more and more visitors, and more local businesses to cater for their needs. There is 20-odd miles of pristine beach front to be built on. Magnificent views over the ocean. The floodplains of the Nerang River will need to be completely cleared for farming. Farms will need to be cut out of the hinterland rainforests, as there will be increasing demand for milk, meat, vegetables, eggs and bananas. The latter are going to play a significant role in the colony. And we must keep the sugar cane fields, not only to sweeten tea but it makes superb rum. I specifically bring Your Majesty's attention to the latter fact.*

In two to three generations' time, the highway will be jammed by weekend visitors. Such will be the growth in popularity that by the 1970s (in only three to four generations) there will be a boom in buildings as high as the Eiffel Tower, sitting right on the water's edge. Foreigners, I expect from the East, will see the money to be made and invest in grand hotels. All sorts of spivs and shonks will speculate in real estate as they are prone to do in rapidly developing areas. Busts will follow booms as night follows day.

There will come to be a large city, the sixth-largest in Australia and millions of visitors will bear down with an ecological footprint of a magnitude not ever experienced on such a delightful sea-side.

Other than the fact that the Governor was not required to prepare an EIS (it was to be 90 years before these were legally required) and we know not of Queen Victoria's interest in matters environmental, the rest is a true if truncated account of the development of the Gold Coast.

Chapter 3 focuses on what has been irreversibly lost. We have some concept, based on modelled reconstruction, of what the Gold Coast landform and various environments were like before James Cook and his scientifically minded companion, Joseph Banks, sailed past and named dangerous or interesting landmarks. One of these, ~30 km from the shore, was Mount Warning, another was Point Danger.

Our comprehension of the pre-European human geography is considerably weaker than our knowledge of ecological matters. We are not certain when the first indigenous Australians arrived in the area, thought to be at least 20 000+ years ago. This would have been close to the start of the thaw that led to dramatic sea-level rise, in the order of 121 m. The extent of land use change in a relatively quick period has left little physical record of the indigenous culture. Their middens disappeared from the 1940s as sand miners dug and scraped rutile, zircon and limenite from the frontal dunes and the beaches. A solitary bora ring remains in the Miami–North Burleigh area while middens remain in Burleigh Head National Park, on Tallebudgera Creek and on South Stradbroke Island. However, from oral histories, we do know a reasonable amount of how the indigenous people lived, what they ate and how the various tribes/clans mixed.

Not only have we lost indigenous material culture, but much of the early settlement culture. We do not use bathing boxes in the 21st century but a few of them, if preserved, would be a reminder of our social evolution. Other examples of lost artefacts are likely to come to the mind of those who value the Gold Coast as part of their personal history.

Chapter 4 adds to the history discussed in the previous chapters. It allows us to understand what induced our exploitation of the natural resources of the Gold Coast area. Some of these drivers, for example the rapid human population growth of the town-cum-city of Brisbane, continue although the rate of growth is much slower than in the past. Another factor, in particular the relatively unsuccessful attempt to grow cotton on the Nerang River floodplains, was motivated by a one-off external event, the loss of cotton to UK mills during the blockade of southern US ports during the American Civil War.

Timber-getting, particularly the exploitation of red cedar, deserves to be dealt with in some detail. The timbermen unintentionally opened up the vast rainforested hinterland mountains to farming. This took place in an era when our environmental science was close to non-existent. Fortunately, the steepness of the very high mountains, particularly Springbrook and Beechmont, saved all but the red cedar and a few other highly valued species from the farmers' axes as they slowly but resolutely went about ring-barking trees. The cleared land would be grassed with paspalum or kikuyu (with clover added) for dairy cows to feed on.

Turning attention to the beaches, we find that as the 19th century wore on an upper class of relatively rich Moreton Bay settlers went looking for health-giving environments, equivalent to the holiday spas of Europe. Beautiful beaches and an ever-present sea breeze were not far as the crow flies from Brisbane. Initially, travelling to the Gold Coast by boat on the calm waters of the inner route in Moreton Bay was the preferred mode. The roads, appropriately called bridle (or horse) tracks, that headed south from Brisbane were very rough, rivers had to be crossed, fallen trees skirted or removed. Overall, the road journey was arduous.

It was not long after Governor Musgrave built his holiday mansion that other dwellings were constructed on the Southport foreshore, and soon the first seawall had to be built to protect them. There was no learning from that: to this very day Mother Nature is regularly fought on the Gold Coast, at great cost to rate-payers.

Technological advances in transport allowed dramatic changes to the Gold Coast. The train came first, then the motor car. In 1925, the Jubilee Bridge crossed the Nerang River and motor vehicle traffic started to flow to the Gold Coast. In the following year bridges were built over the Tallebudgera and Currumbin Creeks. Surfers Paradise, not Southport, was recognised as the village with greatest real estate potential. This excited the entrepreneurs, but the Second World War and concern about Japanese airstrikes and possible invasion brought non-essential travel and tourism to a halt for the duration of the conflict.

The war over, Brisbane-ites discovered a newfound desire to spend and enjoy themselves. Car ownership grew rapidly, and daily or weekend trips to the Gold Coast became very popular. Motels, some of which still exist in near-original form, were constructed along the highway from Southport to Coolangatta. The first high-rise (a magnificent six storeys) was built at Broadbeach in 1956. The idea caught on. The result is modern Surfers Paradise which, from a distance, looks like the visitor is about to enter the CBD of a major capital city, not a conglomeration of holiday units. Massive buildings sit on the flattened frontal dunes. Wealthy home-owners took up the remainder of the ocean-front space; no longer are there undulating sand hills retaining the sea with their native grasses, she-oaks and succulent pig face. Forever and a day there will be an ongoing battle to protect significant tourist and residential investments from collapsing into the sea.

In the same era (the 1950s and 1960s), canal estates were carved out of the Nerang River floodplains. If a seascape was not available or affordable, a water view of engineered canals was the next best thing. Great swathes of agricultural land and mangrove forests were destroyed for housing development. Originally the canals were marine deserts; in due course, benthic communities established and marine life found its way from the remaining natural waterways to colonise new habitat. Nature does not waste space and resources.

As if some of the most splendid beaches in the world were not enough to satisfy holidaymakers, entrepreneurs developed theme parks to attract children, whose families would spend considerable time and money on visits. These entertainment precincts, fortunately, were located in less-than-pristine environments and at some distance from the foreshore, with one exception.

Adults, in particular the increasing number of Japanese visitors, needed more than beaches to occupy their vacation time. Farmland not already taken for residential development became golf courses. To round out the tourist experience, shopping malls as at Surfers Paradise, a shopping centre as at Southport and a casino at Broadbeach were built. Obviously, Mother Nature was insufficient to satisfy the jaded world-weary visitor. However, seekers of natural environments discovered Fraser Island and pitched their tents in the lee of the vegetated dunes, as their parents had done on the Gold Coast in a previous era.

Chapter 5 provides data on the state of the city's forested environment. For Australia's sixth-largest city in terms of human population, the Gold Coast has within its new city boundaries large areas of natural vegetation. We have explained the change of boundaries: the natural vegetation is not only in the hinterland but on the near-shore islands which are now part of the city. These are South Stradbroke Island and several mangrove-covered islands between South Stradbroke and the mainland.

The modern city of the Gold Coast commences with beaches and tidal flats in the east (on South Stradbroke Island) then coastal dunes, the mainland alluvial plains, low rolling hills then high mountain ranges in the hinterland. By referring to broad ecosystems and vegetation types we can classify the Gold Coast as follows: sand dunes and in certain places coastal mangroves; dune woodlands and shrub land (she-oak, wallum banksia, tea trees and paperbarks are dominant); coastal plain wetlands and heath; eucalypt (Queensland blue gum in particular) woodlands and open forest; and rainforests. Most of these ecosystems remain as remnants in selected parts of the Gold Coast.

It has been possible to reconstruct the vegetative cover of the Gold Coast as it was before Europeans arrived and commenced to clear the vegetation (Ryan *et al.* 2003). This has been modelled as at 1750. Based on this model and the new boundaries of the city, it has been estimated that over 50 per cent of all vegetation has been cleared, some types extensively: melaleuca (paper bark) wetlands, eucalypt woodlands along drainage lines and on floodplains, eucalypt open forest on the undulating hills, and Araucanian rainforests (where hoop pines are a distinctive feature, as are thick vines). As we would expect, the majority of clearing occurred along the coastal strip. Fig. 1.2, a photo taken in the late 1800s, shows part of the coastal strip between Nobby headland and Big Burleigh in its original state. The vegetation is dense. It was like this along the whole coastal strip. The area is bare of native vegetation today. What was coastal sand dunes and a complex vegetation cover is now the brick, cement, timber and glass of a linear city, the only significant vegetation being garden trees and shrubs purchased from commercial nurseries established in the interland.

The foredunes are all gone, flattened and built on; most of the coastal heaths and swamps have been covered by residential development and associated urban land uses; the alluvial floodplains have been significantly impacted (destroyed in most places) by clearing, first for farming and then from the 1950s for residential and more general forms of urban development. The vegetation types we associate with these environments have been dramatically decreased. We present the actual figures in this chapter.

Open forests and woodlands (stretching from beyond the coastal heathlands into the rolling hills), with their eucalypt and wattle trees, are as Australian as koalas and common macropods. In fact, these vegetation types existed on the Gold Coast where we would expect koalas, wallabies, kangaroos, possums, echidnas and kookaburras (the laughing jackass). As we have destroyed much of this habitat, we no longer see many of these animals. The absence of koalas, gone from most of the city in under half a century, is most obvious. However, marine fauna communities have fared better, at least in certain parts of the city, as development took place.

Fig. 1.2 Looking south from Nobby headland to Big Burleigh, 1800s. Extensive coastal vegetation can be seen as far and wide as the camera lens permitted. Source: Provided by Gold Coast City Council Local Studies Library. Photographer unknown.

Chapter 6 focuses on the state of the Gold Coast beaches. What have been the environmental impacts on the frontal dunes? We develop in considerable detail the story of the ongoing battle between humans and nature. Attracted to the glorious beaches of Southport, Burleigh and Coolangatta in the late 1800s, we were from the outset building on the foreshore. The first storm gave an inkling of what was to come. The seas crashed over the shore, houses were threatened. Soon a seawall was built at Southport.

The coastal strip was gradually opened up for development in the 1930s and by the beginning of the Second World War a thin line of houses spread from one end of the Gold Coast beaches to the other. However, in a commercial sense, the Gold Coast was still a series of stand- alone villages each with its own shops, a hotel or two, a movie theatre, a primary school, a doctor's surgery and a life-saving club.

During the war years the sand miners came and levelled the foredunes, doing the job for subsequent high-rise developers and beachfront residents who demanded prime real estate and magnificent sea views; when cyclones or severe storms came, as they did when and where Mother Nature determined, the residents also faced the threat of loss. The beaches were in the control of engineers who worked for the benefit of those who built on sand, against all established wisdom. We expect that modern high-rise buildings have their foundations in bedrock. The foreshore houses don't.

Chapter 6 is a major story in itself, capable of filling a whole book. Given the degree of beachfront development today, from one end of the Gold Coast to the other, what do we do when the inevitable severe storms come and, even more troublesome, when the cyclones hit? We could factor in the sea-level rise as a consequence of global warming. Without protective measures, houses would simply tumble over the cliffs. How secure are buildings without seawalls to blunt the force of nature?

Then there is the loss of beaches as a consequence of storms. Sand comes and goes under natural conditions. Training walls were built on the Tweed River and the northern Gold Coast beaches were denied the natural northerly flow of sand. This was addressed by installing a sand bypass system. New ideas have been tried recently, because walls, groynes and the replenishment of sand by pumping and bulldozer grading are simply treating the symptoms. The construction of artificial reefs beyond the surf zone is one such concept. There has been an off-shore artificial reef at Narrowneck for some years and the available evidence is positive. In early 2014, two other artificial reefs were approved. More radical proposals are being made, particularly in the context of expected increased numbers and intensity of extreme weather events. Retreat from the foreshore! This would be troublesome, akin to unpicking a finely crafted piece of intricate lace. We would need to start with a clean slate, putting aside the vast difference in the magnitude of cost.

We have said this previously, but it is worth repeating. If one characteristic is to define the Gold Coast it would be the beaches, among the best in the world. As we write, an application is being prepared to have the beaches formally recognised on the 'world's best' list. Residents and tourists alike swarm to the beaches when the sun is shining, as it does most of the time. Youngsters build sand castles and scramble in and out of the waves gently rolling up the beach; the castle-builders hope that the water will fill the moat around the king's or queen's castle. The castle-builder will be secure, with the help of Mother Nature.

People of all ages play in the surf, many bodysurf or at least make valiant attempts at it. Board riders, these days removed from swimmers and put in their own zone, engage in their hobby, some with amazing skill. There are those who take their Christmas reading to the beach, or the Sunday paper. Beach cricket is as Australian as a meat pie. Soccer is popular among males visiting from nations addicted to this sport. Kite-flying teases all ages to try out their skill.

And yet the beach is even more. Leon Zann, who in 1995 compiled Australia's first and only *State of the Marine Environment Report*, wrote: 'The beach has become a cherished place and is entwined in the rites of passage of many Australians' (p. 29). Undoubtedly, this has been the role of the Gold Coast beaches for significant numbers of Australians and, we expect, many overseas visitors.

Daryl McPhee informs us in **Chapter** 7 that the marine environments of the Gold Coast are some of the most highly modified and heavily utilised waterways in Australia. The dramatic land use changes which were discussed and analysed in previous chapters have had impact on the waterways. The construction of seawalls and river training walls, massive dredging in the Broadwater and engineered canal estates have singly and in combination led to dramatic modification. The rapid residential population increase and the continued growth of tourism have resulted in the high level of use of the waterways, whether for boating, fishing or swimming. Nearly 30 000 recreational boats are owned by Gold Coast residents. Boat-based water spots are very popular in the Broadwater. Canal estate residents can catch fish from their front or backyards. McPhee explores how well the modified environments are coping. Surprises are in store.

Chapter 8, by Shelley Burgin and Daryl McPhee, takes us to the Gold Coast fresh-water environment, rather than the specifically marine (salt-water) environment. Some of the fresh-water environments are in their natural state but in most cases they are engineered environments. These waterways provide shelter and food for an array of animals. The city is alive with animals if we know where to look.

This brings us to **Chapter 9**, also written by Shelley Burgin. In earlier chapters we presented data that shows how much of the original environment has been destroyed in building the city of the Gold Coast. Some ecosystems have been left as tiny remnants, virtually museum pieces suggesting we should be extremely careful and respectful in entering into them. Yet, surprisingly, the near-complete destruction of natural habitat has not led to a reciprocal loss of certain fauna, the well-known casualties excepted. In fact the replacement of government-initiated slash pine forests, which had covered much of the swamp land west of Burleigh and Miami, with urban dwellings and animal-friendly gardens has been a positive outcome in recent years. Remnants of the pine forests are still to be seen, for example on the approach to Bond University.

James Trefil wrote in his informative and enjoyable book *A Scientist in the City* (1994, p. 9):

> *A downtown area ... possesses cliff side habitats and detritus food sources. Any animal that can take advantage of this ecological niche will be able to live and prosper ... The pigeons you see every day ... are living examples of natural selection at work. They originally evolved to fit into a niche (on) ... high rock cliffs ... When a similar niche opened up in cities, they were ready to go. There isn't much difference between the nooks and crannies in a cliff and the nooks and crannies in a church steeple or a skyscraper. This is a rather common scenario for the development of urban wildlife: first it occupies a niche in the wild ecosystem, then it moves in when a similar niche opens up in cities.*

Think of what Trefil is saying and apply it to the Gold Coast:

> *When a city is born, a new kind of ecosystem is created, one that operates according to the same principles as any other and comes with its own suite of ecological niches. Plants and animals that have developed strategies in the wild which would allow them to fit niches created by human beings move into cities and flourish there, while those that do not possess such strategies are forced to move or become extinct (p. 14).*

Be surprised at the wildlife that has made the populated suburbs of the Gold Coast home.

For a significant number of visitors, the Gold Coast is not simply beaches, excellent though they are. Schoolchildren on long six-week summer holidays, do seek a little more; albeit not too much more than swimming, surfing, boogie-board riding and, for some, fishing. The entertainment entrepreneurs came to their rescue some years ago. The Gold Coast's theme parks are the number two attraction for visitors. Some of the theme parks play an important part in environmental education. This is the focus of **Chapter 10**, written by wildlife ecologist Shelley Burgin.

Before there were theme parks on the Gold Coast, there were travelling shows. Itinerant carnival operators turned up at popular camping beaches such as Southport, Burleigh Heads and Coolangatta–Tweed Heads when the school holidays commenced in December. The shows were basically a set of children's rides such as ferris wheels, dodge-em cars, knock-em-down stalls and fairy-floss sellers. After a day on the beach these fairs provided added fun to youngsters on holidays. Fun was their sole focus.

There were two small zoos on the Gold Coast in the mid 20th century, one associated with the Surfers Paradise Hotel and the other at Coolangatta. These played a role in educating youngsters (and some adults) about wildlife. Alex Griffiths' Currumbin Bird Sanctuary (now Currumbin Wildlife Sanctuary) and Fleay's Fauna Reserve (now David Fleay's Wildlife Park) opened, both after the Second World War. They remain today in somewhat different guises. They are part of the building-blocks of the Gold Coast, even though they sit in contrast to the high-rise developments, the casinos, the shopping centres, the theme parks and the clubs. Without the effort of these wildlife pioneers, the Johnny-come-lately theme park entrepreneurs would not have succeeded. People came to the Gold Coast because it was natural. The feeding of lorikeets by Alex Griffith was not considered unnatural. David Fleay was our David Attenborough well before the latter was recognised.

The Gold Coast changed and those who came were different types of people from the pioneering tourists who were happy with camping in tents. As high-rise apartments and motels replaced the tent cities, the dedicated beach campers went to Fraser Island. It was not until 1974 that the Gold Coast got its first theme park, Dreamworld, and not until 1987 that its wildlife display, Koala Country, opened. By then Japanese tourists were coming in large numbers and were willing to pay $10 each for a photo of themselves cuddling a koala. Had their parents visited the Gold Coast a generation earlier, in particular Burleigh Heads, and strolled five minutes west from the beach to the gum trees that surrounded the Burleigh State School, they would have seen a dozen or so koalas in the wild, any day of the week.

Sea World is another Gold Coast theme park with a pronounced environmental theme. It prides itself on being a marine mammal park, with an oceanarium as well as conventional attractions. Its policy of taking in orphaned and injured wildlife for veterinary treatment and rehabilitation earns it considerable public kudos.

A modern theme park is a grouping of entertainment attractions, some with an educational attraction as well. Disneyland in California was not the first modern theme park. That prize goes to Santa Claus Land in Indiana (opening in 1946); however, Disneyland made the concept popular. Surprisingly, given Walt Disney's philosophy of animal conservation, Disney's Animal Kingdom was not opened until Earth Day (22 April) 1998. The importance of nature-based theme parks should not be underestimated. The annual attendance at Disney's Animal Kingdom is ~10 million people. The Gold Coast theme parks are second only to the beaches in visitation rates. Not only do they provide entertainment but, some at least, add to visitors' knowledge of 'wild' animals (even if they are in captivity).

Mention has been made of David Fleay and his extraordinary commitment to the protection of Australian wildlife. Fleay and his family came to the Gold Coast, specifically West Burleigh on Tallebudgera Creek, when the city was still a series of coastal holiday villages for tent-campers. He established a reserve and from that day on played a fundamental role in educating domestic and foreign visitors about the unique fauna of Australia. Bridgette McDougall tells the story of his legacy in **Chapter 11**.

David Fleay and Alex Griffith are two stand-out nature conservationists who made the coastal strip of the Gold Coast their live lecture theatre. Both donated extremely valuable real estate in the interest of conservation. The *Gold Coast Bulletin* (3 January 2012) reported that Alex Griffith could have retired a multi-millionaire, but died with only $8000 to his name. Various members of the Gold Coast's 'white shoe brigade' ended up equally poor – but not by choice. The 'white shoe brigade' is the description commonly afforded to land developers cum speculators who made the Gold Coast their hunting ground. They stood out due to their 'uniform' of white shoes and pale suits, or at the other extreme Hawaiian shirts.

So far we have paid scant attention to the built heritage of the Gold Coast. This is the focus in **Chapter 12**, written by Lynne Armitage and Shelley Burgin. We know we should not expect many old buildings as the city is young, very young by world standards. We hope that this simple fact would lead to a pro-preservation policy for the little that is available to be kept for posterity.

To attempt to understand what the early Gold Coast settlers and city-builders were seeking to do, their architecture should tell us a lot. Unfortunately little is left. This is not uncommon when only the new is deemed valuable. Lynne Armitage and Shelley Burgin look for the human-made treasures that help bring to life the values and attitudes of the pioneers who made the city.

Various heritage organisations (at national, state and local level) exist for the express purpose of protecting the valuable but often they are not powerful enough when those who march to the tune of 'new is better' come with financiers in tow. As we were writing this book the iconic Miami Ice Works was demolished against the wishes of many, including elected representatives of Gold Coast rate-payers.

In **Chapter 13** we look to the future of the Gold Coast's energy footprint. A city in the sun (otherwise 'a sun city') has great scope to utilise sunshine for some, if not all, of its energy needs. At present, the electric power that residents, tourists and businesses rely on is generated by burning coal in distant power stations. As with all coal-fired energy production, greenhouse gases are an unwanted by-product.

Direct sunlight can be, and is being, used to heat water for household needs. Much more use could be made of this free energy. There is potential for the more sophisticated utilisation of sunshine – photovoltaic solar installations either on a small scale or as solar farms. Again, Gold Coast residents and businesses could be doing far more to harvest this free energy.

We can rule out geothermal energy for the Gold Coast, according to geologists, and hydro-electricity which requires steep mountains and the continuous flow of water. While the hinterland mountain ranges get significant rainfall, at best they could be used for local micro-hydro generation. There is a micro-hydro plant below the Hinze Dam. We might guess that a 'surfer's paradise' would provide the possibility of wave power, or maybe tidal power. These have been explored and found not to be feasible options. But there are those ever-so-welcome sea breezes. Is there enough consistent wind to power wind farms? The Gold Coast will be required to pull its weight in reducing greenhouse gases. Sophie Telfer and Tor Hundloe explore these possibilities for the future.

Chapter 14 focuses on the business community of the Gold Coast, in particular the big players and their environmental values. Much is made of the call by Gold Coast civic leaders to position the city as a world leader in sustainability. In a market economy, most of the responsibility for that falls on the business community. The notion of the 'triple bottom line' comes into play. A business is expected to modify a narrow focus on profitability (although this is a prerequisite for its sustainability) by taking a genuine and transparent approach to corporate social responsibility (CSR), in which the environment and social conditions are given equal importance with profits.

In this regard two iconic buildings have set benchmarks, although limited in purpose. One is the School of Sustainable Development at Bond University, the other is the AFL stadium at Carrara. Their achievements are briefly described in assessing the take-up of CSR by some of the major businesses on the Gold Coast. Madelaine Waters made this her research project.

The penultimate chapter, **Chapter 15**, puts the development and planning of the Gold Coast into perspective. Historians talk of path dependency, meaning simply that events that have occurred will structure the future. They can be very difficult to 'undo'; the history of the Gold Coast influences its present urban environment. The Gold Coast as we know it today was shaped by historical events, economics, political forces and, in more recent times, the work of trained town planners. While economics and politics are as old as human societies, town planning is a newcomer.

Town (or urban) planning as a professional discipline is just over 100 years old. The British established the Town and Country Planning Association in 1899, and the first university degree in the field was awarded in 1909. Not until 1951 was a professional body for planners, the Regional and Town Planning Institute, formed in Australia. It changed its name to the Planning Institute of Australia in 2002. By the 1950s, certain development approaches had taken root on the Gold Coast. Professional planners were going to be playing 'catch-up'.

Town subdivision, the major town planning task in the early days of the Gold Coast, became in 1879 the responsibility of so-called Divisional Boards, renamed shires in 1903. These bodies were the creation of the colonial government, that became the Queensland state government at Federation. The shires had nothing more than delegated powers. This remains the case. The governments of Australian states can override decisions made by local governments. They can take decisions on major developments out of the hands of local government; they can and do establish the locations for urban expansion; they can and do form statutory authorities to manage areas within the boundaries of a local authority. The Gold Coast Broadwater is a prime example. State governments can have very significant influences on the formation of cities by the roads they build and the locations of schools and hospitals. No other area of Australia is likely to have been more influenced by state government decisions, and the private sector, than the Gold Coast.

The Gold Coast as we know it today was fashioned and shaped by an imperfect process. Fast-talking entrepreneurs were able to do deals which helped them make extraordinary profits, and sometimes go bankrupt. Undoubtedly, favours (access to land and to finance) to government 'friends' were granted by the Queensland state government during the 1970s and 1980s. That is for another book. However, all government help amounted to nothing if the entrepreneur's project was a dud. And some were.

In 1928 a Royal Commission formed to consider local government boundaries recommended that the whole coastal strip plus parts of adjoining shires be made into a single town council called Nerang. The war intervened and nothing happened until December 1948 when a town, which stretched from Southport to Surfers Paradise to Burleigh Heads to Coolangatta was proclaimed. This is what we refer to as the 'old' Gold Coast. A new shire, Albert, was formed to incorporate the surrounding areas. It stretched from Brisbane through the hinterland to the NSW border.

The land-use policies of the Albert Shire were to have an overbearing approach in how the city of the Gold Coast was formed. Much of what today comprises the city of the Gold Coast was in the city's formative years in the Albert Shire. In the recent past, a 1994 review of the boundaries of the Gold Coast City Council, Albert Shire Council and Beaudesert Shire Council resulted in the amalgamation of the first two into the City of the Gold Coast. This was formalised in 1995. From then on the Gold Coast had the city boundaries we deal with today.

The Gold Coast City Council has very important, far-reaching and complicated responsibilities. They are very important due to the size and nature of the city. It is not a bush town or small seaside resort where local folk can muddle through. Its annual budget is twice that of Tasmania. Well-informed councillors and teams of professional staff face big questions. The biggest: is there a population limit to the city? If it is allowed to grow, where is the residential land to accommodate the growth? What is lost if more land is converted from a near-natural state to housing blocks? What if quality agricultural land is covered with tar and cement? At what stage of growth does the city destroy the clean-green environmental image that its leaders promote?

There are immediate matters needing attention, such as restoring land to something that closely resembles its natural state, and re-establishing wildlife corridors. The Gold Coast City Council gathers money from rate-payers for this purpose. Does it get enough to be effective in pursuing these goals? Animal overpasses could play important roles. One is needed to link Burleigh National Park to the forest across the highway. This overpass was costed at $4.9 million (in 2012). A Bond University study found that 57 per cent of a sample of rate-payers (250 interviewed) would be willing to pay $10–20 per year to the Council's environmental fund for the purpose of constructing the koala overpass (*Gold Coast Bulletin*, 29 June 2012). But there are no animal over- or underpasses on the Gold Coast, although they exist across the border in NSW. Explanations for this lack are hard to come by.

Restoring degraded vegetation (as is being done on Springbrook by the Australian Rainforest Conservation Society, a Queensland government initiative) is a call on the Council's resources where it has acquired land in poor condition. There should also be protection of the city's built heritage, but a recent example of inaction was allowing the destruction of the Miami Ice Works on 12 November 2013. This famous old building, constructed just after the Second World War out of two army huts, produced the large ice-blocks that the tent-city campers of the 1950s and 1960s relied upon for their ice-chests, the 'eskies' of that era.

Our focus turns to what we can do in the future to, in a small way, compensate for the considerable damage done in creating a remarkable city. However, it is extremely important to be mindful of the limited power and influence of professional town planners. They are bound by the political constraints imposed by the elected city councillors, by the decisions of state parliamentarians and, in regard to a few issues covered by international conventions such as the Ramsar Convention, by the political decision-makers in Canberra. Of all modern professions, town planning has not been able to speak with a unified voice when political decisions breach town planning standards. This is the normal experience of young planners.

In **Chapter 16** we attempt to bring together the various strands of our enquiries so to assess and report on the Gold Coast's 'state of the environment'. It is a truism that environmental impact is a function of human population, the population's affluence and the available technology. This is conventionally written as Impact = PAT (population, affluence and technology). All three will play a significant role in determining the future of the Gold Coast. All three have fashioned the city as we know it.

This chapter commences with some elementary human geography, including population densities. We will discover that very few people live in the distant hinterland, and none on the mangrove islands. This simple fact protects those environments. Those who live in high-rise apartments close to their place of work have a small ecological footprint compared to the footprint of those who live in the outer suburbs and travel to work some distance away.

Not only do the half a million residents cause environmental impacts, so do tourists, both day visitors and those who stay longer. The city receives nearly 30 000 visitors on average per day, and near 100 000 on a peak day. Note that this does not account for the visitors' length of stay. Accounting for that, the number is in the order of 80 000 visitors on any day of the year. How does the city's natural environment cope? We present the available data, and note that there could be a serious disconnect between the vision of the city's leaders who support sustainability and what is actually happening on the ground.

It was not that long ago that the city's mayor was proclaiming that the Gold Coast would set the international standard for a sustainable coastal tourist city. Is progress being made or has this ideal been silently discarded? As we write, powerful voices call for 'more': more casinos, more cranes in the sky building more high-rises, more annual 'events', a cruise ship terminal and a 24 km sky-rail along the coast at the city's northern end. If any or all of these come to pass, there would need to be a significant increase in tourist numbers to justify the investment, and a significant increase in the permanent population to provide the services the tourists demand. How long would the presently preserved natural environments remain intact? How much larger would the city's ecological footprint become?

Our task has been to determine the environmental impacts that have resulted from building a modern, relatively large tourist city in virgin territory. Much has been lost. There is potential for even greater impact if the city is allowed to grow. Limits to growth are features of biological systems. We are slowly starting to realise they are features of social and economic systems. With regard to the latter, diseconomies of large-scale are evident and well known. We will know that we have come to understand this fact if the city of the Gold Coast retains its unique status as the world's premium nature-based city. Attempt to do more than nature makes possible, and the game is lost. Drawing a line in the sand somewhere sensible is a necessity.

We are a group of optimistic scientists, economists, sustainability experts and town planners. We have made the sustainability of the Gold Coast our goal. We have decided to bring this book to an end by suggesting a means of enjoying the Gold Coast's environment that none should overlook. We have titled **Chapter 17**, the ultimate chapter, 'Something to chew on: natural plant foods of the Gold Coast'. It is written by Simon Grigalius and Daryl McPhee. We attempt to entice you.

Subtropical waters and rainforest teem with life. The indigenous folk who for 20 000 years made the Gold Coast home, whether on the beaches, the river banks or rainforests, had the following choices on their menu: pipis, oysters, mud crabs, sea mullet, tailor, whiting, turtles, dugongs, stingrays, lizards, goannas, echidnas, parrots, scrub turkeys, pigeons, koalas, possums, wallabies, bandicoots – and this before the fruits and nuts of the forest![1]

We describe in Chapter 17 the range of naturally produced foods that, with a little imagination, can provide delightful bush tucker in the modern era. While many on the list of indigenous foods are no longer available, there is an exciting range, particularly of fruits and nuts waiting to be tried and, we expect, enjoyed. A city with its own culinary delights should not be denied its place in the sun.

Note

1. We are mindful that there is some debate about the inclusion of koalas.

References

Hundloe T, Hamilton C (1997) *Koalas and Tourism: An Economic Evaluation.* With contributions from L Wilkes. Discussion Paper No. 13, Australia Institute, Canberra.

Ryan TS, Bean AR, Hoskins BB, Wilson BA, McDonald WJF (2003) *Gold Coast City Council 1998 Nature Conservation Mapping Review Stage 1.* Queensland Herbarium for the Gold Coast City Council.

Chapter 2

The Gold Coast: a snapshot

T. Hundloe

We know the city's boundaries as they are today (they have changed dramatically over time) and that is all we need to answer the question: what is the size of the city? The city's boundaries today are shown in Plate 3. As noted previously, the Gold Coast was a lot smaller in a geographical sense a couple of generations ago. When it was known as the 'South Coast' (or simply 'the Coast'), its northern boundary was at Lands End, north of Labrador. Coolangatta to Lands End established the south–north limits. Beenleigh in Logan City was considered the half-way mark[1] between Brisbane and the Gold Coast. Just south of Beenleigh is the tiny town of Yatala, famous for its meat pies (the food of choice for Australians at sporting events or when travelling by car). Many a traveller to the Gold Coast stopped at Yatala to purchase the famous pies. Today the northern boundary of the Gold Coast stretches to Yatala and Beenleigh, home of one of the largest breweries in Australia. If the Gold Coast manufactures anything on a large scale it is beer.

The western boundary has also changed as the Queensland government amalgamated local government areas, called 'shires' if rural, otherwise 'cities'. These political boundaries do not always make sense from a citizen's perspective. Community of interest or economic geography determines how local residents, both urban and rural, define and think about localities. This applies to the Gold Coast as much as anywhere else. This we need to explore.

The southern hinterland, from the old town of Nerang along the Nerang River as it meanders into Numinbah Valley, between Springbrook on the east and Beechmont on the west, has always been considered part of the Gold Coast, although this area was for a long time in a separate shire. Follow the Beechmont road south-west into the Lamington Plateau and you will come to a long-established eco-tourist venture, Binna Burra Lodge. Travel via Canungra on to the plateau and you will find O'Reilly's Guesthouse. Today these rainforest retreats are placed outside the Gold Coast boundaries. The tourist literature suggests otherwise, local people think otherwise.

The farming land in both the Tallebudgera and Currumbin valleys was, in the past, thought of as part of the Gold Coast. What was not the Gold Coast was the extensive area north, north-west and north-east of Southport. The extensive Southern Moreton Bay Islands were not considered part of the city. The sugarcane growing area around Jacobs Well has been added, as has the sugar mill from which Beenleigh Rum is a by-product.[2] Further east, South Stradbroke Island and several uninhabited mangrove-covered islands of southern Moreton Bay are now officially part of the Gold Coast. In the north-west, the east of Tamborine Mountain is included but the rest of the mountain is in another shire. Who are we to argue with those who draw up political boundaries?

A Gold Coast community?

The close association of economic and social interests of the 'old' Gold Coast has been diluted by the city's geographic expansion and by the loss of identifiable rural villages which have merged into suburban centres. A city with over half a million residents and millions of tourists per annum cannot be expected to sustain a community spirit. There are simply too many people with diverse interests. It is not just the 'them' and 'us' so typical of tourist towns, the local residents are a far from homogenous group. Suburbs have varying status. Some have a large percentage of tourists. Some are solely residential. Some are enclaves for the rich. Some working-class. Residents in the north of the city are just as likely to travel to Brisbane for work, shopping and leisure as to the Gold Coast's CBD of Southport. To what city do these people 'belong'?

To add a personal touch as a means of explaining the urbanisation of rural areas, when the author was a child growing up on a small dairy farm in The Pocket in Numinbah Valley, the town of Nerang was where monthly shopping for foodstuffs and farm supplies took place. Only certain foods had to be bought; much food (vegetables and fruits, poultry and occasional game meats) were produced on the farm or sourced from the nearby rainforests. For clothing, shoes, hats and major household items a trip was made to Southport, the major commercial centre. As it was common to have retired family or friends living in the coastal villages such as Surfers Paradise or Burleigh Heads, regular visits would be made to the beach areas. The hinterland and the beach formed a community. Today Nerang is a mix of small-scale industry, suburban living and semi-rural residential areas on which the mandatory horses graze.

What does the Gold Coast look like? Its landforms

The Gold Coast is a city approximately half covered by forests of various types, including small patches of near-pristine ancient rainforest, mangrove-covered islands, and patches of coastal heathlands and farmland with areas of uncleared eucalypt forest. There are tiny remnants of the plantation pine forests that were planted in the 1950s and 1960s, when commercial forest planting for tax minimisation was encouraged by the Commonwealth government. Vast areas of natural forest and native animal habitat were destroyed as a consequence of this ill-considered program. The remaining near-pristine forest is very special. You would have to search far and wide to find another city with so much high-quality non-urban land.

While the city is Australia's premier tourist destination, the majority of tourist accommodation has been built in a very narrow strip between the coastal Gold Coast Highway (this is not the Pacific Motorway further west) and the beach. This means only a small percentage of the city is devoted to tourist accommodation. If not on the east of the highway, the remainder of the motels and holiday units are on its immediate west, within walking distance of the beach. The bulk of the high-rise tourism accommodation is concentrated in an area encompassing Surfers Paradise and Broadbeach. This is the glittery and glitzy end of town. There are other concentrations of high-rise apartments at Southport, Burleigh and Coolangatta.

The actual headland at Burleigh (locals tend to omit the second part of its name) is Australia's tiniest national park, declared in 1947. It, like a few other places on the Gold Coast, had a name change some time ago. Originally it was Koala National Park, with a 'Koalas Cross Here' warning sign on the highway which cuts the rainforested headland from a forested corridor which, with human-made breaks in its continuity, reaches the rainforests in the hinterland. The hinterland is where the Gold Coast gets formal UN recognition for its World Heritage status subtropical rainforests. Springbrook National Park is part of the Gondwana Rainforests, recognised by UNESCO as a World Heritage property (see Box 2.1). This recognition puts these subtropical rainforests on par with the Great Barrier Reef and Fraser Island in Australia and with Yellowstone National Park in the US. That a proportion of the rainforests are in a city is something very special.

More canals than Venice

The Gold Coast has 35 km of continuous beach if the few rocky headlands are dismissed as nuisances, or welcomed as sculpted nobs breaking the city's beaches into segments (one is called Nobby). These headlands play a fundamental role in producing great surfing waves. There is more to the water environment of the city than beaches. Behind Surfers (using the name locals prefer), Broadbeach and Burleigh, the city comprises a myriad of canal estates. More canals than Venice. These have been carved out of mangrove forests and coastal scrub that existed on the floodplains of the Nerang River and, to a lesser extent, Tallebudgera and Currumbin Creeks. More recently canal estates have extended into the new northern coastal and river environments.

Smart real estate developers discovered that battle-axe blocks were the optimum configuration of housing lots on canal estates (see Fig. 2.1). Think of two battle axes put together. One has its head facing the water of the constructed canal, with space for a private boat-ramp; the other has the axe-head facing the street, but the handle runs down to the canal and, if nothing else, the owner can boast of a water frontage ('backage' would be the more appropriate description if the English language allowed such a term). At the end of the block there is enough space for a small jetty on which to tie a small boat.

Only so much waterfront

Canal estates became the solution to a specific Gold Coast development problem that occurred as people moved to the city in ever-increasing numbers. Consider new

Box 2.1: Gondwana Rainforests

The Gondwana Rainforests of Australia were listed as a World Heritage area in 1986, and in 1994 the protected area was increased.

The rainforests have a combined total area of 366 507 ha, only a small part of which is in the city of the Gold Coast.

The rainforests meet three of the four natural criteria for World Heritage listing. They:

- represent a major stage of the Earth's evolutionary history;
- are an outstanding example of ongoing ecological and biological processes;
- contain the most important natural habitats for conserving biological diversity.

The Gondwana Rainforests are the most extensive area of subtropical rainforest in the world.

More frog, bird, snake and marsupial species are found in the Gondwana Rainforests than elsewhere in Australia.

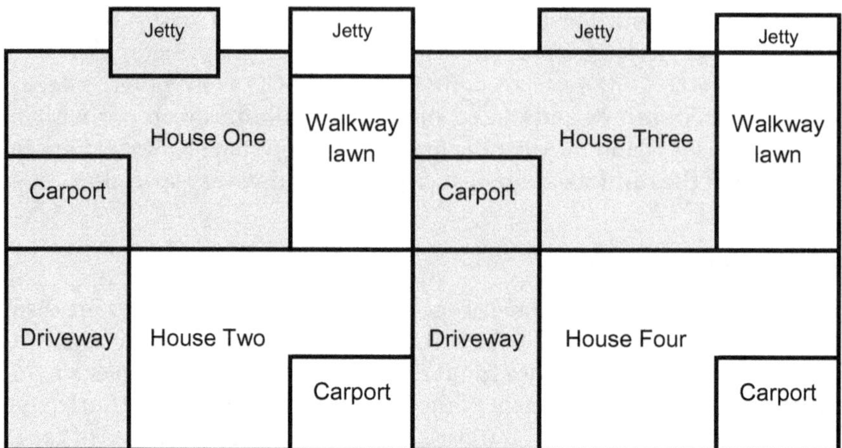

Fig. 2.1 Battle-axe housing blocks on canal estates. The shaded ones (here, blocks 1 and 3) face the canal. Blocks 2 and 4 face the street.

development in the following context. There is only so much beachfront land with water views, and only a few wealthy individuals can afford to purchase land and build houses there. This is illustrated by the beachfront at Hedges Avenue, Broadbeach being known as 'Millionaires' Row'. The next best thing to a beachfront house is to 'improve on nature' and carve canals out of floodplains. Once the blocks with ocean views were all sold there was no shortage of millionaires eager to purchase the largest battle-axe blocks in the engineered canals. No points for guessing where the axe-head was located for the more wealthy.

Much of the rest of the urban area of the Gold Coast is conventional, modern residential housing. Most of it is located between the Gold Coast Highway and the Pacific Motorway, with the rest pushing into the lower foothills of the hinterland. Very little of the residential accommodation is old. In mid 2013, one of the city's few remaining 'beach shacks' was sold to be demolished. The house had the wonderful name, ironic in the sense it did not linger on longer, 'Linga Longa'. It had been built not long after the beachfront land at Currumbin was released for sale in 1923. The selling price today for this shack? $1 million.

Once more into the hills

Let us leave the urban areas and venture into the major river valleys and cleared rainforest hills that were once important farming communities, as was the Nerang River floodplain around what is now known as Carrara. Dairy farming dominated the hinterland until a generation or two ago. Numinbah Valley contained dozens[3] of viable small farms. There were dairy properties in both the Tallebudgera Creek and Currumbin Creek valleys. Banana growing was a profitable business on cleared steep land that was formerly rainforest.

Before dairy farming, there was timber-getting as we discussed previously, and some not-so-successful attempts at cotton-growing during the American Civil War. Sugarcane farming came early but today is confined to the flat north-east country around Jacobs Well; considerable cane land remains south of the Queensland border. All the dairies have gone, with most of the remaining farms now running small herds of beef cattle. Hobby farms have been developed, each with its mandatory few well-bred, much-loved horses. There is limited horticulture. Garden-product nurseries exist. Otherwise about the only other sign of human activity in the hinterland is eco-tourism, a few accommodation places and night-time tours to view the glowworms at Natural Arch (Bridge).

Residents

At the time of writing the Gold Coast's population was over half a million, over 400 000 of them aged 15 and over. This age group is important as we will use it to make comparisons with visitors (day-trippers, holiday-makers, folk visiting friends and relatives, business visitors) where the conventional reference point is those aged 15 and over. Another important age cut-off is 65 and over, as a proxy for retirement age. Australian readers will know that for a long time 65 has been the retirement age for males, while for females it has been 60. However, the rather dramatic increase in life-spans and changes in the law which make it somewhat harder than previously for employers to dismiss employees at these arbitrary ages means that there is now no mandatory retirement age (except in certain professions) and that we have now no rule of thumb for determining who is or is not retired. ABS census data is the best we can do, but be mindful of rather rapidly changing patterns of employment. The most recent census (in 2011) indicated that the retired population of the Gold Coast was 71 000. With those figures, it is far from being the 'retirement village' some coastal cities have become.

Population growth

At the turn of the century (2001) the city's population was 387 102. For the first decade of the 21st century, population was growing very fast, at 2.2–4.3 per cent per annum. However, the population growth has not been uniform across the city. The northern parts of the city, following the motorway north into the recently greenfield areas of Pimpama, Coomera, Upper Coomera and Kingsholme, have had the highest population increases as young families moved in. It should be noted that these are not 'near-the-beach' suburbs normally associated with the Gold Coast. We keep bumping up against perceptions of the city and boundary changes.

Also in the north but nearer the water, Hope Island experienced high growth from retirees making it their home. Two major centres of the 'old' Gold Coast – Coolangatta and Burleigh Heads – experienced decreased population over the same period. We will not spend time on population growth here other than to present Table 2.1, which needs little discussion. We have selected three villages/suburbs to report official population numbers over a long period. For the village-cum-suburb of Southport the increase over 130 years has been more than 100-fold. It is probably easier to relate to the population growth in Surfers Paradise from 1961 to 2006. This is from pre-population-boom times to the present. The suburb's population has grown more than four-fold. What the data in Table 2.1 cannot illustrate is the expansion of population west of the coastal villages where new suburbs stretching into the hills of the hinterland have come into existence.

The changing skyline

One of the most noticeable features of the Gold Coast is its variable skyline, from densely clustered high-rise in the Surfers Paradise area, to one- to two-storey beachfront units and houses sweeping north and south from Surfers Paradise, occasionally interrupted by small clusters of high-rise. Size matters. Only Gold Coast real estate developers would boast of having the highest residential building in Australia (they call it a 'tower', appropriately). It has the unimaginative name 'Q1'. One assumes this means 'Queensland's first'. The concept

Table 2.1. Population growth

Suburb	Year	Population
Burleigh Heads	1875	8
	1921	343
	1933	556
	1947	1048
	1961	2692
	1981	6497
	1991	7997
	2001	7351
	2006	7606
Surfers Paradise	1875	14
	1954	2402
	1961	4319
	2006	18 501
Southport	1875	30
	1881	230
	1901	1230
	1921	3551
	1933	4218
	1954	8134
	1961	12 746
	1986	18 930
	2006	24 097
	2011	28 315

Source: Various ABS census counts; Longhurst (various histories).

of the Tower of Babel has remained alive for millennia and shows no sign of exhaustion. The push into the sky isn't limited to residential buildings. Pacific Fair shopping centre is, as we write, being redeveloped to become Queensland's 'largest' shopping centre.

Where it borders the Pacific Ocean, the Gold Coast is a high-density city. Both affluent residents and holiday-makers want a beach view. If not that, then walking-distance proximity to the beach. If neither of these is affordable, a canal estate residence. Mother Nature did her best in providing a strip of continuous beach of 35 km;[4] engineers constructed more canals than in Venice. Once these were full, housing development was forced west, away from the much-prized beaches and canals. Hence, building into the sky has been the solution for the richest. Air-space becomes more expensive the closer to the ocean.

Houses, apartments and high-rises

The following data, taken from the most recent census (2011), tell part of the Gold Coast housing story. Just over 50 per cent (56 per cent to be precise) of Gold Coast dwellings are separate houses. This might not raise the eyebrows of visitors from the UK or other crowded parts of the world, but in Australia this is an unusually low statistic. In Australia, three-quarters (74 per cent) of dwellings are separate houses. Large houses on large blocks of land in sprawling cities define urban Australia. The Gold Coast is very different in this regard.

Nearly one-quarter of dwellings on the Gold Coast are medium-density, what we would call flats, units, apartments, townhouses, generally in blocks of one or two storeys. The old highway motels, still popular in the Mermaid Beach, Nobby Beach and Palm Beach areas also fit this description. These are for down-market tourists and visiting academics.[5] High-density dwellings – apartments and flats of three or more storeys – comprise 18 per cent of the city's dwelling stock, more than double the national average for this type of residence. Geography (the desire for an ocean view) and economics (the ability to pay for an ocean view) combine to define much of the building stock of this unique city.

At this point we should raise a question of sustainability even though the next chapter deals with this subject in formal terms. Here we confine it to the built environment. A building named 'Iluka', often touted as the first high-rise on the Gold Coast beachfront (much depends on the definition of beachfront), was recently demolished. It was not 50 years old! The first private high schools of the Gold Coast are about twice that age and very much functioning. Visit Rome, Athens, Istanbul and numerous other famous cities (which are never short of cashed-up tourists) and contemplate the age of their buildings. In any of those cities, you can stay in an expensive tourist lodging which is hundreds of years old. What is it about tourism in modern cities and built-in obsolescence?

Viewed impartially, a sizeable proportion of the Gold Coast economy has made itself dependent on built-in obsolescence. This includes tourist accommodation, tourist entertainment venues and large shopping complexes. We are referring to what could be called a 'fetish of the new'. Rather than compete with laid-back Fiji, the Cook Islands, Bali and Honolulu for cashed-up beach-goers, the Gold Coast city leaders aim to compete on the basis of flash hotels, casinos, shopping centres. It is as if nature has lost its value in comparison to neon lights and the clatter and clinking of the casino.

The tourists

Tourists, here defined as people travelling for pleasure, have been coming to Gold Coast villages at least from the day Burleigh Heads was promoted as the equivalent to the spa towns of the coastal European cities, in the late 19th century. England also had health-restoring spa towns, such as the appropriately named Bath.

The spa town concept floated for Burleigh in the 1880s was not (at that time) a resounding success. The village was quite difficult to get to by Cobb & Co. coach. The bush tracks from Brisbane were not engineered for comfort. Rivers had to be forded and fallen trees circled or removed. Rail transport, however, eventually made a significant difference and it played a central role in transporting Brisbane holiday-makers until the private motor car became affordable for the masses in the late 1950s.

In the late 19th century, what drew affluent Brisbane 'society' to the Gold Coast, in particular to Southport, a competitor to Burleigh Heads and Coolangatta, was the decision by the Governor of Queensland, Sir Anthony Musgrave, to build a summer holiday house in Southport, then known as Nerang River Heads. Governors were the peak of the pile in the British-ruled Australian proto-states (otherwise colonies); what those 19th-century 'celebrities' did set a trend for those lower in the pecking order.

Little has changed in the economic drivers of tourism. Put photographs of a celebrity (movie star, singer, model) on the front pages or television news and we flock to where they were seen. We don't expect many to recall Norma Ann Sykes (Honorary DLitt), but some might recognise the name Sabrina. She visited the Gold Coast in 1959 on an extended tour of Australia. She was a genuine celebrity – anything she did was photographed and splashed across the newspapers and television screens. More tourists came. Gold Coast promoters, whether real estate developers or friendly politicians, still rely on celebrity culture to draw visitors (see Plate 6).

Having introduced Gold Coast tourism, we will leave the subject as it will be explored more fully later. However, here is as good a place as any to list the city's tourist attractions (Box 2.2). We will include a few that no longer exist or that have been radically changed, to illustrate a little of the dynamics of tourism. Some of the iconic attractions listed are not within the present boundaries of the city, yet are more closely related to it than to anywhere else. Hinterland eco-tourism accommodation houses south-west of the defined city boundaries are cases in point. They are places where visitors to the Gold Coast would go. But two historic facts warrant noting.

In 1925, a road east of the old bush tracks from Brisbane to Southport was opened. Because it was close to the coast (Moreton Bay) it was known as the Coast Road, and was called that until a generation ago. The second matter of significance was the building of the Jubilee Bridge across the Nerang River at Southport. It was opened in 1925. These two pieces of public infrastructure were crucial to the growth of the Gold Coast villages, growth which accelerated after the Second World War, with the significant increase in private car ownership. Prior to the road infrastructure and the bridge, rail transport had to suffice. Go even farther back in history, before rail, and horse and buggy or coastal passenger boats took holiday-makers to and from Brisbane (see Fig. 2.2).

A noteworthy feature of the tourist attractions listed in Box 2.2 is that only four are 'green', meaning environmentally focused. In addition to that list, comprising mainly theme parks, there are special yearly events that bring select groupings of tourists to the

Fig. 2.2 Touring the Gold Coast at four horse-power. Source: Provided by Gold Coast City Council, Local Studies Library. Photographer unknown.

Box 2.2: The events and people who 'made' the Gold Coast

1925: Jim Cavill built the Surfers Paradise hotel in the village called Elston. The hotel burned down in 1933 and was rebuilt in 1936 with a very small zoo attached.

1926: O'Reilly's Rainforest Guesthouse in the rainforested hinterland was opened. Today it is a celebrated eco-tourism establishment with a tree-top walk. The O'Reilly family, pioneer eco-tourism operators, remain the owners.

1933: Binna Burra Lodge was opened as another hinterland accommodation house promoted to 'escape' city life and enjoy nature. Pioneer conservationists, Romeo Lahey and Arthur Groom (a *Courier Mail* journalist) were the founders. Binna Burra is local Aboriginal for 'where the (Antarctic) Beech trees grow'.

1933: Elston, where Jim Cavill built his hotel, was renamed Surfers Paradise.

1947: Alex Griffiths, a bee-keeper and flower grower at Currumbin, decided to feed the flocks of wild lorikeets to stop them eating his flower crops. This became the Currumbin Bird Sanctuary, renamed the Currumbin Wildlife Sanctuary in 1995.

1952: David Fleay brought his zoological skills to West Burleigh where he purchased land to establish a fauna reserve. He was the first person to successfully breed a platypus in captivity. His legacy lives on: the reserve was renamed the David Fleay Wildlife Park in 1997. It is now owned and operated by the Queensland National Parks and Wildlife Service. Its major visitor groups are schoolchildren.

1958: Keith Williams opened the Ski Gardens on the Nerang River. Williams was one of the first of the 'white shoe brigade'. His most recent development was the very controversial Port Hinchinbrook marina and residential area adjacent to Hinchinbrook Island and the Great Barrier Reef Marine Park. Keith Williams died in 2011 and his business, now in the hands of his son, is in serious financial trouble.

1965: The first Meter Maids, young bikini-clad women who fed money into parking meters on the streets of Surfers Paradise, were introduced. This was 'pure gold' (the colour of their bikinis) publicity for the emerging Gold Coast.

1967: Bruce Small, one-time bicycle manufacturer (of Malvern Star bikes), Gold Coast real estate developer and salesman, was elected Mayor of the city. He served on two occasions, 1967–73 and 1976–78. He was also elected to the Queensland parliament. There is a bronze statue of Bruce Small erected at the corner of Orchid and Elkhorn Avenues, Surfers Paradise. Those streets are named after common rainforest plants.

1971: Keith Williams' Ski Gardens was relocated to The Spit near Southport.

1972: The Ski Gardens became Sea World, a completely different type of tourist attraction, basically a water-based theme park with trained dolphins plus various activities and shows to interest young children.

1976: The Currumbin Wildlife Sanctuary was given to the Queensland National Trust after being offered to, and declined by, the Queensland Conservation Council.[6]

1981: The Dreamworld theme park was opened.

1984: Cade's County Water Park was opened. It was renamed 'Wet'n'Wild' in 1987.

1988: Sea World Nara resort was opened.

1988: Ripley's Believe It Or Not was opened.

1991: Warner Bros Movie World was opened.

2004: Paradise County was opened.

2006: WhiteWater World was opened at Dreamworld. The Australian Outback Spectacular was opened.

2009: The Rainforest Skywalk at Mount Tamborine was opened.

Gold Coast. There is a car race, Schoolies' Week (for secondary students who've just finished Year 12), music festivals (the Big Day Out and Summafieldayze), plus international surf carnivals. We will discuss some of these ever so briefly. While they are important in understanding the character of the Gold Coast, they play no significant role in our primary goal of tracing and understanding the environmental impact caused by building the city.

The car race is held within the confines of a few streets in the high-rise part of Surfers Paradise. The streets are closed for the weekend. The race commenced in 1991 as the Gold Coast Indy 300. Since then it has had two name changes to coincide with changes in focus. The event has not always been popular with the elected council. Past Mayor Ron Clarke (one of Australia's all-time great distance runners) was quite hostile to it. As with many special events in Australia and the Gold Coast in particular, government support has been provided over the years. This benefits local businesses during the event. Without taxpayer support the economic viability of many events would be questionable.

There is an annual horse sale. In January 1986, the first Magic Millions yearling sale was held at a race track owned by the Gold Coast Turf Club. The following year a race, the Magic Millions (a two-year old classic) was held. Other big prize-money races were to follow.

Schoolies' Week is actually two to three weeks in November. Graduating high school pupils, in significant numbers, converge to party on the Gold Coast, mainly in the area around Surfers Paradise. They come from Queensland, NSW and Victoria and a few from further afield. One week, one state. Over-indulgence for any longer would be hard to tolerate, even for the young who can manage to sleep all day after a night of partying. Major surfing events (board-riding not body-surfing) occur throughout the year, commencing with the Quiksilver and Roxy Pro in March at Snapper Rocks. The Gold Coast beaches are part of the World Tour of Surfing (see Fig. 2.3 and Box 2.3).

What do tourists do? Few go to the mountains, many to the beach

The number of tourists to the Gold Coast is impressive. Tourists come for the beach and the theme parks. Few 'discover' the ancient Gondwana Rainforests, the truly exceptional natural feature of the Gold Coast. The beaches are long, the surf can be fantastic and the water is warm for most of the year, but a few other places could be considered genuine competitors along those lines. There is no competitor for the ancient forests.

About one-sixth of the World Heritage Gondwana Rainforests are in Queensland, the remainder is in northern NSW. Of the 59 223 ha in Queensland, only a small percentage is in the city of the Gold Coast, with Springbrook the major location. Nearly all the planet's

Fig. 2.3 Locations and dates of surfing's World Tour, 2013.

Antarctic beech trees are found at Springbrook, Beechmont and Lamington National Park. Some are thousands of years old.

Other than the fantastic flora and fauna of these mountains, one small mosquito-like fly has captured the imagination of tourists. Not as a fly but in its larval form. Each year over 250 000 visitors travel to Natural Arch (Bridge) at the top of Numinbah Valley at night to see the bioluminescence (the ability to glow in the dark), of the critters commonly called glowworms.

Tourist data

We will close this introductory chapter by presenting a few statistics pertaining to tourism. They will help put into context the environmental impacts that have resulted from the day the Queensland colonial governor decided to holiday at Southport, about 130 years ago.

In counting the number of tourists, the convention is to use three mega-categories with several divisions within each. The overriding groupings are day-trippers (people who travel 40 km or more for the purpose of pleasure and return home that same day), domestic (citizens of the country in question) overnight visitors, and international visitors (who cease being tourists if they stay in the same country for more than 12 months).

Box 2.3: The six surfing sisters

Peter Drouyn, now known as Westerly Windina, christened the surfing 'points' from Burleigh south to the NSW border the 'six surfing sisters'.

They are:

Burleigh Point
Currumbin Alley
Kirra Point
Greenmount
Rainbow Bay
Snapper Rocks

Nicole Glennon wrote an application to have the southern Gold Coast beaches and their wave breaks recognised as a World Surfing Reserve (surfers' highest accolade for a constant wave break):

> *Thanks to consistent and perfect wave foundation and a clean unpolluted ocean, the southern Gold Coast has become the preferred destination for surfers from around the world. This has enabled an iconic surf culture to not only become mainstream, but to define a community and the greater city in which it resides ... The southern Gold Coast's prime surf conditions were recognised early. In 1915, Hawaiian Duke Kahanamoka arrived at Greenmont. No doubt Duke's influence rubbed off on all those who witnessed his feats ... (The Gold Coast) has become the spiritual home to Australian beach and surf culture.*

Duke's full name is Paoa Mokoe Hulikohola Kahanamoka. He is regarded as the father of modern surfing.

Source: McKinnon (2014).

At the time of writing the number of day-visitors to the Gold Coast, most of whom travelled from Brisbane, was 7 566 000.[7] The number of domestic overnight visitors was 3 651 000. This count is from March 2012 to March 2013. International visitors amounted to 764 000. To make an 'apples to apples' comparison we need to convert overnight visitors to per-night stays. The average number of nights for a domestic visitor to the Gold Coast is four. Hence, there were in the order of 14 600 000 visitor nights accounted for by domestic tourists. As the average length of stay for international tourists was 10 nights, their total number of nights was in the order of 7 600 000. Visitor nights in total amounted to just over 22 million. On a daily basis we would expect ~80 000 visitors to be on the Gold Coast. Add this number to the residential population and there are over 600 000 people on the Gold Coast every day. This would be a starting point if we were to attempt to estimate the human ecological footprint of the Gold Coast. What do these people consume? Where does it come from? What waste and pollution is created by this?

Combining the number of visitors to the Gold Coast with local residents, on an annual basis there are about 7 million who use the beaches.[8] This estimate is based on a count of nearly 20 000 people (tourists and local residents) being on the Gold Coast beaches daily. This is an interesting figure. The same numbers of people, 20 000, were camping along the beach between Big Burleigh and North Burleigh in 1936 (Ginis 2014). Today, the most popular beaches are Surfers Paradise (over 3000 beachgoers per day) and Burleigh Heads including North Burleigh (at about the same number). Between them these two beaches account for ~30 per cent of beach users. The major board-riding beaches are Rainbow Bay, followed by Burleigh (180 surfboard riders per day). We estimate that 1.7 million day-visitors use the beach, 3.6 million overnight domestic visitors (making about two beach trips per visitor) and 1.9 million international visitors go to the beach (with three beach visits on their holiday).

We have some data on visits to the theme parks. The combined number of visitors to the Warner Village theme parks (otherwise Village Roadshow Ltd) was 2.3 million in 2011.[9] Three of the theme parks listed in Box 2.3 are not included. It is clear from these data alone that the theme parks have, in recent years, become a basic attraction on the Gold Coast. This is a major difference between it and its nearby rival, the Sunshine Coast where, except for Australia Zoo (a superb nature-oriented attraction a considerable distance from the coast), there is nothing comparable in large-scale theme parks. In fact, there is no other Australian beach location that compares to the Gold Coast in terms of theme parks.

With these scant statistics we conclude our snapshot. Much more detail, including discussion of subject matter omitted in this chapter, is to be found in following chapters.

Notes

1. There is a creek in the Yatala/Beenleigh area named Halfway Creek.
2. Two brands of rum are produced in Queensland, one at Beenleigh and the other at Bundaberg. As we would expect, they're called Beenleigh rum and Bundaberg rum.
3. The number ranged from 40 to 50 dairy farms.
4. If the beaches stretching from the NSW border to Couran Cove on South Stradbroke Island are included, there are 57 km of beach, according to the Gold Coast City Council.
5. One of this book's editors, Tor Hundloe, stays in one of these old motels if the commute home to Brisbane from his office at Bond University is ruled out.
6. One of the editors, Tor Hundloe, was at the time President of the Council and after considerable thought and discussion by the executive of the Council the offer was declined.
7. Visitor data were sourced from Queensland Tourism and Events, *Regional Snapshot 2013*.
8. Marc Lebreton (undated).
9. No breakdown of adult and children numbers is available. Data were sourced from the *Gold Coast Business News*, 2012 annual edition.

References

Ginis L (2014) Camping: the classic Australian experience. *Australian Geographic*, 14 June.

McKinnon A (2014) Submission to the World Surfing Reserves Executive to have the beaches/wave breaks from Burleigh Heads to Snapper Rocks declared the Gold Coast World Surfing Reserve. 10 May 2014.

Chapter 3

The Gold Coast before Cook named Mount Warning

T. Hundloe

We could and should ask, where does the Gold Coast sit on a scale from 'good' to 'bad' in environmental terms? Sustainable or unsustainable? Is it progressing or regressing? It is far too early in the book to attempt to answer this. Maybe at the end of the book you will feel confident to make your own assessment. What we do in this chapter is to make obvious a small number of seemingly irreversible changes that have occurred since the first escaped convicts walked the Gold Coast beaches.

We know that indigenous Australians have lived on the Gold Coast for a very long time, possibly over 20 000 years. We take as given that James Cook was the first European to sail close to its beaches. He named various obvious landmarks. It was some years later that European explorers, such as John Oxley, and escaped convicts put their feet on the Gold Coast beaches.

From that time to the present, the dramatic increase in both residential population and tourist numbers has led to very significant changes in the physical environment of the Gold Coast. Most noticeable has been the construction of canal estates and the building of high-rise apartments on the foreshore. The success of tourism has radically transformed the beachfront environment at Surfers Paradise and, to a lesser extent, that at some other places with New York-style high-rise buildings. The tourism and residential construction on the foredunes, most mined in the 1940s and 1950s for rutile, zircon and other black sands, has led to a battle with nature and the need to harden the beachfront with rock walls and groynes. In the hinterland, rainforests were destroyed to permit dairy-farming and horticulture; today the demise of farming has resulted in farms becoming rural-residential blocks.

Go back before European settlement and we would discover a different Gold Coast. European intrusion saw the demise of red cedar in the rainforests and the gradual carving-out of farms in the forests and floodplains. On the latter, lining the river banks, were extensive mangrove forests. Most are now gone. If you wish to imagine the coastal sand dunes and the beaches as they would have been before they were mined then built on, visit the natural, ever-changing beaches on World Heritage-listed Fraser Island. 'Ever-changing' is the key to beaches and dunes moulded by longshore drift, currents, waves, wind and the work of the moon and tides. The occasional severe storm or more ferocious cyclone will be even more determined in sculpting the beach. If we wanted to, we could live with these natural occurrences at the Gold Coast, we do on Fraser Island and parts of the Sunshine Coast. That would require a vastly different attitude from the one we brought to the Gold. We decided we knew better than nature, and now pay the cost.

In the long sweep of geological time, what we have done to the forests, the floodplains and the foredunes is not irreversible. If humans were to pack up, leave and allow nature to reclaim these environments, reversibility would be possible. Much time would have to elapse; a few years for the beaches to return to natural conditions, longer for the mangroves to re-establish forests, hundreds of years for the red cedars to dominate the rainforest canopy. Readers might know the book by Alan Weisman, *The World Without Us*, where he engages in a thought experiment, imagining what the planet would be like if people vanished. This is the type of thinking involved in dreaming up the pre-European Gold Coast.

Indigenous cultural losses

On the topic of lost indigenous culture, we are truly in the sphere of irreversible losses. Yet these losses are the least obvious because there is no Gold Coast equivalent to Fraser Island where it is possible to view massive middens and be able to assert this is 'what it was like before the Europeans came'.

We are dealing with the loss of a very old culture, that of the local Aborigines. The first Australians, as we know, had no written language. They left only orally conveyed stories of the past, and a few places of material and spiritual culture. Construction of residences and other buildings, plus the mining of mineral sands, destroyed much of the indigenous material culture. A little remains, but you need to know where to look. There is one reminder of a past culture known to those who grew up on the Gold Coast, but that few newcomers or visitors would know about – the kink in the coastal highway north of Burleigh Heads is there because it protects a 'bora', a small circular indentation in land where Aborigines performed initiation ceremonies (see Fig. 3.1).

Beginning late in the 19th century, the local Aboriginal people gradually lost their lifestyles, their favourite waterholes and the rainforest habitat that was home to wild game, fruits and nuts. In Numinbah Valley, between Springbrook and Beechmont, the Nerang River flows north-east towards Surfers Paradise and the Broadwater at Southport. In its southern upland reaches, the river is home to fresh-water mullet, eels and platypus and is the feeding place of shags, ducks and kingfishers and a variety of other less common birds. Snakes swim its waters. Wallabies drink from its banks. It would have been a bountiful and pleasant resting place for the local people, providing a range of nourishing foods.

Within three generations of the European settlement of the penal colony of Brisbane, which occurred in 1824, timber-getters, land-clearing farmers and pioneering tourists had overwhelmed the local indigenous people. As with all such acts of colonisation, there were tragedies but some good. There were murders and there was intermarriage, there were farm jobs and there was complete dispossession. This is a major story deserving a book of its own. We can't pursue it here. However, we ask readers to ponder the meaning of sustainability, the paradigm of the 21st century, in situations of dramatic social and cultural change. This, of course, is the Australian story as experienced by those who first came to this continent, some as early as 50 000–60 000 years ago.

Environmental losses

We can explore in considerable detail, because we know much more on this topic, the case of lost physical environments as Europeans came to the Gold Coast in search of resources

Fig. 3.1 204 Jebbribillum Bora, Burleigh Heads. Photograph by Bridgette McDougall.

they valued. Fortunately, not all environments were totally lost; we deal with this in following chapters. Steep-country rainforests survived. The 'green beyond the gold' of the Gold Coast beaches is the magnificent subtropical rainforests in the hinterland.

The beaches were not the original drawcard for Europeans. The first free settlers (pardoned convicts and immigrants) were too concerned with sustenance or, if wealthy, becoming more so by acquiring land for farming, to think of the Gold Coast beaches as would a British aristocrat who sought sun and sea for health-giving purposes. It was not until late in the 19th century that the idea took hold that these magnificent beaches might have the same rejuvenating qualities as the sunny 'spa' villages of coastal Europe.

As we have already established, it was the 'green', in particular the 'red gold' (red cedar), which brought the first Europeans to the Gold Coast.[1] In asserting that they were the first Europeans, we exclude the few escaped convicts who traversed the beaches in their search for fellow British. Convicts escaped from most penal colonies. Those who escaped from Brisbane tended to head south. It must have been extremely lonely in this enormous country to have escaped from penal servitude but not know where to go to remain free yet somehow connect with fellow humans. Heading south towards Sydney was the decision most would make. Humans are extremely social animals and a life in the great Australian wilderness was unlikely to appeal to a poor soul wrenched from crowded London or Dublin.

Turning our attention to the natural environment, wander in the Gold Coast hinterland today as a bush-walker or scrub-scrambler and you are unlikely to see many red cedar trees. To see an old giant of this species would be a matter of extreme good luck. Timber-getters were unlikely to miss anything of size, and therefore of considerable monetary value. Where to find red cedar today? If we closely inspect the furniture in the few remaining old farmhouses in the Gold Coast hinterland, we are likely to discover much of it was crafted from cedar and other highly prized rainforest timbers such as black bean and silky oak. This farmhouse furniture would be very valuable if cleaned, polished and put on the market.

The timber-getters came in the middle of the 19th century. The major Gold Coast river systems (the Nerang River, Tallebudgera and Currumbin Creeks) and the Tweed River over the border in New South Wales provided a route to the rainforested mountains of the McPherson Range. Follow the rivers into the low hills, past the foothills to the high mountains and we reach the source of the rivers in one of the wettest parts of Queensland. This is what the timber-getters did. And they found what they came for. The two large rivers, the Nerang and the Tweed, were much more convenient than bullock-snigging tracks for the transport of large logs to coastal 'ports'. I use inverted commas to ensure that coastal harbours are not visualised. A considerable distance from the Nerang River's outlet to the Pacific Ocean was the 'port' of Nerang, now a suburb of the Gold Coast. Visit Nerang today and visualise it as a port. In a later chapter we mention a famous boat that used Nerang as a port.

The cedar trees were found in the high mountains (Springbrook, Beechmont and other mountains in the McPherson Range). Tough, wiry mountain men with nothing more than axes felled magnificent giant trees (see Fig. 3.2). The logs snigged by bullock teams from within the dense rainforest were floated downstream to Nerang. Many did not complete the journey, getting caught in overhanging riparian vegetation or emergent creek boulders. From Nerang the timber would go to Brisbane by boat (through the calm waters of Moreton Bay); that which was not used in the developing town of Brisbane was transported to the much larger town of Sydney or shipped to distant London. The golden beaches of the Gold Coast were yet to catch the eye. Timber-getters were not tourists.

The beach

The sand that has formed, and will continue to form at its own glacial pace, the Gold Coast beaches is the result of eons of erosion of the mountains of the Great Dividing Range, where the northern New South Wales rivers have their origins. The current moves the sand north. Over a time-span beyond human comprehension, sand has built up on the southern side of the few craggy headlands we have given highly descriptive names to; for example, Burly Heads (now with a more 'attractive' spelling). Other descriptive names given to craggy headlands include Nobby, Point Danger, Point Lookout on North Stradbroke Island and Indian Head on Fraser Island.

Sand movement is not a linear process and, as explained earlier, the Gold Coast beaches are subject to various natural forces such as the daily tides, high spring tides, tidal surges, winds, rainfall events (which influence water flows in the creeks that traverse the beaches) and significant but irregular occurrences such as cyclones. Many a visitor ignorant of beach dynamics has, when driving on a southern Queensland beach, been surprised to find that the beach has changed shape dramatically since the last visit (which could have been the day before). If they're unfortunate, they can be brought to grief by a beach creek changing course and depth overnight.

Fig. 3.2 Timber-getters and their admiring families on the Numinbah Plateau (now Springbrook). Provided by Gold Coast City Council, Local Studies Library. Photograph by A.H. Burbank.

Once, we as beachgoers knew about beach dynamics. This was a time, recent enough for all but the very young to remember, when camping was popular and so were boogie-boards. Tent sites were well chosen, near the beach but over the ridge of the foredune to escape the wind, near a creek for fresh water and trees from which to hang the clothes line. Each morning the walk to the surf to clean the frying pan would show if, or how, the beach had changed shape overnight. Visitors worked with nature and loved it.

Numerous Gold Coast developers of high-rise apartments, plus residential home-owners, realised too late that building on the foredunes was not a wise move. Magnificent ocean views and backyard-to-beach access came with a price beyond that recorded in the sales price. Considerable public and private money has been spent in building rock walls (artificial barriers) in an attempt (often unsuccessful) to control the movement of sand and protect these buildings from collapsing into the sea. This issue is dealt with in considerable detail in Chapter 6.

This brings us to a consideration of the historic value of the Gold Coast's built environment, some of which has been lost forever. Not only was loss of the natural environment a foregone conclusion, but the destruction of once-famous landmarks was an inevitable consequence of 'development'. We simply note lost icons: the theatre on Southport Pier, the Southport Pavilion, the Pink Poodle Motel, the Birdwatchers Bar, Magic Mountain, the Playroom and the Chevron Hotel. We could add Jack Evan's pool at Rainbow Bay, the pool at Burleigh Heads, the Burleigh Heads movie theatre, the original 'Koalas cross here' sign on the highway at Burleigh Head National Park and the Miami Ice Works.

In summary

A very old culture has been lost, although attempts are being made to revive aspects of it, such as the local language. We are reminded daily of that language by place names: Tallebudgera, Currumbin, Numinbah, Mudgeeraba and many more. A variety of ancient trees, including red cedar, have been reduced to a lucky few that escaped the timber-getters. Considerable amounts of ancient rainforest have gone, with patches struggling to reclaim once-farmed areas.

The concept of sustainability came too late for old peoples, old forests and old human constructs. It is as if there is in the DNA of 'development' the need to destroy once healthy and valued aspects of the 'old'.

Note

1. It was many decades before the golden sands attracted the nearby residents of Brisbane. Today those sands are an internationally recognised drawcard. The Gold Coast ranks in recognition with Nice, Santorini, Florida and Hawaii. Yet too few know the story of its hinterland, much of which is now a UNESCO World Heritage-listed site, part of the Gondwana Rainforests. So old are these forests that the scientific evidence indicates they existed when Australia was joined to South Africa, South America and the Asian subcontinent. People practised in piecing together jigsaws would have little difficulty in making the fit.

Chapter 4

A brief history of discovery, settlement and development

T. Hundloe and C. Page

Once there were koalas

If we can rely on anecdotal data, the answers to what is truly Australian will start with mention of the koala, go to kangaroos and then include the rest of Australia's peculiar (to foreigners) fauna. The only exception might be that if we asked a male from the Asian subcontinent (India, Pakistan, Sri Lanka and Bangladesh) what he identified Australia with, he might answer 'Cricket'. Putting that aside, the Gold Coast is very likely to be in the mix of Australian icons. To capture the essence of the Gold Coast, we need to talk about its history in more detail.

Recapping a little history[1]

From the day that Brisbane (Moreton Bay, as the penal settlement was called) was chosen as the site for a northern convict settlement in 1824 it was inevitable that the Gold Coast's natural resources would play a significant role in the future of the nation.

Location matters, and not only to real estate agents

Today the Gold Coast is about one hour from Brisbane by motor vehicle. In 1824 and for many years after there was no road or designated track connecting Brisbane to the Gold Coast. There was, however, a 'freeway' provided by nature – the sheltered waters of southern Moreton Bay. The large sand islands, North and South Stradbroke (then joined as one island), protected the bay waters from the wind and waves of the Pacific Ocean. This sheltered waterway was the route for the first commercial trade between the Gold Coast and Brisbane.

When John Oxley put ashore at Mermaid Beach on the Gold Coast in 1823 he was, as far as the history books relate, the first European to walk on Gold Coast ground. Cook had sailed past many years earlier and given various prominent places, for example Point Danger and Mount Warning, appropriate names to guide future sailors.

The first Europeans to gain an appreciation of the area south of Moreton Bay were escaped convicts, on the run from the law. They scurried south through bush, scrub and, once on the coastal strip, along beaches. In fact, no sooner had the penal colony in Brisbane been established than escapees passed south through the Gold Coast. That was as early as 1824. So serious was the problem of escaped convicts that the authorities, in an attempt to recapture prisoners, established a military post at Point Danger in 1828. This could be considered the first European 'settlement' on the Gold Coast.

Not long after that the local rivers including the big one, the Nerang, were discovered. The Nerang was key to the early exploitation of one of the Gold Coast's most valuable resources – timber, needed for construction in the rapidly growing colony and much prized back in Britain. There was arable floodplain land on the lower parts of the Nerang River where a variety of farmed products were tried, some successfully and others not.

A century and half later, the Nerang River and its vast floodplain provided the natural infrastructure that real estate developers could exploit by digging the unique canal estates that are a central feature of the Gold Coast (see Fig. 4.1). Visitors who gaze at the rolling waves of the Pacific Ocean rather than westwards at the Nerang River would not realise that there are more human-made canals on the Gold Coast than there are in Venice. Venice is a marvel of engineering. The Gold Coast canal estates required far less imagination, some luck (in that the human-made canals were not seriously flooded) and a complete lack of understanding of the role and value of mangrove ecosystems. The major flood in 1974 put canal-building on hold for a year as research into flooding potential was undertaken. That aside, the canals provide a much more serene residential environment than what was to become the high-rise glitter of Surfers Paradise. Surfers Paradise was to become the drawcard for the less-adventurous tourist and high-rise accommodation was built for them. These folk would not consider camping which required finding a torch-lit way to a

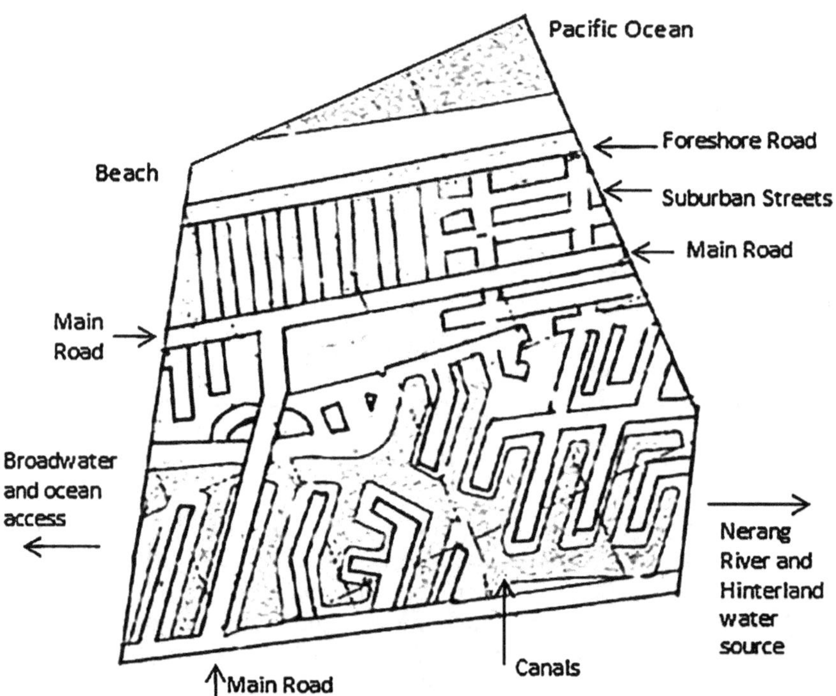

Fig. 4.1 A simplified depiction of a Gold Coast canal estate. Note the varied shapes of the blocks.

public toilet and washing the frying pan in the surf. The latter is still the norm for campers on Fraser Island.

The canals, when first dug, were marine deserts but a range of fish and crabs have now colonised them. The adaptability and resilience of nature makes predictions of sustainability (or unsustainability) a difficult scientific exercise. Residents can fish from their jetty or attach crab pots to the structure and, with luck and at minimal cost, enjoy the freshest seafood. However, residents do not swim in the canals as bull sharks capable of killing adults have taken up residence, due to the abundant prey.

The canals are, in the main, for residents. The tourists in high-rise apartments overlooking the vast Pacific Ocean can only wonder what fish swim in its waters. A seafood meal has to be purchased in one of myriad restaurants that sit cheek-by-jowl below the high-rises. Residents in the canal estates can ascertain the species of fish in their front/back yards according to their catches.

Red gold

The exploitation of rainforests opened up the Gold Coast hinterland. The timber (which included other rainforest species, not just red cedar) was exploited throughout the subtropical rainforests that range from Sydney north to Brisbane and beyond. The taking of these large trees pockmarked the magnificent rainforests. Now that many decades have passed and other tree species, as well as a few cedars, have filled the niches and partly healed the scars in the scrub caused by the crash of giant trees, the original destruction is not noticeable except to the trained botanical eye.

Bullock teams snigged the felled trees from the forests to local rivers which flowed out of the rainforests to the Pacific coast. The Nerang River was nature's free transport route from the local rainforests. The timber was floated to the wharf at Nerang town. From there, the logs were loaded on boats and taken via Moreton Bay to Brisbane. Boats were able to travel as far upstream as Nerang. In the latter part of the 19th century, Southport was called Nerang River Heads and was yet to play its catalytic role in drawing a different type of person to the Gold Coast, the tourist.

In 1839, Robert Dixon and two other surveyors were sent to Moreton Bay to prepare for the establishment of free-settler land ownership. Dixon was the first person to sketch the Gold Coast and its hinterland. He recorded coming across a commercial cedar-getting party on the Tweed. Edward (Neddy) Harper, who according to Longhurst was the European pioneer of the Gold Coast, arrived in 1842 in this area, immediately south of the Gold Coast, and established cedar-getting teams. It was not long before the yet-to-be Queensland border was crossed and timber was being felled in the Numinbah, Beechmont and Springbrook rainforests. From then on cedar was worked until no large valuable trees were left in the magnificent rainforests.[2]

As the cedar-getting was selective logging done by hand (axes and cross-cut saws) there was limited damage to the rainforest ecology. The forests that remained untouched except for cedar-getting were deemed of such quality that they are today part of the World Heritage-listed Gondwana Rainforests, some of which is included in the city of the Gold Coast.

As tends to be the case worldwide, after the timber-getters came the farmers. In the Gold Coast hinterland, the logging tracks allowed horse and cart travel. Farmers were able to shift their produce to market along timber tracks, some of which became roads in due course. This is still the case throughout the developing world and is the reason why selective-logging is viewed as the 'thin edge of the wedge' in destroying forests.

The Gold Coast was part of the global economy by 1865

The Queensland population was about 2000 in 1850 when timber-getters were the only Europeans active on the Gold Coast; by the time the new colony was declared in 1859 the population was 23 520. This was a dramatic increase. Farming was spreading rapidly in proximity to Brisbane-town. Even more dramatic, but distant, events made for an interesting initiative on the Gold Coast.

In 1861 the American Civil War broke out, with major consequences in the UK and minor ones on the Gold Coast. It heralded the start of the Australian cotton-growing industry. The Australian cotton industry began with the clearing of lowland melaleuca and mangrove forests around present-day Surfers Paradise. Cotton required plantation-size blocks, not the small paddocks that pioneering Australian farming families cultivated for garden crops.

The American Civil War put an end to UK importation of American cotton as the cotton-growing South soon found its ports barricaded by the naval forces of the North. No longer could UK mills in Oldham, Bolton and other towns obtain cotton that had been grown by slave labour. Desperate UK mill owners, who employed nearly half a million workers, looked elsewhere for tropical lands suitable for cotton production. India, a British colony, featured. Egypt was another candidate. However, the cotton grown in those countries proved not to be a substitute for the American variety, hence the experiment on the Gold Coast. What was tried on its floodplains was tiny in scale and by the end of the American Civil War was recognised as a failure. And once the war was over, there was no need to look outside the US for cotton. Put into modern-day perspective, the extent of cotton production in Australia in the 1860s was small enough that it would take only 10 hours for the entire crop to be ginned in a 21st-century gin, such as the one at Cecil Plains on the Darling Down. Today, the cotton industry in Australia is big enough that this gin has to work 24 hours a day for months at a time – and there are numerous other gins in Australia.

Sugarcane, an industry stretching to the present, replaced cotton; however, it grew better further north (in the Jacobs Well area) and south (in the Tweed area), rather than around the Nerang floodplains where cotton had been planted. The major sugarcane plantations were to develop in the tropics, Mackay to Mossman. Until the invention of mechanical harvesters, sugarcane harvesting was hard dirty work done by hand. The subtropical and tropical climates made this very unpleasant work for Europeans not accustomed to the sun and heat.

Putting aside cotton and cane growing, farming for the domestic market commenced in the Gold Coast before the start of the American Civil War. Dairy farming grew along with colonial settlements, wherever they were. Milk and butter were daily foods. Beef and mutton were not far behind. As squatters moved ever northward from Sydney, settling one river basin and then the next, it was inevitable that the Gold Coast area, particularly the less-hilly plains, would be turned into farms. Where there was grassland or less densely wooded eucalypt forest, establishing a farm was not as difficult as in the rainforest country that covered the Gold Coast mountains. Wherever farmers went, trees beyond the size of saplings were ringbarked, left to slowly die from lack of sap, their blood. Dead and on the ground the trees were hauled to be heaped and burned. Small amounts of dried timber would be saved for use in the kitchen stove.

The floodplains east of Nerang, now the Carrara area, were an obvious choice for experimental cotton farms. The original ecosystem was similar to the small paches of remnant bushland dotted around the Nerang River floodplains. The vast majority of this land became dairy farms in the years following the demise of cotton growing. As dairy country it retained a semblance of near-natural land, particularly where significant clumps of trees were saved for animal shade and along the river banks, where riparian vegetation often remained.

The farmers of the 19th century knew virtually nothing about the value of the ecosystems that they changed radically. We expect that even if they had some understanding of the role of nature in providing ecosystem goods and services, they would have been comforted by the knowledge that not far away there were many more ecosystems like the one they were destroying. Australia was (and remains) a very big country with very few people seeking sustenance from it. This has had, and continues to have, a pro-development influence on its citizens.

When recent generations again began dramatically altering the Nerang coastal plains, there were not many ecosystems similar to the one they focused on. Population growth has changed Australia. We live in large cities and virtually all fertile land in close proximity is farmed. The extensive farming on the rain-fed soils of the eastern coastal plains has resulted in these becoming scarce. All the pristine areas, if not completely lost, have felt the force of 'development'. Their economic value has increased due to scarcity; however, their ecosystem goods and services value is yet to be fully recognised.

Today the Nerang River floodplain is covered with residential housing, golf courses and the road infrastructure that goes hand-in-hand with urbanisation. A small amount of farmland remains. The area is home to a major AFL stadium, a sign that the Gold Coast is truly part of Australian football culture.

From the late 19th century, grazing and dairy farming took command of the wide Nerang floodplain. Until the idea of canal estates was acted on in the 1950s and 1960s, it remained farming country. In 1956 approval was given for the first canal estate, Florida Gardens. From then on virtually anything could be done to this alluvial floodplain. Keith Williams, a Gold Coast entrepreneur, turned a large area of farmland into a race track for 'hotrods'; it was eventually bought by one of the many developers of residential land and golf courses.

What had been good-quality farming land, reaching virtually to the Pacific Ocean with only the meandering Nerang River dividing agriculture from the coastal villages such as Surfers Paradise, became housing land. The best farming land in close proximity to cities is destined to be lost to urbanisation, anywhere in the world. The economics are flawed.

On the Gold Coast the process of change in land use was initially gradual, then as demand grew from the promotional efforts of the real estate brigade, land was quickly cleared (as if the money would run out tomorrow), dug up and recontoured. The Nerang River was diverted into finger-like contorted (in some instances) backwater tributaries – our canals. But this is getting well ahead of our story.

On the coast, next to the Pacific Ocean beaches, the small townships of Surfers Paradise, Burleigh Heads and Coolangatta and the 'big town' of Southport had consolidated as self-contained villages by the end of the Second World War. In these urban proto-holiday towns cooking was done on wood-fired stoves, water came from rainwater tanks, refrigeration was supplied by kerosene-powered refrigerators, supplemented when visitors from Brisbane arrived at Christmas by ice from local iceworks. An iceworks remained at Miami/North Burleigh until it was destroyed in late 2013 (see Plate 7). Away from the canal estates the typical conversion of land from farms was into so-called integrated resorts, where there was the mandatory golf course, a resort (accommodation and dining) and residential housing on the periphery.

Once again, we have taken the story to the present era and must return to the latter part of the 19th century. Farming was not going to make the Gold Coast Australia's premier tourist resort. That would have its own fashionable beginning.

High society comes to Southport: tourists follow

Our journey, moving on from the time of the timber-getters and the early farmers, should start with the catalytic role of the supreme person of the colonial aristocracy, the Governor of the colony of Queensland. In 1885, Governor Sir Anthony Musgrave decided that his summer residence would be at what is now Southport rather than in the cool-climate mountain range of Toowoomba. His residence was grand in comparison to the dwellings of most settlers. Farm families lived in what the Americans would call log cabins. Only the more affluent businesspeople, publicans, shopkeepers and professionals such as doctors lived in dwellings we would recognise today.

The Governor's summer residence was a sign to the moneyed class and to status-seekers that Southport was where one should holiday, or at least visit. In 1882, a little before the Governor's house was built, Goy-te-lea school had opened. It later became St Hilda's School, the most fashionable girls' school on the Gold Coast, if not Queensland. It is not surprising that in the era we are discussing 'coming out' balls were held at the Southport School of Arts. This part of the Gold Coast was 'high society' but it lost that status on the journey to becoming a major tourism destination, with the attendant baggage. Southport was different in its heyday as a prestigious holiday destination. The other original villages (Burleigh Heads and Coolangatta) catered for simpler, less pretentious tastes.

In the late 19th century there were many other catalysts for the changes that were coming, some more important, as time went on. Technological advances in transport played a crucial role, as they have done throughout human history. With relatively fast and comfortable transport, by both rail and car, the Gold Coast became accessible to many more than the rich or adventurous Brisbane holiday-makers. It became a seriously popular destination, the first place considered by Brisbane-ites when the annual holiday season arrived.

As transport continued to improve during the 20th century so did the number of day-trippers increase. After the Second World War, with the development of the Australian domestic airline industry, wealthy southerners could holiday on the Gold Coast without spending days travelling. A few came by flying boat, which landed in the Broadwater.

By the 1980s, the Japanese had discovered that the Gold Coast was in the same time zone as Japan and that it offered numerous photo opportunities in unfamiliar environments: beaches, rainforests, glowworms, theme parks for cuddling koalas, other parks where multi-plumed parrots would land on your head. Japanese tourists could finish work on a Friday afternoon and be in a hotel at Surfers Paradise next morning for an early breakfast or a pre-arranged tour. Time was not to be lost.

Other exogenous factors, as economists say in referring to events outside the control or influence of the subject, played significant roles in changing the Gold Coast. These we will weave into the story as we go back in time and follow events through to the present.

Population growth and the spread of farming

In 1859, the new colony of Queensland was created by excising it from the colony of New South Wales. Rapid population growth had started before then as a consequence of immigration; transport of convicts had ceased in 1839. The 1861 census recorded 32 838 people in Queensland, excluding an unknown number of indigenous inhabitants. By then, a few pastoral leases had been granted, often over significant areas. Demand for food increased in proportion to population growth, as did the need for building materials, clothing and all sorts of farm, industrial and household machines and tools. The domestic market for food was provided by an increasing number of small-scale local farmers and, as already discussed, the Gold Coast floodplains and cleared rainforest hills developed into farming communities. The variety of products was considerable and people were generally healthy and hard-working. Dairy farms provided milk, cream and butter as well as meat from bull calves. Pigs and poultry were common supplementary products from the dairies. All sorts of vegetables and fruits were grown, mainly for the subsistence of the farming families. Paddocks of potatoes and corn provided food for home consumption and sale. Banana plantations were cut into the forested mountain sides.

Burleigh Heads: the first tourist attraction

In 1871 (four years before Southport was surveyed and many years before the Queensland Governor built his summer residence at Southport), the Burleigh area was declared a town reserve, and in 1872, 65 town allotments were put up for auction. The sales blurb stated that Burleigh Heads was to become a 'fashionable watering place'. 'Watering place' suggests a colonial-style Australian hotel, a large rooming-house above a very large ground-floor bar. Notwithstanding urging by the early developers, the first hotel was built at Burleigh Heads only in 1883.

'Watering place' alluded to more than a building in which to drink, dine and recline. It was a 'sanatorium', according to the advertisements. The idea of Burleigh as a sanatorium which the wealthy residents of Brisbane-town could visit for rest and invigoration was borrowed from the promotion of the sunny parts of France, Spain and Italy (as ideal settings for health-restoring vacations for the weather-weary British). It worked in Europe. In Australia, a healthy outdoors glow, respite from respiratory illness and simple relaxation was at everyone's doorstep, if a little difficult to access via bush roads riding in Cobb & Co. coaches. The importance of location – 'at your doorstep' – underpinned the growth of the Gold Coast tourism from the late 19th century until international tourists started to arrive in numbers in the 1970s.

Referring to Burleigh, a vision was reported in the tourism literature of the time:

> *I can see ... the white villas rising tier upon tier on the surrounding hill slopes ... the bronzed visitor drinking in the sea breezes, and forgetting fever and ague.*

The white villas would eventually be built on the hill slopes, but not for nearly 100 years.

As noted, venturing to the Coast for a holiday was an adventure in its own right until the railway line between Brisbane and Nerang, and a few years later to Coolangatta (and the Tweed), was opened. The latter was achieved in 1903. Prior to that, horse and buggy, Cobb & Co. coach, or boat travel through the southern Moreton Bay island passages were the means of getting to Southport. When a bridge was built at what is now Cavill Avenue (then Myer's crossing) it became possible to take a wheeled horse-drawn vehicle along the beach all the way to Coolangatta. Skill in judging the tides at the craggy outcrops, such as Nobby Beach, and the entrances of the Tallebudgera and Currumbin Creeks was essential.

Burleigh was closer to Brisbane than the creeks; the less adventurous could stop there. This gave Burleigh an advantage before the opening of the rail line to West Burleigh (a village in its own right), some distance along sand tracks to the Burleigh Heads beach. Burleigh then lagged behind Southport and Coolangatta, due to the rail route.

A modern history

We now move on to the more modern history of the Gold Coast. Some books start their discourse earlier than 1925, the year we have chosen, and for good reason – much detail is missed by overlooking the late years of the 19th century and the first two-and-half decades of the 20th, but space does not allow for that here.

In the largest of the valleys, Numinbah Valley, there is a fascinating history of farming pioneers. The iconic Australian travel book company, Lonely Planet, describes Numinbah Valley as the prettiest in south-east Queensland. It is best viewed from Rosin's Lookout on Beechmont Road.[3] The farming pioneers deserve their own book.

In 1925, Jim Cavill, whom we might label a 'pioneer developer', built the Surfers Paradise Hotel in the village then known as Elston. With the support of local residents, he got the village's name changed to Surfers Paradise in 1933. Ironically, the beach at Surfers Paradise, although seemingly endless as it joins with Broadbeach in the south and Main Beach in the north, was not then and is not now a 'paradise' for surfers (either bodysurfers or board surfers). Burleigh Heads and Rainbow Bay were, and are, considered the picks of the beaches.

The Second World War broke out in 1939 but it was not until after the Japanese bombing of Pearl Harbour in 1941 that the US entered the war. Soon after, US servicemen began visiting the Gold Coast on R&R leave. Some also trained in the Canungra rainforest in the Gold Coast hinterland as it was a military training ground for servicemen who were to be sent to tropical jungle battlefields in New Guinea, the Solomon Islands, the Philippines, Indonesia and Malaysia. Their dense rainforests had much in common with those of the Gold Coast.

The cultural values and attitudes of the Americans had a noticeable, if not immediate, impact on local beach customs and the recreational culture. The most obvious impact eventuated after the end of the war. The local real estate developers and agents had been quick to borrow from the US beach scene. Some had visited the US and came back with visions of Florida and California. Others may have spent too much time watching Hollywood movies.

Should we blame the US servicemen for the naming of suburbs, streets and motels after US locations? Miami! Florida! El Dorado! Three examples which contrast with the English names: Southport! Burleigh! Ashmore! And with Aboriginal names: Tallebudgera! Mudgeeraba! Currumbin! The answer is 'No'. It was an Australian idea to adopt those names.

Tent cities

Before getting too far into the recent history, we must recognise a particular feature of the Gold Coast holiday as undertaken by those of modest means and with a preference for outdoor and beach activities. As early as the beginning of the 20th century, camping in tents was the preference of the average citizen – not a 'blue blood', as the Queensland status-seekers were inclined to assert of their heritage. The average citizen was not rich and could experience considerable fun and pleasure in the summer tent cities.

While the moneyed and/or social elite wanted to be seen at Southport, following the Governor's lead, adventurous and less wealthy holiday-makers went to Burleigh Heads or Coolangatta. With camping there was no need to destroy the coastal vegetation, although some was cut for firewood when dead trees were not available. Tent camping has remained basically unchanged for those who prefer their holidays in natural settings. Today, Fraser Island is the preferred south-east Queensland location.

The long Christmas school holiday period was the peak time for camping. Australian school-age children enjoy a six-week break from school from mid-December to the end of January. Families who were wealthier or less adventurous could find lodgings in the few elaborate guesthouses built in the early years of the 20th century at Coolangatta. They became fashionable for young holiday-makers in the 1960s and 1970s.

Until the 1960s, tent cities continued to dominate the near-beach landscape, particularly over the six-week summer school holiday. However, times were changing. The more affluent sought motel-style accommodation. As a consequence, from the 1950s motels,[4] mainly brick, single-storey one-bedroom, appeared as a built environment verge along much of the Gold Coast Highway, which was then the only road. It was a long time before the inland freeway (the M1) was constructed to bypass the increasingly clogged coastal road, particularly as it meandered through the centre of Surfers Paradise and Burleigh Heads.

Still in the immediate post-war era, people with a little spare disposable income purchased housing blocks on either side of the highway, where vast areas of coastal forest and swamp had been cleared. Fibro shacks, as they were called (a realistic description), were built as holiday homes. These tended to be basic, with two bedrooms (one for parents and one for children and their friends) and a living room–kitchen. Most living was done outside, playing cricket on the lawn or on the beach. There was no television in Australia until the Melbourne Olympic Games of 1956.

The creation of waterscapes

The 1950s saw the first canal estates dug out of the lower Nerang River floodplains. Artificial islands were created. The availability of land on the foreshore with direct views over the Pacific Ocean was limited: as more and more residential and tourism development occurred and the cost of beachfront land increased significantly, real estate developers came up with another avenue to make profits from those who valued waterscapes – engineered canals. These were a South Seas Venice without any need to build the foundations on which the buildings would sit. Cut the land into slices, and then carve fingers into them. Ignore the fact that the land was barely above sea level and subject to regular flooding from the Nerang River. The developers had limited ideas (some would say, intelligence) in naming and building them. The first were called Paradise Island, Chevron Island and the Isle of Capri. Some canal estates flooded, as the wise old-timers predicted, in the heavy rains of 1974. The flooding of McIntosh Island, then farmland, in 1954 should have been a warning. On 19 February 1954 a tropical cyclone crossed the coast at Coolangatta. Cars were washed off the road at Kirra. Fifty families were evacuated from the Broadwater and 22 residents of McIntosh Island were stranded for eight hours before being rescued. In the hinterland, Springbrook received approximately half of its annual rainfall in 24 hours.

Purchase land on the banks of a man-made canal, build a house and you had a waterview without searching for an elusive and expensive block of land on a flattened sand dune with direct views onto the vast Pacific Ocean. When the canals were created, they were marine deserts. The flora and fauna, on which fish, crustaceans and molluscs depend, had been bulldozed away. Bare sand, and rocks where hardened banks were required, enticed no plant or animal, at least until years had passed. Originally, there was considerable uncertainty about the possibility of life ever returning to the new waterways.

The canals linked into the Nerang River and the river had a considerable tidal flux, as well as being fed by rains from the rainforested mountains. These two natural features provided, in the form of detritus and deposited vegetable matter, food and habitat for marine life to colonise the canals. Not all was lost. We discuss this in Chapter 10.

After the canal estates, golf courses were built on the remaining farmland. Today there are 30 golf courses on the Gold Coast. The fact that Japan became a major country of origin for tourists goes a long way to explaining this – tee fees were much cheaper on the Gold Coast than in Japan. There is anecdotal evidence that Japanese businessmen found it cheaper to fly to the Gold Coast for a few weekends of golf then to pay course fees in Japan.

The concept of an integrated land conversion project became popular. One component of the package was residential real estate, argued to be the profitable part of the business. The campus of Bond University, which at the time of writing is celebrating its 25th birthday, was intended as a drawcard for adjoining residential land sales. The university succeeded, but the original real estate development failed.

Resorts and golf courses (and universities) were necessary inducements for real estate sales but not very profitable in their own right. Considerable foreign money flowed into these projects. Until the late 1980s, a foreign developer needed an Australian partner with a half-share in the business. Geoff Burchill (2005) said that many of the Australian partners were stooges, not genuine partners. The policy was revised when Paul Keating was Treasurer. Another impediment faced the land speculators who had a keen eye not only for Japanese money but for money from Hong Kong, Malaysia and Singapore (and later Russia). People from these countries wanted to own residential properties on the Gold Coast, but existing housing stock was not allowed to be sold to foreigners. The concept of residential properties as a component of an integrated resort development was used as the way around this prohibition. A foreigner bought a part of a resort and ended up with the sought-after residential property. There is another book to be written on this topic. We mention it here to suggest the flavour of land deals, speculation and 'beating the system'.

Dredging of canals notwithstanding, the Gold Coast which we know today was not conceptualised or begun until the first high-rise tourist resort was constructed. It was Lennons Broadbeach, built in 1956 and reaching a fantastic six storeys (see Plate 8). It sat in a bare sand environment with a few planted palms, altogether a curiosity for locals. The Brisbane Town Hall of three storeys was the tallest building (in Brisbane) until Lennons Broadbeach was built. There are those who assert that a building known as 'Kinkabool' was the Gold Coast's first high-rise. They are wrong. That was built in 1959. The Q1 was opened in November 2005 and stands at 78 storeys.

Theme parks, shopping and a casino

The surf scene with all its permutations from riding waves to kite-flying, other recreational activities such as playing golf, or partying and simply enjoying life on a private deck watching the boat traffic on a canal estate is only a part – although a big part – of the Gold Coast in the early years of the 21st century.

A family with young children (through to teenage years) holidaying on the Gold Coast is likely to visit one or more of its well-known theme parks. These were listed in Chapter 2 and are discussed in more detail in Chapter 10, but a few words are warranted here. The concept of a theme park is relatively new. Go back two generations and the specialised theme park did not exist in Australia. Holiday and tourist destinations were likely to have small zoos (on the Gold Coast there was one at Surfers Paradise and one at Coolangatta). Travelling side shows and circuses provided entertainment when they visited town. They had ferris wheels, dodge-em cars and fairy-floss stalls and would set up over the summer vacation period. There was adequate parkland in all the coastal villages to locate them.

When youngsters were not spending their pocket money at sideshows, there were roller-skating (and some ice-skating) rinks to visit. There was one west of Miami in what is now suburbia, another in the Coolangatta–Tweed Heads area. On Saturday afternoons there were cinema matinees. Each major village had a theatre. The façade of the one at Burleigh Heads still stands. The era of side shows, skating rinks and Saturday movies has well and truly gone.

Let us keep the narrative running. The first modern shopping centre on the Gold Coast opened in 1969, at Southport. It was called Sundale Shopping Centre. It closed in 1989 after the larger Australia Fair Shopping Centre opened nearby. For some Brisbane residents a visit to Sundale became a specific part of a trip to the Gold Coast. Economists have some difficulty explaining this as there are equally good, if not better, shopping centres in Brisbane. We place this in the hands of psychologists. Today the Gold Coast is very well served with large shopping centres: Biggera Waters, Southport, Broadbeach, Robina, West Burleigh and Elanora.

Shopping is not the only activity that demands serious enquiry. The research is yet to be done on whether humans are hard-wired to gamble. While we wait for the results we can rely on observation. Many purchase an instant prize 'scratch-it' card for $2; a sizeable number will purchase a Lotto ticket; only a small minority will engage in serious betting on the horses, on poker-machines, at the craps table.[5] The Gold Coast has had a casino since 1986 and as we write there is a proposal for another one.

Notes

1. The early history, from European settlement to the 1950s, is mostly drawn from Longhurst's historical accounts. The recent history has been 'lived through' by the authors.
2. As a youngster in the 1950s, I (Tor Hundloe) would wander, barefoot, through the rainforests of Numinbah Valley without ever seeing a red cedar tree. I did, though, see various pieces of red cedar furniture in local farmhouses. The story of red cedar is similar to that of other once abundant, unpriced gifts of nature. Exploited to near extinction.
3. The senior author spent the first six years of his life on Rosin's farm, which his parents share-farmed.
4. 'Motel' is a word of recent construction, derived from 'hotel' and 'motor' as in 'motoring to the hotel'.
5. We can leave out the stock-exchange gamblers, of whom there are a considerable number. They don't think of buying and selling of shares as gambling. They are wrong in most cases.

Reference

Burchill G (2005) *Passion, Power and Prejudice.* Golden 12, Gold Coast.

Chapter 5

The impact on the Gold Coast's terrestrial environments

T. Hundloe

We tend to think of the Gold Coast as a water environment. As tourists know, it sits on the shore of the vast Pacific Ocean. That is why most come. They have seen the magnificent photographs. If not perched on flattened dunes looking east to the ocean, a significant part of the urban Gold Coast environment is located around natural and human-made water environments. Of these we will say little here, other than to note their extent. The focus of this chapter is the city's terrestrial environments, reporting on and ultimately, after describing the environments, discussing what proportion of them that existed before European settlement still remain today. This will allow us to make our first assessment of the environmental impact of the construction the city of the Gold Coast.

There are 480 km of rivers/creeks/streams in the city of the Gold Coast. This is close to an order of magnitude greater than the length of the city's beaches. As explained, the floodplains of the lower reaches of the rivers/creeks were converted from natural swamps into farming land then to canal estates. Such is the extent of the canal estate development and other engineered waterbodies that there are 774 ha of lakes, canals and water impoundments. There are also natural coastal wetlands which over the eons have provided habitat for native animals plus resting grounds for migratory birds. In this chapter we put aside consideration of these environments and turn to the Gold Coast's vegetation cover now compared to its pre-development state. A great deal has been lost. We provided an insight into this in Chapter 1. Plate 3 shows that the coast and near-coastal area has been cleared almost completely.

Let's look at a reminder of the natural Gold Coast. Fig. 5.1 is a photograph taken nearly 100 years ago. Three people walk towards the beach along a golden sand track freckled with leaves from the overhanging, shade-providing native trees. That track is now Cavill Avenue, undoubtedly the best-known street on the Gold Coast.

The Moreton Bay Islands

We shall commence on the east of the city, even though it is difficult to think of virtually uninhabitable islands as part of the city. Including nearby islands in city boundaries is a recent change of government policy in Queensland. (These islands are depicted in the north-east, in dark green, in Plate 5). Before that occurred, the islands in Moreton Bay were a 'no-man's land' in terms of governance and all sorts of illegal real estate deals were

Fig. 5.1 Pre Cavill Avenue, c. 1918. Provided by Gold Coast City Council, Local Studies Library. Photograph by Herbert Arundel.

done, including selling housing blocks that were partly underwater at high tide. A major criminal trial took place in the early 1980s to ascertain guilt or otherwise in the sale of partly underwaterl housing blocks on Russell Island, which is just outside the northern border of the Gold Coast. The trial ended without a conclusion, due to the illness of a juror. The government realised that it could no longer permit uncontrolled land dealings and all the Queensland islands were incorporated into adjacent local government authorities. As an aside, it is interesting to note that Russell Island was named after Earl Russell, twice UK Prime Minister in the mid 1850s and grandfather of Bertrand Russell, arguably the 20th century's most eminent philosopher. Australian place names are a fascinating subject.

Until 1896, South and North Stradbroke Islands were joined. In that year the Pacific Ocean cut a passage at what is now known as Jumpinpin Bar, where the north-eastern boundary of the Gold Coast is today. South Stradbroke Island is typical of the sand islands along the southern Queensland coast, islands reaching as far north as Fraser Island.

South Stradbroke Island is mainly bush and coastal dunes, with very limited tourism and residential development. Other than the resort and residential development at Couran Cove (initially an eco-tourism and sports complex), there are small quasi-tourist operations catering for boat owners. There are a few residential blocks. Much of what Ron Clarke, the instigator of the development at Couran Cove, had in mind no longer exists. Eco-tourism on the Gold Coast's coastal environment did not attract enough paying consumers. This could suggest that the nature-based tourism on which the Gold Coast was founded, no longer appeals to the type of tourists that come to the city in the 21st century. We should ponder this as we consider the Butler Cycle discussed in Chapter 1.

Let us return to South Stradbroke Island. In the early days of the 20th century cattle grazing took place on South Stradbroke Island but it was not economic given the costs of moving stock to the mainland. Ringbarked trees and the occasional stump are evidence of partial clearing for grazing purposes. In the 1950s and 1960s, limited sand mining occurred on the beach. It was not a major source of rutile, zircon and ilmenite.

Today the land cover of the island includes coastal dunes, tidal wetlands, heath, eucalyptus forests and remnants of Livistona rainforests. The common trees are melaleuca, banksia, black wattle, dune cypress (Bribie Island pines), cabbage tree palms, brush muttonwood and mangroves, with sedges on parts of the sheltered western shore. Spinifex is common on the dunes. These habitats provide food and shelter for a diverse range of fauna: the golden swamp wallaby (endemic), the agile wallaby, bandicoots, flying foxes, a variety of snakes including the dangerous red-bellied black snake, brown snakes and death adders, and significant numbers of birds including the jabiru, ibis, kingfisher, heron, mangrove warbler, little tern, brahminy kite, osprey, spangled drongo, quail, pheasant coucal, pale-headed rosella, rainbow lorikeet, rainbow bee-eater, noisy friar bird, scrub turkey and various native doves.

Several areas of the island are Ramsar Convention sites protected for the benefit of migratory birds. In fact, most of Southern Moreton Bay is protected by this treaty. Notwithstanding the human impact (cattle grazing, mining on the beaches, resort and residential development) much of the island is worthy of protected status for its natural attributes. It has been afforded status as a Conservation Park.

West of South Stradbroke Island are the mangrove islands Cobby Cobby, Eden, Kangaroo, Woogoompah and Coomera. These, plus Willes Island, outside the city of the Gold Coast, contain half the remaining mangrove forests in Moreton Bay and the bulk of the remaining mangroves in the city of the Gold Coast. This is noteworthy. Moreton Bay and its eastern oceanic environment are significant commercial and recreational fishing grounds. A variety of prawns are caught, as is the local delicacy, the Moreton Bay Bug (not actually a bug but a small crayfish). Finfish are plentiful, so are sand crabs and mud crabs. Oyster leases exist. Mangroves are as necessary to these fisheries as mulch is to a garden.

It was through the foresight of Don Young, Deputy Co-ordinator General in the Queensland government in the 1970s, that a study of coastal land use in the Gold Coast–Moreton Bay region was undertaken. One of the topics was the economic value of mangroves. This was an era when the remaining mangrove forests in the Moreton Bay area and the Gold Coast were threatened by further development of canal estates. The study pointed to the significant economic value of mangroves and led to the protection they now receive. The mangrove islands comprise the Southern Moreton Bay Islands National Park. Mosquitoes, sandflies and mud crabs are common. Humans, except those fishing in adjacent waters, are not evident. A small win for the environment.

National parks and other protected areas

Moving westwards to the mainland, there is a large remaining forested area near the urbanised part of the city, just north-east of Nerang. We emphasise that this abuts an industrialised and residential area and it's not far into the hinterland where the major forests remain. The protected forests are in the Nerang National Park and the Nerang State Forest. This is eucalypt country, with a predominance of grey gum, blue gum, stringybark, tallowwood and small patches of rainforest in the gullies.

Also in the urbanised area, there a few other much smaller areas set aside for conservation: Burleigh Head National Park, Burleigh Knoll Conservation Park, Nerang Conservation Park, Pine Ridge Conservation Park and David Fleay Wildlife Park. Only in the mountainous hinterland, far removed from the urban areas, do we find the large national parks and World Heritage rainforests.

One of the small conservation areas has a special place in my memory. In the late 1970s, I was Chair of an Evaluation Panel advising the national government's Australian Heritage Commission. My panel's area of responsibility was the subtropical part of Queensland south from Rockhampton to the New South Wales border, and west to the Northern Territory and South Australia borders. All national parks plus other land that had been assessed as having national park values but not so designated (because the then government was reluctant to remove land from potential development) were put on the Register of the National Estate by my panel. This action gave the Commonwealth government a degree of power to exercise if the Queensland government sought to open these areas for development.

Occasionally we would become aware of special cases, land which was small in size or simply overlooked but clearly worth protecting in its natural state. One such area, and one I took a personal interest in, was an area of remnant wallum banksia immediately to the north of rapidly developing Southport. I visited the site. It reminded me of the bushland of the Gold Coast I knew as a child. In particular, it was very much like the Burleigh Swamp and the Merry Mac[2] Swamp, large lowlands which before the bulldozers arrived stretched north from Burleigh Heads State School to Miami and west to the lower hills.

Pine Ridge Conservation Park is a heath and paperbark swamp with banksias and bloodwood trees throughout. By placing it on the Register of the National Estate we saved a tiny fraction of typical Gold Coast coastal country. For those interested in how dramatic the change in environments has been over the past 50 years, Pine Ridge is a reminder. It is a genuine museum piece which asks us to imagine an earlier era – albeit only two generations ago – when most of the Gold Coast west of the Gold Coast Highway was similar to it. For those who are inspired by our research to construct in their mind's eye the Gold Coast as Mother Nature made it, I suggest a visit to Pine Ridge Conservation Park followed by a walk around Burleigh Head National Park. You will experience totally different ecosystems and ecological relationships.

Burleigh Head National Park is a tiny 27 ha. It is home to rainforests, eucalypt forests, groves of pandanus, coastal heathlands and mangroves. It is mainly littoral rainforest. A variety of birds are to be seen, and snakes, but koalas are not seen there any more. I do not discount the possibility that some still reside in the headland. However, the Gold Coast Highway (the busy main coastal road) cuts the national park from the small amount of koala habitat on the road's west. Many animals have lost their lives in attempting to make this hazardous crossing. Warning signs alert motorists to the fact that 'koalas cross here' (see Fig. 5.2). But in 2014, we expect they don't cross any more.

The Gondwana Rainforest

We now come to the major rainforests within the city's boundaries, again drawing attention to the fact that these forests were not formally in the city until its boundaries were changed in 1995. Notwithstanding, well before then both Gold Coast residents and visitors from Brisbane thought of these rainforest environments as 'belonging' to the city.

These rainforests are found in Springbrook National Park, a small component of Australia's World Heritage-listed Gondwana Rainforests. The national park covers more than Springbrook Mountain as Natural Bridge (Arch) at the very top of Numinbah Valley is included, plus forests in the southern part of Numinbah Valley (commencing just north of the land inundated by the Hinze Dam), and not forgetting Mount Cougal to the east. Lamington National Park, which is typically thought of as part of the Gold Coast hinterland, is not within the city boundaries. It is a much larger part of the Gondwana Rainforests, the largest undisturbed subtropical rainforest remaining in Australia.

The Gondwana Rainforests acquired their UNESCO status as a World Heritage property on the basis of meeting three of the four criteria established by UNESCO (see Chapter 2, Box 2.1). As a whole, the Gondwana Rainforests were the most extensive rainforests in Australia before European settlement. Today, virtually all the planet's Antarctic beech is found in these forests. And there is more: the forests are home to more bird, marsupial, snake and frog species than anywhere else in Australia.

What is truly fascinating and exciting (for scientists at least) is the lineage of the wide range of flora and fauna species in these rainforests, traceable as far back as the ancient days of Gondwana as a continent. Some of the oldest of the world's ferns are to be found. The Araucarian conifers (hoop pine) are the most ancient and primitive of Earth's conifers. The rainforests' songbirds such as lyrebirds, scrub-birds, treecreepers, bowerbirds and catbirds belong to the oldest lineages of passerines. There is considerably more of ancient lineage.

Much of what was rainforest before settlement is gone. And so it is across Australia. It has been estimated that no more than one-quarter of the rainforests that existed in Australia in 1770 remains. Considerable amounts of the commercially valuable timber has been removed, starting with the red cedars but involving a wide range of beautiful trees (and timber). Hoop pine was being felled in Gold Coast hinterland and taken to local sawmills up to the Second World War.

The environmental impact: a dramatically changed ecosystem

Having described the forested areas of the city, we can now make an assessment of the environmental impact of the formation of the city of the Gold Coast (see Table 5.1). It comprises a list of the major forest communities in the city of the Gold Coast at two periods, pre-clearing (at 1750) and the present. Many minor forest types are excluded,

Fig. 5.2 Koalas Cross Here sign at Burleigh Heads, adjacent to what was the Koala National Park (now Burleigh Head National Park). Photograph by Bridgette McDougall.

including three subgroupings of vine forests that decreased nearly 60 per cent from 7824 ha to 3228 ha. Of course, taking axes and cross-cut saws (and in recent times, bulldozers) to vegetation is only the first cut in terms of environmental impacts.

Natural and near-natural vegetation is animal habitat. Biodiversity values reflect the interdependence of fauna and flora. Genetic, species and ecosystem biodiversity is, in the nature of things, that which makes for the resilience of planet Earth. We need to seek correlations between loss of habitat and the health and size of animal populations. While at general level we are relatively confident in identifying what types and how much of a particular habitat can support one animal of a given species, it becomes an immensely difficult task to do the sums for a specific location and a variety of species, as we would like to do for the Gold Coast.

What the data in Table 5.1 illustrate is the extent of clearing of the Gold Coast lowlands. This is country that existed just beyond the coastal dunes and stretched far westward through the swampy plains onto the low hills. These were the melaleuca forests that flood during heavy rainfall, otherwise commonly known as swamps. Only 8 per cent of the original vegetation of the swamps remains. The melaleuca and heathlands that were the Burleigh Swamp and the Merry Mac Swamp have been completely destroyed.

The degree of clearing of the eucalypt-dominated and open forest woodlands that range from near the beachfront into the foothills of the high mountains is also obvious. In absolute terms, less of these forests remain than of the melaleuca swamps. The other forest type to take a major hit as the city grew was the coastal heath community.

By combining the various types of vine forests (the 6062 ha pre-clearing shown in Table 5.1 plus the other 7824 ha discussed previously), we have an indication of the loss of a certain type of rainforest. Approximately 50 per cent has gone. As we find throughout Australia, only the very steep high mountains provided an impediment to the timber-getters and the farmers who followed. Springbrook and upper Numinbah Valley and parts of Beechmont are prime examples of very steep land that survived.

Yet another perspective: today there is more land on the Gold Coast given over to golf courses than there is in remnant melaleuca forest. That forest type was one of the dominant types on the Gold Coast pre-development, and the one that took the biggest loss in transforming a once natural environment into a city of half a million plus. It is claimed by the golfing fraternity that there are more golf courses per head of population on the Gold Coast than anywhere else in the world. Given the difficulty involved in checking the accuracy of this assertion, we accept it on face value. It is not a claim we are necessarily proud of. That is not to denigrate the game of golf. We do not need this many courses to

Table 5.1. What is left of Gold Coast forest communities

	Pre-clearing, 1750 (ha)	Today (ha)	% remaining
Moist to dry open forest and woodland	50 739	20 104	40
Melaleuca, seasonally inundated	19 151	1517	8
Eucalypt woodland on basalt, usually high-altitude	14 018	8823	63
Wet tall open forest, above 200 m	9249	6385	69
Eucalypt-dominated open forest and woodland	8971	1094	12
Vine forests on volcanics	6062	3596	59
Mangroves	5654	5051	89
Coastal heath communities	4627	1005	22
	118 471	47 575	

Source: Based on Ryan *et al.* (2003).

produce world-class golfers. As we write, the Gold Coast is home to 30 golf courses and a champion golfer, Adam Scott.

In 2005, the Gold Coast City Council commissioned a study to identify the conservation significance of the Gold Coast's remnant natural and near-natural vegetation. An expert panel, led by Alan Chenoweth, was formed and the work undertaken. Some of the more important recommendations are summarised next.

The panel recommended that various environments be designated as having 'state significance', which means they are significant for their biodiversity values at a bioregional or state scale. These obviously include areas assessed as being significant at national or international scale. If they have been assessed as meeting the higher-level status (e.g. World Heritage listing) they are already protected. The areas that need to be recognised and protected are the ones which have not previously been given formal conservation status but deserve it. It has been estimated that 82 per cent of the remaining naturally vegetated land in the city of the Gold Coast is of state significance in terms of its biological-diversity value (Francis *et al.* 2005).

Table 5.2 lists these valuable areas according to type.[3] It should be noted that there are some quite specific environments, not listed in the table, which require protection; for example, the Horseshoe Bay area of South Stradbroke Island, which is a narrow band of beach vegetation (sedge, sheoak and cotton trees) and the only known nesting site in Moreton Bay for the little tern.

The expert panel identified five major 'bioregional corridors'. These are areas of high ecological significance; for example, in providing the food sources for animals that travel significant distances. They are the Burleigh/Bonogin/Springbrook corridor, the Currumbin/Cobaki/Border Track corridor, the Springbrook/Lamington corridor, the Springbrook/Darlington/Beenleigh corridor and the Mt Wongawallan/McCoys Creek corridor. These are areas where the purchase of land for conservation purposes is paramount.

In summary, the available data suggest that approaching 47 per cent of the Gold Coast city remains vegetated in a near-natural state. But keep in mind that today the city incorporates near-natural South Stradbroke Island, plus several mangrove-covered protected islands plus World Heritage rainforests in the hinterland. In its present boundaries, the city of the Gold Coast is not just an urbanised area. If we were to calculate the amount of

Table 5.2. Gold Coast environments that need to be designated of state significance

Vegetation type	Rationale
Riparian wetlands and wetland floodplain	Habitat value for priority fauna: grey goshawk, Coxen's fig-parrot, barking owl, painted pitta, black-necked stork, platypus
Rainforested communities including wet sclerophyll communities	The Gold Coast hinterland supports the highest concentration of threatened plant species in Australia
Marine habitats north of the Coomera River and south of Couran Cove, South Stradbroke	Core habitat for the false water rat (a vulnerable species)
Grey-headed flying fox camps	Vulnerable under Commonwealth legislation
Habitat of spotted-tailed quoll	Vulnerable under Commonwealth and state legislation
Wader roosting and foraging sites	For obvious reasons

Source: (Francis *et al.* 2005).

near-natural forest in the 'old' Gold Coast boundaries, the situation is one of significant destruction of flora and consequently of fauna habitat, leading to a significant reduction in wildlife. We have made an attempt to illustrate this in Plate 3. Except for small remnant, isolated pieces of land (Burleigh Head National Park and a few others) we can note that the 'old' Gold Coast is denuded of natural vegetation.

As mentioned previously, the future of koalas is a major issue. The expert advice to the Gold Coast City council is that ~15 per cent of the koala population is isolated in subpopulations east of the Pacific Motorway. The experts note that 'none ... have a guaranteed future' and report that the remaining 85 per cent 'survive in an increasingly fragmented habitat matrix bisected by roads and water barriers ... with threatening processes that range from development pressures at the urban/bushland interface, road strike, ongoing habitat loss and increases in fire frequency and intensity' (Biolink Ecological Consultants 2007).

It is important to note that the highest-quality koala habitat comprises only 2548 ha, the majority in the ridges and slopes of the Springbrook–Numinbah–Lamington region where stringybark and tallowwood grow. The preferred tree species for koalas are forest red gum, tallowwood, grey gum and swamp mahogany. In Table 5.3 we present a reasonably comprehensive list of koala trees.

When we look to the historical records of koala sightings, we get a patchy picture of the abundance and scarcity. For example, an expert's report to the Gold Coast City Council (Biolink Ecological Consultants 2007) indicates that the earliest records came from Numinbah Valley where in 1927 there were three sightings, although the study author believed that the sightings were likely to be of the same animal. On the other hand, historical notes from the pre-widescale farming era suggest great abundance. Carl Lentz in *Memoirs and Some History* (1961) wrote that he saw '9 bears in a little gum tree' in Numinbah Valley. Another pioneer of the district, Henry Stephens, reported that he saw

Table 5.3. Trees for koalas

Scientific name	Common name
Eucalyptus camaldulensis	River red gum
Eucalyptus crebra	Narrow-leaved red ironbark
Eucalyptus drepanophylla	Grey ironbark
Eucalyptus exerta	Queensland peppermint
Eucalyptus microcorys	Tallowwood
Eucalyptus orgadophila	Mountain coolabah
Eucalyptus populnea	Bimble box, popular gum
Eucalyptus propinqua	Grey gum
Eucalyptus raveretiana	Black ironbox
Eucalyptus resinifera	Red mahogany
Eucalyptus robusta	Swamp mahogany
Eucalyptus siderophloia	Grey ironbark
Eucalyptus signata	Scribbly gum
Eucalyptus tereticornis	Forest red gum
Eucalyptus thozetiana	Mountain yapunyah
Lophostemon confertus	Brush box

Source: DPI Qld (1995).

Table 5.4. Gold Coast endangered flora

Species	Conservation Status
Southern ochrosia	Endangered
Brush cassia	Vulnerable
Southern corynocarpus	Vulnerable
Springbrook pinkwood	Endangered
Smooth Davidson's plum	Endangered
Jointed baloghia	Vulnerable
Southern fontainea	Vulnerable
Pink cherry	Near threatened
Brush sophora	Vulnerable
Silver leaf	Near threatened
Rose walnut, Crystal Creek walnut	Endangered
Stinking cryptocarya	Vulnerable
Velvet laurel	Vulnerable
Black walnut	Near threatened
Onion cedar	Vulnerable
Mountain wattle, nightcap wattle	Near threatened
Veiny lace flower	Near threatened
Ardisia	Near threatened
Sweet myrtle	Endangered
Red lilly pilly	Vulnerable
Durobby coolamon	Vulnerable
Giant ironwood	Near threatened
Southern velvet myrtle	Near threatened
Smooth scrub turpentine	Least concern
Shrubby jasmine	Endangered
Ball nut	Vulnerable
Red bopple nut	Vulnerable
Macadamia nut, Queensland nut	Vulnerable
Rusty helicia	Vulnerable
Tree waratah	Near threatened
Spiny gardenia	Endangered
Small-leaved tamarind	Endangered
Long-leaved tuckeroo	Near threatened
Fine-leaved tuckeroo	Vulnerable
Shiny-leaved coondoo, Eerwah plum	Endangered
Rusty plum	Vulnerable
Ormeau bottle tree	Endangered
Small-leaved hazelwood	Vulnerable
Richmond birdwing vine	Near threatened
Large-leaved wonga vine	Near threatened
Arrowhead vine	Vulnerable
Shaggy-leaved plectranthus	Endangered
Giant stream lily	Near threatened
Rainforest sedge	Vulnerable

Source: Based on GCCC (2010a).

29 koalas while he was on a horse ride a few kilometres from the Pine Creek Bridge to The Pocket (Hall *et al.* 1988).

The habitat that remains in near-natural condition, some of World Heritage status, some of regional conservation status and the remainder needing some degree of maintenance and/or restoration, provides the habitat that makes for the high biodiversity status of the Gold Coast. The fact that more than half the city has had its vegetation cleared emphasises the increased value of that which remains. This fact applies throughout the world as natural environments continue to be destroyed.

Table 5.4 is a list of the flora and Tables 5.5–5.8 list fauna on the Gold Coast that are rare, endangered or vulnerable. Rare species of flora and fauna should alert us to possible losses in the future. In Chapter 16, where we are forced to think about a future with a much increased human population, we need to be mindful of the damage already done and the prospect of more damage.

A matter that cannot be overlooked is the significant area of vegetated land that is in private hands, approximately one-third of the total. Here is a challenge for society if maintenance and restoration are to play a role in reversing damage done to the natural environment. How do we encourage conservation by private land-holders?

Table 5.5. Gold Coast threatened frogs

Vulnerable	Endangered	Rare
Freycinet's frog	Pearson's frog	Green-thighed frog
Olongburra frog	Fleay's barred frog	Revealed frog
Tinkling frog	Giant barred frog	Marsupial frog
		Loveridge's frog
		Fletcher's frog

Source: Based on GCCC (2010b).

Table 5.6. Gold Coast threatened birds

Vulnerable	Endangered	Rare
Red-tailed tropicbird	Herald petrel	Cotton pygmy-goose
Marbled frogmouth	Little tern	Black-necked stork
Beach stone-curlew	Regent honeyeater	Square-tailed kite
Black-breasted button-quail		Grey goshawk
Powerful owl		Lewin's rail
Rufous scrub-bird		Sooty oystercatcher
		Australian painted snipe
		Eastern curlew
		Sooty owl
		Albert's lyrebird
		Red-browed treecreeper
		Olive whistler

Source: Based on GCCC (2010a).

Table 5.7. Gold Coast threatened mammals

Vulnerable	Endangered	Rare
Spotted-tailed quoll		Indo-Pacific hump-backed dolphin
Long-nosed potoroo		
Brush-tailed rock wallaby		
Dugong		
Humpback whale		

Source: Based on GCCC (2010a).

Table 5.8. Gold Coast threatened reptiles

Vulnerable	Endangered	Rare
Green turtle	Loggerhead turtle	Rainforest cool-skink
	Leathery turtle	Three-toed snake-tooth skink
		Short-limbed snake-skink
		Common death adder
		Stephen's banded snake

Source: Based on GCCC (2010a).

One private Gold Coast land-owner whom readers will immediately recognise is Germaine Greer. In 2001, she came across an abandoned dairy farm adjacent to the national park (and World Heritage Gondwana Rainforests) at Natural Bridge (Arch) at the top of Numinbah Valley, on Cave Creek, a tributary of the Nerang River. Greer purchased the farm and with the help of her botanist sister Jane, plus a group of workers, set about re-establishing the rainforest. In 2013, she published a book, *White Beech*, that explains her project in great detail.

Many feel about nature as Germaine Greer does but do not have the money to put into practice what they would surely like to do. Greer is of the view that governments will fail in their duty to nature, and hence it is up to individuals.

Notes

1. The land was tidal mangrove swamps, exposed at low tide and promoted as 'dry' blocks. Much of this land was sold sight-unseen to people in the southern Australian states.
2. This is the old spelling of Merrimac. Some refer to the Burleigh Swamps as the Burleigh Forest.
3. Note that the terms 'endangered' and 'vulnerable' meet the definition of 'threatened' under international criteria. 'Vulnerable' status is of greater importance than 'rare' status in Queensland legislation. We can but hope that common terminology is soon adopted in respect of identifying fauna and flora that are in serious trouble.

References

Biolink Ecological Consultants (2007) *Koala Habitat and Population Assessment for Gold Coast City LGA*. Uki, NSW.

DPI Qld (1995) *Trees and Shrubs Forest Resources Division*. Revised edn. Department of Primary Industries Qld, Brisbane.

Francis D, Searle J, Chenoweth A (2005) *Nature Conservation Mapping Review: Stage 2 Significance Mapping*. Report for the Gold Coast City Council. Chenoweth Environmental Planning and Architecture Pty Ltd, Brisbane.

GCCC (2010a) *Flora of the Gold Coast Local Government Area*. Gold Coast City Council, Gold Coast.

GCCC (2010b) *Vertebrate Fauna of the Gold Coast Local Government Area*. Gold Coast City Council, Gold Coast.

Hall P, Yaun D, Gilmont N (1988) *Numinbah Valley: A Social and Natural History 1840s–1988*. Numinbah Valley Bicentennial Committee, Numinbah Valley.

Ryan TS, Bean AR, Hoskins BB, Wilson BA, McDonald WJF (2003) *Gold Coast City Council 1998 Nature Conservation Mapping Review Stage 1*. Queensland Herbarium for the Gold Coast City Council.

Plate 1 Gold Coast erosion 1967. Photograph by Harry Willey.

Plate 2 Gold Coast erosion 2013. Tor Hundloe and Craig Page explaining the problem to AUSAID postgraduate students. Photograph: *Gold Coast Bulletin*.

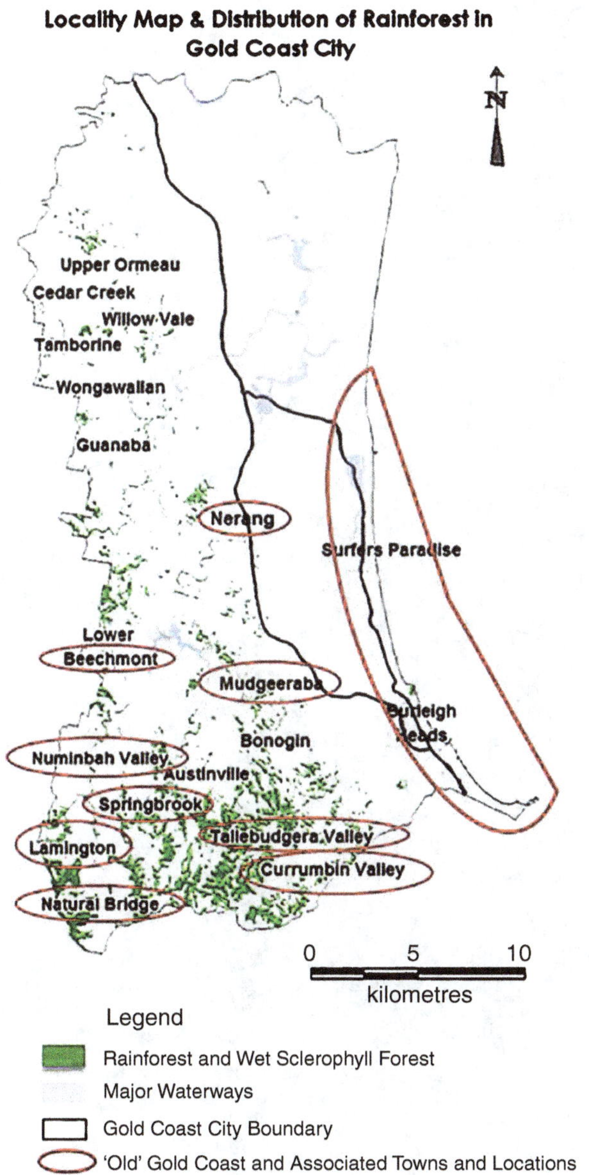

Plate 3 Gold Coast city boundaries, old and new.

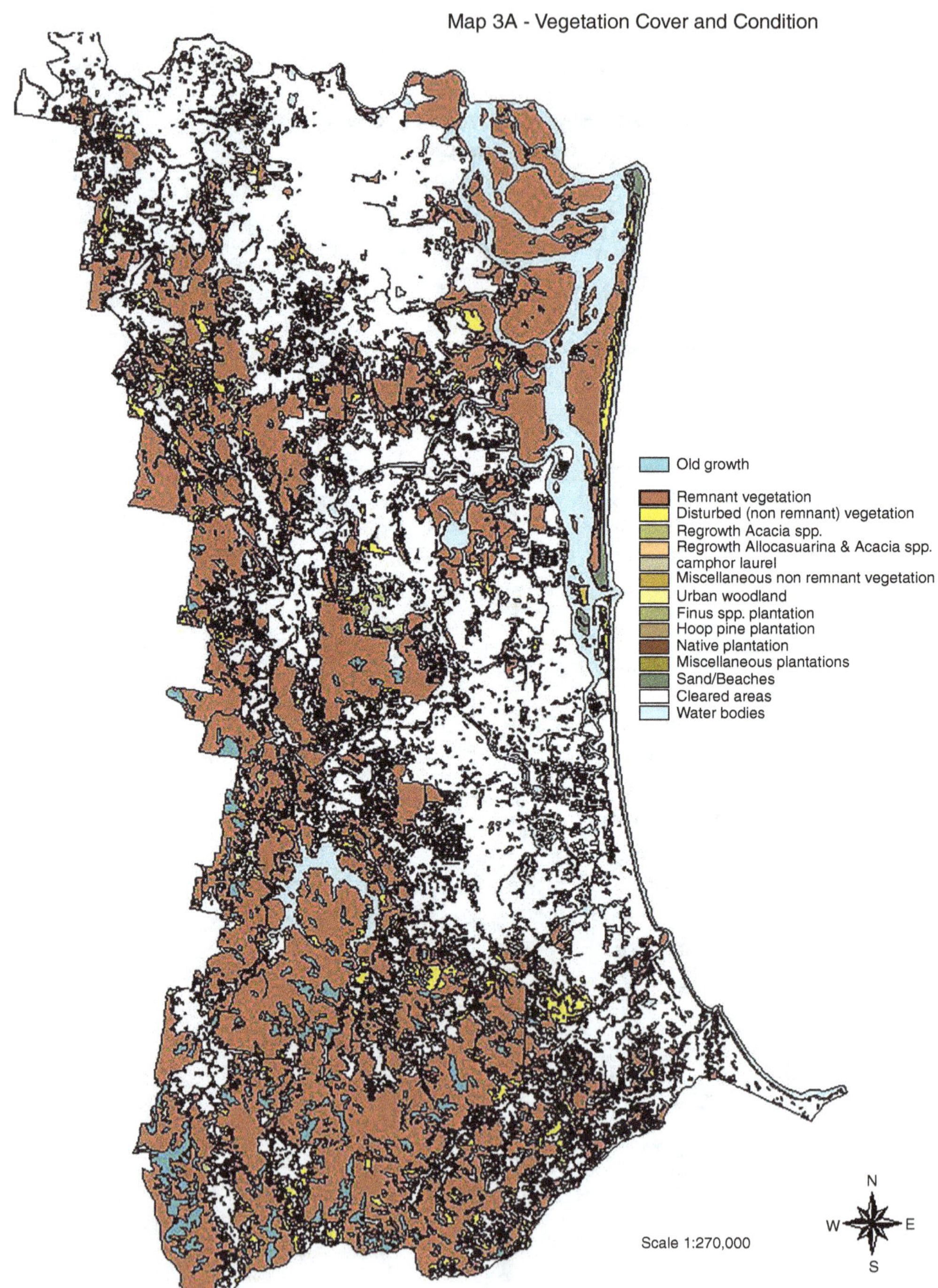

Plate 4 Vegetation cover and condition.
Source: Ryan *et al.* (2003).

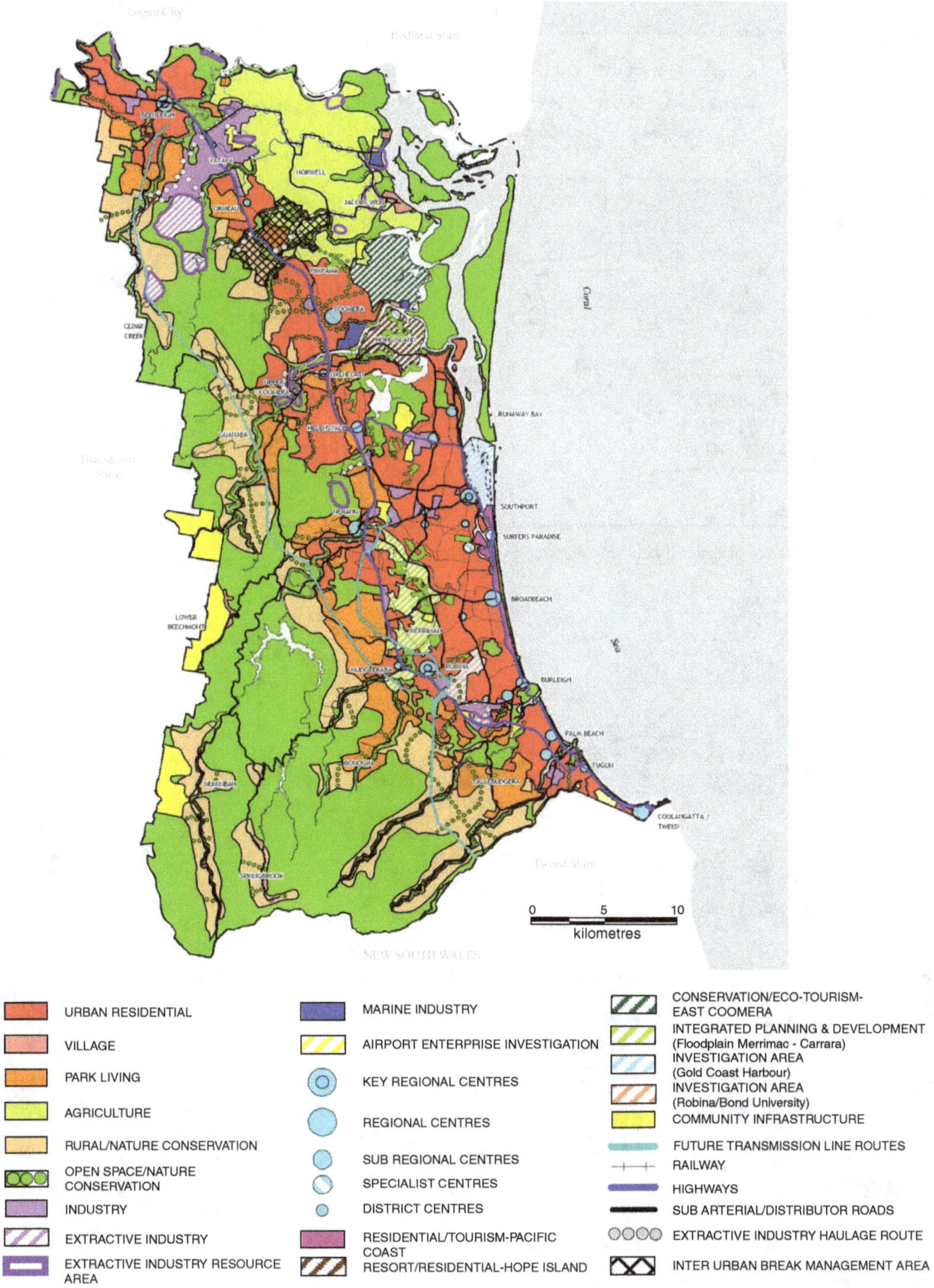

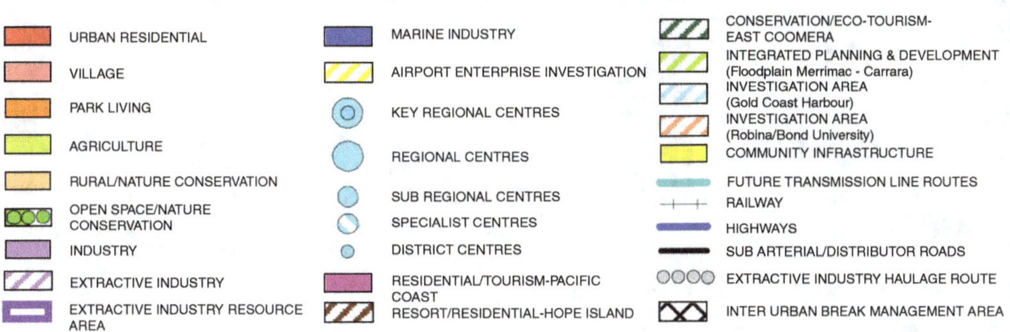

Plate 5 The Gold Coast City Council land use strategy map, 2011.

Plate 6 The importance of celebrity culture in attracting tourists.

Plate 7 Miami Iceworks before demolition in 2013. Provided by Gold Coast City Council, Local Studies Library. Photograph by Bill Chivers.

Plate 8 Lennons Broadbeach Hotel, built in 1956. Provided by Gold Coast City Council, Local Studies Library. Photograph by Peter Huddy.

Plate 9 Alex Griffiths at Currumbin Bird Sanctuary. Provided by Gold Coast City Council, Local Studies Library. Photographer unknown.

Plate 10 Small-leaved tamarind *Diploglottis campbellii*. Photograph by Glenn Leiper.

Chapter 6

The beaches

C. Page and T. Hundloe

The Gold Coast beaches are, of course, the key interface between the terrestrial and marine ecosystems of the city. The fine-textured golden sands are one of the possible reasons for the city's name. Prior to European settlement, the beaches were a source of seafood for the indigenous people. A favourite food was the pipi (or eugary); there were also oysters, mud crabs and sea mullet during winter when the schools ran. Before the sand miners took their toll, midden heaps of pipi and oyster shells were common at places where the local people gathered to feast.

Townships surveyed

Burleigh Heads was surveyed in 1871, and in 1874–1875 the site that would become the township of Southport was surveyed. The most southerly port from Brisbane could rightly be called Southport. Its primary role was that of a 'port' from which red cedar was taken by boat to Brisbane. The first settler was Richard Gardiner, who built a house and then a wharf. Other selectors took up farming properties. Stories of excellent fishing and extensive rock oyster grounds brought numerous fishermen to Southport.

As discussed previously, the decision by the Queensland colonial governor to build his summer residence at Southport in 1885 transformed the port into a holiday destination for the 'rich and famous' of Brisbane-town. So successful was it that by Federation in 1901, Southport had a resident population of 1230, up from about 200 in the 1880s. The railway line between Beenleigh and Southport opened in 1889. Prior to that the transport options were a four-hour boat trip from Brisbane (relatively fast for the era) or the Cobb & Co. coach service which commenced in 1879.

In 1877, the first house was built on Marine Parade at Southport. It was named 'Balaclutha'. The owner was concerned enough about protecting the foredunes that he retained native vegetation while clearing enough to gain that much sought-after water view – the dilemma faced ever since by beachfront property owners. Others followed, building houses in locations where they were threatened by the next cyclone or even major storm and high tide. Many were rented out at holiday periods or as weekenders. Visitors who could not afford rental accommodation camped in tents adjacent to the beach. Some simply preferred camping to holidaying in a house. Beach camping became the holiday of choice for the growing working and middle classes of Brisbane.

In 1878 the Southport Hotel was constructed, then guesthouses were built. Visitors kept increasing in numbers. The Governor's summer house had shifted perceptions significantly. Southport was the place to be seen. Burleigh Heads and Coolangatta suffered due to their distance from Brisbane and the sheer difficulties of dealing with tides, crossing rivers and travelling on sand tracks. Notwithstanding these impediments, allotments began to sell in Burleigh Heads in 1884.

In 1886, the Grand Hotel was opened at Broadwater. Guesthouses lined the waterfront, bathing pavilions and bathing boxes sat on the beach. Even though this was the era of very demure 'neck to knee' bathing costumes, if someone was really modest or their religion demanded it, a beach box would allow them to change into their costume and enter the water without anyone seeing more than an ankle. The local nuns (Sisters of Mercy who taught at the Star of the Sea Convent) had their own beach box. Other popular beaches had bathing boxes: the ones at Burleigh were removed in 1937.

By 1889, there were six hotels and 12 guesthouses in total at Southport and across the Nerang River on the ocean-front. Swimming in the surf rather in the calm water of the Broadwater was a developing interest. Early warnings of the destructive force of nature came in 1890 and 1893, with cyclonic weather destroying beachfront facilities.[1] The breaking asunder of Stradbroke Island into its North and South parts in 1896 changed the marine dynamics in the southern part of Moreton Bay and the Broadwater, where considerable tourism and residential development already existed. A build-up of sand produced the Southport Spit and led to even calmer swimming and boating water in the Broadwater.

The Broadwater developed as the model for 19th-century seaside resort towns. There was safe bathing, plentiful fish catches and boating. The aesthetics, a sea view and the comfort of an evening sea breeze, with houses, hotels and guesthouses facing the waterfront, some with their own jetties, made for an ideal holiday setting except … except when the cyclones came. Longhurst informs us that in 1890 'A series of cyclonic storms battered the foreshore, the pier baths were destroyed … and not replaced for some two years, only to be destroyed again in 1893.' Something had to be done about this, and it was.

The first seawall

To counter the threat to property built on denuded and flattened foredunes, in 1901 a seawall was constructed at Southport. The engineers thought it would stem erosion. Not so. The seawall had the unintended consequence of dramatically reducing the size and shape of the former sandy beach. As time passed, more and more engineering took place along the foreshore of Marine Parade. Today a human-made grassed park and playground has replaced the once dynamic beach environment. A small component of the original seawall can be seen near the Jubilee Bridge. Here school children practise archaeology by digging in search of the remainder of the seawall. Television has clearly made the discipline of archaeology interesting.

Beach rock walls eventually stretched along great swathes of the Gold Coast foreshore, all for the purpose of protecting property built on sand. For example, the rock wall along Burleigh beach was built in 1935. As rock walls were constructed on other Gold Coast beaches, the same mistake was made. If seawalls were not constructed by the government or council, private land-owners spent considerable money in having their own built. The extent of privately built walls is difficult to ascertain without undertaking a residence-by-residence inspection. In the present era, a prospective wall-builder needs approval from the Gold Coast City Council.

Don't mention Matthew

'The wise man builds his house on the rocks, the foolish man builds on the sand' – to paraphrase St Matthew. Houses and hotels did not have to be built upon the beach. There was a choice. They could have been situated some distance inland from the foredune, on land high enough to permit the ocean view so highly valued. There are parts of the Sunshine Coast, such as Perigian Beach, where this approach was taken. But development on the Gold Coast came well before that of the Sunshine Coast, and at that time there was a degree of ignorance of how Mother Nature worked.

There was more to the reckless development than ignorance. Let us learn from Geoff Burchill, in decades past a major developer–planner–engineer. He wrote, 'Australia's first local Government 'Strategic Plans' were tailor-made by Gold Coast council … to respond to the overwhelming push of new growth and projects. These ensured that few of the town planning conventions of the major cities would frustrate creative ideas' (Burchill 2005, p. 32) The Gold Coast was to be different, even if the cost of protecting private property would be high and continue indefinitely. Basic town planning practices were to be ignored, much of the cost of protecting beachfront properties were to be paid by rate-payers regardless of where they lived. There are no Pacific Ocean views to be had at Nerang.

The role of sand mining

Flat coastal foreshores facing the rolling Pacific surf were 'sites to die for'. They became available as a result of sand mining. The first mining (a rather overstated description of digging in beach sand with shovels) took place at Byron Bay in 1934 (Sweet 2008).[2] The miners were seeking the black mineral sands rutile (from which titanium is made), zircon, ilmenite and monazite. In 1941, mining began on the North Burleigh foreshore. Much beach and foreshore land was mined along the Gold Coast in the 1940s and early 1950s. There was wartime demand for rutile and the few objections to the destruction of the frontal dunes were trumped by support for the war effort. Rutile plays a key role in the manufacture of armaments and military equipment.

Sand mining, the threat of limestone mining and oil drilling on the Great Barrier Reef were the catalysts for the formation and rapid growth of the conservation/environmental movement in Australia in the 1960s and 1970s. In fact, the Great Barrier Reef conflict could be said to have heralded the commencement of environmentalism in Australia, in the mid 1960s. The protests against sand mining at Burleigh in the 1940s have gone unrecognised. It was not until the sand miners targeted Cooloola, Inskip Point, Fraser Island, Moreton Island, Deepwater and Agnes Waters that sand mining became headline news. North Stradbroke Island was mined early, and is the only remaining Queensland source of the black mineral sands.

Sweet (2008, p. 11) wrote that 'In the 1950s, the Gold Coast City Council favoured mining because, apart from the economic benefits, miners were required to flatten … the dunes, leaving them ripe for development'. Another historian, Andrew McRobbie (1984, p. 50), mades the same point: 'the local authorities regarded it as an excellent way of having land cleared for development … at no cost to the Councils'. A another who was awake to the situation, Peter Neumann (Director of Currumbin Minerals), said that '(We) were …

doing Council a favour. We would flatten out the dunes leaving them ready for development ... Much of the Gold Coast is built on mined land' (in Sweet 2008, p. 11).

Laissez-faire beach-building

Other things happened on the foreshores of the Gold Coast that would not be permitted today. In the early 1950s, Jack Evans built a 'porpoise pool' on Snapper Rocks at Rainbow Bay. He then built a swimming pool on the rocks at Burleigh. The latter survived numerous cyclones and was replaced in 1987. A skating rink was constructed in the same area at Burleigh in 1947; it was destroyed by a cyclone in 1954. This illustrates the force of nature that the Gold Coast beaches can expect. In the present era, neither the pools nor the skating rink would be approved. But to local councils and devil-may-care 'entrepreneurs,' the 1950s to the 1980s was a unique era, never to be repeated. It was the Gold Coast's 'Wild West' era. The best known of the 'white shoe brigade' – Christopher Skase, Mike Gore and Keith Williams – have passed away, as has the controversial Local Government Minister of that time, Russ Hinze.

Eventually the Queensland government recognised the risks to properties built on the Gold Coast foredunes. Cyclones and other less extreme weather events occurred frequently enough to indicate that beach erosion and accretion were natural phenomena. There would be relatively long periods when the beach would disappear. The sand would move and settle in off-shore bars, returning to form a beach only when nature determined. This we understand today, but our recent knowledge has come too late to minimise the cost of foreshore protection.

What has to be done?

What was to be done? The chance to call a halt to building on the flattened foredunes before enormous sums of money were put into residential dwellings was missed. Tor Hundloe recalls a senior civil engineer with the Queensland government, Don Young (the same chap concerned about mangrove destruction) repeatedly calling for an end to building on the foreshore and for it to be reserved for public use. Few listened. He was before his time: his early wisdom is the conventional wisdom today.[3]

Looking back to that period, it is difficult to determine why the authorities did not step in and require all buildings and roads to be constructed well west of the frontal dunes. Was optimism the prevailing attitude: a cyclone won't hit the Gold Coast again? Were the authorities short-sighted in not anticipating the expansion of foreshore development and the enormous amount of money at stake? If they could have foreseen the massive complexes built at the very edge of the beach at Surfers Paradise, would they have been as blasé as they appear to have been in the 1950s and 1960s? Did the authorities have the power, even assuming they had the will, to say 'Stop'? In fact, it is not clear who had the power to control beachfront development in that era. Could local government engineers and town planners have said 'no' and had that command followed by the local government politicians? Was the promise of a growing rate base too good to overlook? This may have been the motivation of the elected councillors. So many questions to ponder. It is late in the day to identify and question those who might have answers as to what was happening in this early period.

From 1962 to 1964, 'training walls' were built at the Tweed River mouth in New South Wales. There were unintended consequences, but these should have been predictable as by then our knowledge of coastal dynamics had improved considerably. The Tweed River construction played havoc with the Gold Coast beaches to the north. The northward movement of sand on which the beaches relied was impeded. Groynes were built in an attempt to remedy this. There was some learning from this experience. In 1994, the Queensland and New South Wales governments jointly financed a sand bypass system to return the northward movement of sand. By the time that training walls at the surf entrance to the Broadwater, at Southport, were contemplated, engineers were wise enough to install sand bypass pipelines which permitted the north-bound sand to find its way to South Stradbroke Island.

In 1967, devastating cyclones plus flooding in the Nerang River was – or should have been – a wake-up call for Gold Coast councillors, town planners and engineers. This was a big year for extreme weather events. Between late January and early August, four cyclones (Dinah, Barbara, Elaine and Glenda) hit the Gold Coast beaches, causing serious erosion and economic loss. In June, three east coast lows added to the destruction. It is estimated that about 33 345 000 km^3 (8 million cubic miles) of sand was moved off-shore by these cyclones. Houses fell into the sea at Mermaid Beach, Nobby Beach and Palm Beach. Parts of the esplanade collapsed at Surfers Paradise. As Harper wrote, 'unrestricted development within active beach zones have robbed the beach of its natural buffer against storm attacks and those areas remain chronically affected for many years' (Harper 2001, p. 4.7).

Attempting to protect foreshore properties by shovelling wrecked cars onto the beach was the best that we could do in this era. Wrecked vehicles were transported from as far

Fig. 6.1 Old cars used for beach protection in the 1960s. Provided by Gold Coast City Council, Local Studies Library. Photographer unknown.

away as Sydney for this purpose – a more dignified end to life than being left to rust in a wreckers' yard (see Fig. 6.1).

The Delft Report

The Queensland government's response to the threats to beachfront properties was to ask the best professionals in the world for advice on coastal protection. No prizes for guessing the experts were Dutch. In 1963, Delft Hydraulics Laboratory was asked to provide advice and then commissioned to undertake a major investigation. This commenced in 1966. We have documented above what happened a year later, in the form of extreme weather events. The government took legislative action, although to what ultimate good can be debated, by passing the *Beach Protection Act 1968*. Beaches not previously walled by rocks, sandbags or car-wrecks were deemed suitable for similar treatment. The impenetrable walls forced the waves to halt, but the waves then dragged great quantities of sand out to sea where they formed underwater sandbanks. The sand eventually returned to the beaches, but in the meantime the beaches were barren for months and tourist numbers fell.

By 1970 the Delft Report, as it was known, was finalised. The construction of several groynes followed. One was built at Kirra Point to restore Coolangatta Beach, another connected Currumbin Rock to the mainland. Following extensive erosion at Kirra Beach after the 1974 cyclone, the Miles Street groyne was constructed. In 1977–79, the Tallebudgera Creek groyne was built to stabilise the northern end of Palm Beach. In 1981, small training walls were built at the mouth of Currumbin Creek. As noted previously, in 1984 training walls were built at the mouth of the Nerang River to facilitate navigation. This is what we now call 'The Seaway'.

In 1995, the *Beach Protection Act* was superseded by the *Coastal Protection and Management Act*. From 1999 to 2001 something new was tried to avoid further beach erosion – an artificial reef off-shore at Narrow Neck. The Gold Coast City Council has funding from the Queensland government and the Commonwealth government to construct two more artificial reefs.

The cost and solutions

Putting aside the environmental consequences (from an ecological perspective, the Gold Coast beaches and foreshore are no longer habitat for native animals or typical coastal plants), the financial cost of beach 'restoration' to Gold Coast rate-payers was approximately \$20 000 per day in the first half of 2013. Severe storms had dragged the sand offshore and properties perched precariously on 5 m cliffs. Engineers with the Gold Coast City Council estimated that \$30 million needed to be spent on reinstating sea-walls, importing sand and constructing more artificial reefs. Except for the latter, the 'solution' remained one of treating the symptoms. Constructed reefs decrease the impact of waves which otherwise batter the beach and drag sand out to sea. The radical proposal of restoring the foreshore to the dictates of nature will remain off the agenda unless (until) the cost of restoration becomes too high. The financial cost of removing foreshore properties and compensating owners is beyond the resources of the Gold Coast City Council and the Queensland government.

Notes

1. The 1893 cyclone crossed at Yeppoon on 1 February.
2. Some claim that sand mining on Gold Coast beaches was occurring in the first decades of the 20th century, but there is no indication of what minerals were sought.
3. The eminent 20th century economist, John Maynard Keynes was convinced that a generation or two had to pass before new ideas (whether valuable or not was not the issue) were accepted.

   The second author is a beneficiary of titanium metal, having had rods inserted to correct spinal degeneration and injury, likely to have resulted from playing Australian Rules football on the rock-hard ovals in Brisbane and the Gold Coast. The ovals are much improved now.

References

Burchill G (2005) *Passion, Power and Prejudice.* Golden 12, Gold Coast.

Harper B (2001) Natural hazards and the risks they pose to south-east Queensland. In *Flood, Tropical Cyclones, East Coast Lows and Severe Storms.* (Eds K Granger and M Hayne). Geoscience Australia/Bureau of Meteorology, Canberra.

McRobbie A (1984) *The Fabulous Gold Coast.* PAN News Ltd, Surfers Paradise.

Sweet C (2008) *Lines in the sand.* Honours thesis. University of Queensland, Brisbane.

Chapter 7

Marine environments of the Gold Coast: out with the old, in with the new

D. McPhee

Introduction

The marine environments of the Gold Coast comprise one of the most highly modified and heavily utilised waterways in Australia. Chapters 2 and 3 discussed changes in the historic land use patterns. Just what has this meant to the marine environments of the Gold Coast? In this chapter the contemporary marine habitats of the Gold Coast are described, along with the fauna that those habitats support. We talk about how the current status of the habitats compares with various historical points in time, and the role of novel habitats. Given the importance of recreational fishing to both tourists to and residents of the Gold Coast, knowledge of the condition and trends of marine habitats is of significance.

Overview of significant changes

The Gold Coast marine environments are affected by a suite of impacts that are common to coastal cities. This includes reclamation of saltmarsh, mangroves and tidal flats, increased nutrients and pollutants from both point (e.g. sewage treatment discharge) and non-point sources (general run-off), hydrology and sedimentation and the general increase in human usage of waterways.

Change in the marine environment of the Gold Coast can be categorised as event-based (e.g. construction of the Gold Coast Seaway), with these events overlaid on continuous and cumulative impacts from urbanisation in general. A major feature that sets the Gold Coast apart was the creation of the Gold Coast Seaway and Wavebreak Island in the mid 1980s. This altered the tidal flow of the region. Then there was the large-scale creation of a series of residential canals that are most pronounced in the Nerang River, but that also occur in the Coomera River, Tallebudgera Creek and Currumbin Creek. This series of residential canals was modelled on the Florida region.

The Gold Coast Seaway

Prior to the creation of the Gold Coast Seaway, the Southport Bar was a highly mobile surf bar that varied significantly and unpredictably in depth, making navigation across it potentially dangerous at times. This difficulty of access resulted in the Gold Coast offshore reefs being generally lightly fished in comparison to other close-by locations. Prior to construction of the Gold Coast Seaway, the Southport Bar, at least since the breakthrough which resulted in the separation of North and South Stradbroke Islands, had progressively moved north. That is, the area now known as The Spit expanded northwards, while the southern end of South Stradbroke Island regressed.

The Gold Coast Seaway and associated sand bypass system was constructed between 1984 and 1986 to facilitate safe entry for commercial and recreational boats. Wavebreak Island was constructed at the same time, directly in-shore of the modified entrance using dredged sediments, its function being to block storm waves and protect the western shores of the Broadwater (Coughlan and Robinson 1990). Areas such as the old Southport Bar are known to be preferred spawning locations for many estuarine species of fish, including important recreational and commercial species such as yellowfin bream (*Acanthopagrus australis*) (Pollock 1982). While such habitat has been lost, the addition of a large amount of rock has created a man-made habitat that supports a significantly different assemblage of fish and provides amenity for recreational fishing and diving.

Gold Coast canals and tidal lakes

The history of the construction of the Gold Coast canals was dealt with in some detail in Chapter 2. This chapter focuses more on the canals' impacts on natural habitat and their role as modified habitat themselves. The construction of the canals occurred principally through the reclamation of wetlands (mangroves and saltmarshes), although in several instances canal systems replaced ostensibly terrestrial environments. Many of the canals are directly attached to the marine environment, while others have tidal flows restricted by tidal gates and locks. While the bulk of the canal systems on the Gold Coast are in the Nerang River, less extensive developments also occurred in the Coomera River, Tallebudgera Creek and Currumbin Creek. Residential canals tend to be free of seagrass and fringing mangrove habitat (Morton 1992). Maintenance dredging is undertaken to maintain channel depth and to provide a source of sand to replenish beaches within the canal system. Floating rubbish (e.g. plastics) are regularly scooped up by a specially designed boat to address visual amenity and environmental impacts from marine debris.

Several artificial tidal lakes have also been constructed. The Burleigh Lake system that covers 280 ha represents the world's largest aggregation of artificial estuarine lakes (Waltham and Connolly 2013). These tidal lakes are separated from the downstream estuary via tidal control structures and represent an engineering approach to expand waterfront residential land while not increasing the tidal prism of the estuary, which can cause erosion of downstream properties (Zigic *et al.* 2005).

Key habitat types

Despite the significant and varied human disturbances to Gold Coast waterways, there still remains or has come to be re-established a diversity of marine habitats, including seagrass, mangroves, saltmarsh and ocean beaches. Coastal development itself has in many instances contributed to the diversity of available habitat. Marine habitats generally function as a mosaic with the faunal value of an individual habitat patch being influenced by the presence of other nearby habitat patches (Pittman *et al.* 2004; Skilleter *et al.* 2005). In simple terms, a patch of seagrass that is associated with a nearby mangrove area may have higher faunal value than a similar seagrass patch that is not associated with nearby mangroves.

Seagrass habitats

Seagrasses are flowing plants related to terrestrial lilies and ginger; they are not a true grass at all. Seagrass is a highly productive habitat type and the decomposition of seagrass material drives a detritus-based food web. Seagrass beds also play several other significant ecological roles: they provide a structurally complex habitat for juvenile fish and invertebrates and food for dugong and green turtles, and they stabilise the seabed through trapping and binding sediments. Organic matter from seagrass meadows is important at the base of food webs for fish on adjacent unvegetated mudflats (Melville and Connolly 2005).

There are six species of seagrass commonly encountered in the Gold Coast region, *Zostera muelleri*, *Halophila ovalis*, *Syringodium isoetifolium*, *Cymodocea serrulata*, *Halophila spinulosa* and *Halodule uninervis* (Cuttriss *et al.* 2013). *Z. muelleri* is the dominant species recorded within the Broadwater and it is dominant to depths of ~0.7 m below mean sea level (MSL) although *H. spinulosa* or *H. ovalis* tend to dominate deeper water (0.7–2 m below MSL) (McLennan and Sumpton 2005). Despite the significant increases in pressures that are known to cause declines in seagrass beds, Cuttriss *et al.* (2013) identified that seagrass cover did not decline in the Southport Broadwater between 1987 and 2005, although the beds themselves became more fragmented. Cuttriss *et al.* (2013) identified that seagrass in the Southport Broadwater covered approximately 860 ha in 1987 but had increased to 1208 ha in 2005 – an increase of ~40%. This occurred after the construction of the Gold Coast Seaway.

In terms of utilisation of seagrass beds by fauna, seagrass in the Broadwater is less studied than that in Moreton Bay, but available information suggests similarities in terms of the structure of the assemblage. Guest *et al.* (2003) examined the structure of the fish assemblage in *Z. muelleri* beds in the vicinity of Coomera Island and found it to be numerically dominated by the trumpeter *Pelates sexlineatus* and the perchlet *Ambassis jacksoniensis*. The crustacean assemblage was dominated by the eastern king prawn *Penaeus plebejus* with lesser numbers of greasyback prawn *Metapenaeus bennettae* and brown tiger prawn *Penaeus esculentus*. These three species are found in seagrass in Moreton Bay more generally (Masel and Smallwood 2000).

Mangrove habitats

Mangroves are found throughout most tropical and subtropical regions of the world. Mangroves protect coastal areas from erosion, support marine food chains in areas both adjacent to and remote from the mangrove areas themselves, maintain coastal water quality, provide significant structurally complex habitats for invertebrates and juvenile fish, and provide habitat for birds (Laegdsgaard and Johnson 2001; Manson *et al.* 2005).

While declines of mangroves at a local scale have occurred in Australia (Duke *et al.* 2005) mangrove areas in many parts of Australia have increased in extent, but often at the expense of saltmarsh habitat (Saintilan and Williams 1999; Breitfuss *et al.* 2003; Harty and Cheng 2003). Within Moreton Bay, the net loss of mangrove habitat has been relatively small, with significant losses occurring on the western foreshore, but those losses are being offset in the southern bay islands and elsewhere through natural expansions (Manson *et al.* 2003). On the Gold Coast, mangroves can be found in the Coomera River (4.58 km^2), Coombabah Creek (3.37 km^2), Currumbin Creek (0.27 km^2) and Tallebudgera Creek

(0.18 km^2). The Nerang River is now largely absent of mangrove habitat. There is inadequate information on which to determine the extent of decline in mangroves on the Gold Coast but, given their virtual absence in the Nerang River which historical photos show as previously having extensive mangroves, the loss is likely to be significant.

There are four species of mangroves found on the Gold Coast – grey mangrove *Avicenna marina*, red mangrove *Rhizophora stylosa*, river mangrove *Aegiceras corniculatum* and orange mangrove *Bruguiera gymnorhiza*. The grey mangrove is generally the most common species. Examples of all four species can be found at Jabiru Island in the Coombabah Creek area.

Saltmarsh habitats

Saltmarsh is a term used to describe a diversity of salt-tolerant bushes, herbaceous plants and grasses that grow in intermittently low-gradient inundated areas in the upper intertidal region of estuaries and creeks. It is a harsh and physiologically demanding environment for plants and animals, and those that reside there possess various adaptations to that environment. Common species of saltmarsh plants in south-east Queensland include *Sarcocornia quinqueflora*, *Sueada australis* and *Sporobolus virginicus*; these are also generally the dominant saltmarsh species on the Gold Coast (Hollingsworth and Connolly 2006). Saltmarsh in Australia generally occurs at the landward edge of mangrove forests. Coastal saltmarshes around Australia are diminishing and the Gold Coast is not an exception, although the magnitude of the decline cannot be determined as historical records of the extent of the habitat are lacking. Compared to mangrove and seagrass habitats, the marine environmental value of saltmarsh, particularly from the fisheries perspective, has been assessed as lower (Connolly *et al.* 1997). On the Gold Coast, saltmarsh can still be found in the Coomera River (0.76 km^2), Coombabah Creek (0.91 km^2) and Currumbin Creek (0.14 km^2). The Nerang River and Tallebudgera Creek are now largely absent of saltmarsh habitat.

Where saltmarsh is adjacent to urban development, it can be subject to the introduction of invasive species (weeds), increased nutrients which reduce the competitive advantage of saltmarsh species over other plants, and mosquito control measures, whether through pesticides or other methods such as runnelling (digging small trenches for drainage which alters the hydrology and hence the function of the system) (Breitfuss *et al.* 2003; Connolly 2005; Laegdsgaard 2006; Dale 2008). Despite a limited period of inundation, saltmarsh habitats make a contribution to fisheries production and marine biodiversity in general (Thomas and Connolly 2001), although in terms of usage by juvenile fish of commercial and recreational significance the direct contribution they make to fisheries habitat is potentially lower than that of seagrass and mangrove areas. The more landward edge of saltmarsh provides habitat for freshwater and brackish-water fishes, which highlights how saltmarsh is a transitional habitat between ecosystem types (Morton *et al.* 1988). Saltmarsh habitats are also used extensively by various bird species for feeding and roosting (Laegdsgaard 2006).

Ocean beaches

Viewed as an area for tourism and recreation, ocean beaches are not generally considered important marine habitats from an ecological perspective (James 2000), but they nonetheless have ecological value. The ocean beach as a habitat starts in the foredunes, although as a result of the coastal development of the Gold Coast very little functioning foredune habitat remains, with the exception of the Southport Spit and South Stradbroke Island.

The dune habitat along most of the Gold Coast ocean beaches has been highly modified through retaining walls to protect beachfront residential and commercial property, which alters the pattern of sand erosion and accretion. Remnant functioning areas of coastal dune habitat still occur on South Stradbroke Island and parts of the Gold Coast Spit; this habitat consists of spinifex grass (*Spinifex sericeus*), coastal she-oak (*Casuarina equisetifolia* subsp. *incana*), coastal banksia (*Banksia integrifolia*), coastal hibiscus (*Hibiscus tilaceus*), coastal jack bean (*Canavalia rosea*) and pigface (*Carpobrotus glaucescens*). These plants represent the typical plants that would have been found along the coastal dunes of the Gold Coast as a whole before European settlement. Conspicuous by their burrows, ghost crabs (*Ocypode* spp.) are a key faunal inhabitant of the foredunes and their foraging in the intertidal zone of the surf beaches provide a direct link in the food web between the marine environment and the adjacent terrestrial environment. Beaches backed by wider dunes that are more densely vegetated are better habitats than the beaches with severely modified dunes (Noriega *et al.* 2012).

The surf zone itself is a highly dynamic environment that is influenced by tides and weather conditions. The fauna of the surf zone is generally low in species diversity, patchily distributed at several different spatial scales, but it can be high in biomass. Species that occur in the surf zone have specific adaptations to persist and utilise the high-energy environment. For example, the swash-riding moon snail *Polinices incei* has a much heavier and flatter shell than its relatives that occur in protected waters; the adaptation is thought to assist the snail maintain its position within the swash zone (Morton 2008). Two benthic animals that reside on the Gold Coast surf beaches are important for supporting recreational fisheries, the surf worm (*Onuphis* spp.) and the pipi (*Plebidonax deltoides*).

Fish species in ocean beach environments can be classified (Bennett 1989) as:

- residents – species which are present in the surf zone as adults and juveniles throughout the year;
- juvenile migrants – species which are represented primarily by juveniles present either throughout the year or seasonally;
- adult migrants – species which are present seasonally primarily as adults;
- sporadics – species represented by few individuals showing no consistent seasonal pattern of occurrence.

The fish fauna of the Gold Coast beaches has not been quantitatively studied although, like beaches in south-east Queensland in general, it is dominated by adult migrants – sea mullet *Mugil cephalus*, tailor *Pomatomus saltarix* and yellowfin bream *Acanthopagrus australis*. These species form the basis of recreational and commercial fisheries in the surf zone of the region (McPhee 1999). The main resident species is the swallowtail dart *Trachinotus coppingeri*, which contributes significantly to recreational fisheries in particular (McPhee *et al.* 1999). The surf zone habitat itself has undergone little in the way of modification, although the pattern of sand supply was altered due to the Gold Coast Seaway and the rock walls at the Tweed River, as well as several groynes which may have a localised impact through small-scale changes to sand movement. As discussed, the foredune habitat throughout most of the Gold Coast has been removed or highly modified.

Man-made habitats

The development of the Gold Coast has resulted in the destruction of marine habitat, but it has also resulted in the creation of habitat. This tends to be overlooked by many non-experts. The residential canals of the Gold Coast represent man-made habitats at a large scale. In comparison to the marine habitats that they replace, these waterways tend to have poorer water quality because of greater depth, limited circulation and the input of untreated storm water (Waltham *et al.* 2011). They also generally lack vegetation or extensive intertidal areas, and are depauperate in terms of macrobenthos (Maxted *et al.* 1997; Waltham and Connolly 2006). In terms of hydrology, water quality, sedimentation and faunal utilisation, residential canals do not represent homogenous marine habitats, and the variation in water quality (oxygen, temperature, pH and salinity) can be higher than in comparable natural waterways (Morton 1989, 1992). When residential canals replace terrestrial environments, they can be viewed as providing additional marine habitat (Morton 1992). Canal estates in the Nerang River have increased the linear extent of the Nerang River estuary from ~20 km to over 150 km (Waltham and Connolly 2006). This expansion is implicated in increasing the tidal prism (the volume of water entering and exiting the river), which causes erosion to downstream properties (Zigic *et al.* 2005). To prevent further exacerbating the erosion problem while still allowing the expansion of residential waterfront property, new residential expansions on the Gold Coast have tidal gates which create artificial estuarine lakes.

Fish utilisation of the residential canals on the Gold Coast has been well investigated and changes in the structure of food webs is clearly evident. Overall, the same species tend to be present in canal environments compared to relatively unmodified riverine habitat, but the relative abundances of species differ (Morton 1989, 1992). Compared to unmodified environments, the fish assemblage of the Gold Coast canals tends to be numerically dominated by planktivores (e.g. Families Clupeidae and Ambassidae) and microbenthic carnivores (e.g. Family Gerridae), while macrobenthic carnivores such as yellowfin bream and the common toadfish *Torquiner hamiltoni* are reduced (Morton 1989, 1992; Waltham and Connolly 2007). Despite the artificial nature of the waterways, the Gold Coast canals have grown in prominence as a location for sportfishing. Various recreational fishing websites and publications laud the area as it produces consistent captures of large predatory fish such as tarpon *Megalops cyprinoides*, mangrove jack *Lutjanus argentimaculatus*, and various trevallies such as big-eye trevally *Caranx sexfasciatus* and giant trevally *Caranx ignobilis*. These and other species support an expanding tourist industry focused on guided fishing. The presence of the various sportfish species tends to have been underestimated or absent in the studies of Morton (1989, 1992) and Waltham and Connolly (2007), perhaps in large part due to the sampling gear used which is not overly effective at catching larger and more mobile fish and/or fish closely associated with structure.

The artificial estuarine lakes represent habitats that have some similarities with the residential canals that open directly and permanently to the Nerang River estuary, but also some differences. Like canals, estuarine lakes generally lack vegetation and extensive intertidal areas, and are depauperate in terms of macrobenthos (Waltham and Connolly 2013). They too contribute to a net gain in fish habitat if they replace terrestrial environments (Waltham and Connolly 2013). They differ from canals in that they can be much larger individual bodies of water and in part have much greater depths (up to 27 m). Additionally, hydrological difference in the design of lakes compared to open canal estates results in much longer residence time as a result of tidal restrictions. This reduced flushing time can result in the accumulation of metals and pesticide contaminants in the water and sediments (Waltham *et al.* 2011).

Waltham and Connolly (2013) analysed the fish fauna of the Burleigh Lakes system and identified that the tidal gates allowed the passage of estuary fish upstream of them. Fish were found along the shallow waters at lake margins but were absent from deeper areas, potentially as a result of low dissolved oxygen. Overall, Waltham and Connolly (2013) found that the fish fauna in the Burleigh Lakes system consists predominantly of a subset of species reported from nearby natural estuarine habitats, although there were exceptions: the predominantly freshwater and brackish water species *Philypnodon grandiceps* and *Hypseleotris compressus* occur in the lakes but have not been recorded from the natural wetlands of the region (Johnson 2010).

The Gold Coast Seaway and the rock walls on Wavebreak Island in effect function as an artificial reef and support both recreational fishing activities and diving. A large number of species that have been recorded at these locations would not have been found there before the introduction of a significant amount of rock into what was an environment of shifting sand. These includes reef-dwelling fish species belonging to the Families Labridae (wrasses), Lethrinidae (emperors) and Chaetodontidae (butterfly fishes), as well as the various seabed fauna such as sponges and soft corals. Diving websites proclaim the Gold Coast Seaway as the best dive in any Australian city! However, construction of the Gold Coast Seaway resulted in the loss of habitat within the Southport Broadwater itself. Prior to the Gold Coast Seaway being constructed there was an area at the southern end of Crab Island known as The Deep Hole, which was low-profile rocky reef. This was rapidly infilled by the movement of sand following construction of the Seaway. As fishers would say, 'there are swings and roundabouts'.

Conclusion

The development of the Gold Coast has seen the loss of important marine habitats but also the creation of new habitat. Although not well quantified, the loss of mangrove and saltmarsh habitat in the Nerang River is almost total, although such habitat still persists in the Coomera River and Coombabah Creek. Between 1987 and 2005 the cover of seagrass within the Southport Broadwater increased, although trends outside that period are unknown. The seagrass beds have become more fragmented and this has implications for their use by fauna. The extensive series of residential canals has created a greater linear extent of marine habitat in the Nerang River than existed previously. While the species diversity and abundance of the fish assemblages in the canals are comparable to the river environment and the same species generally occur, they differ in the comparative importance of species. The Gold Coast Seaway provides significant amenity for recreational fishing and diving related to the novel habitat provided and the suite of reef-dwelling species that reside there which otherwise would have been absent in the habitat that occurred there before construction. Swamps and Roundabouts!

References

Bennett BA (1989) The fish community of a moderately exposed beach on the southwestern Cape Coast of South Africa and an assessment of this habitat as a nursery for juvenile fish. *Estuarine, Coastal and Shelf Science* **28**, 293–305. doi:10.1016/0272-7714(89)90019-X.

Breitfuss MJ, Connolly RM, Dale PER (2003) Mangrove distribution and mosquito control: transport of *Avicennia marina* propagules by mosquito-control runnels in southeast Queensland saltmarshes. *Estuarine, Coastal and Shelf Science* **56**(3–4), 573–579. doi:10.1016/S0272-7714(02)00207-X.

Connolly RM (2005) Modification of saltmarsh for mosquito control in Australia alters habitat use by nekton. *Wetlands Ecology and Management* **13**, 149–161. doi:10.1007/s11273-004-9569-z.

Connolly RM, Dalton A, Bass DA (1997) Fish use of an inundated saltmarsh flat in a temperate Australian estuary. *Australian Journal of Ecology* **22**, 222–226. doi:10.1111/j.1442-9993.1997.tb00662.x.

Coughlan P, Robinson D (1990) The Gold Coast Seaway Queensland, Australia. *Shore and Beach* **58**(1), 9–16.

Cuttriss AK, Prince JB, Castley JG (2013) Seagrass communities in southern Moreton Bay, Australia: coverage and fragmentation trends between 1987 and 2005. *Aquatic Botany* **108**, 41–47. doi:10.1016/j.aquabot.2013.03.003.

Dale PER (2008) Assessing impacts of habitat modification on a subtropical salt marsh: 20 years of monitoring. *Wetlands Ecology and Management* **16**(1), 77–87. doi:10.1007/s11273-007-9058-2.

Duke NC, Bell AM, Pederson DK, Roelfsema CM, Nash SB (2005) Herbicides implicated as the cause of severe mangrove dieback in the Mackay region, NE Australia: consequences for marine plant habitats of the GBR World Heritage Area. *Marine Pollution Bulletin* **51**, 308–324.

Guest MA, Connolly RM, Loneragan NR (2003) Seine nets and beam trawls compared by day and night for sampling fish and crustaceans in shallow seagrass habitat. *Fisheries Research* **64**, 185–196. doi:10.1016/S0165-7836(03)00109-7.

Harty C, Cheng D (2003) Ecological assessment and strategies for the management of mangroves in Brisbane water – Gosford, New South Wales, Australia. *Landscape and Urban Planning* **62**, 219–240. doi:10.1016/S0169-2046(02)00151-2.

Hollingsworth A, Connolly RM (2006) Feeding by fish visiting inundated subtropical saltmarsh. *Journal of Experimental Marine Biology and Ecology* **336**, 88–98.

James RJ (2000) From beaches to beach environments: linking the ecology, human-use and management of beaches in Australia. *Ocean and Coastal Management* **43**, 495–514.

Johnson J (2010) Fishes of the Moreton Bay Marine Park and adjacent continental shelf, Queensland, Australia. *Memoirs of the Queensland Museum* **54**(3), 299–353.

Laegdsgaard P (2006) Ecology, disturbance and restoration of coastal saltmarsh in Australia: a review. *Wetlands Ecology and Management* **14**, 379–399. doi:10.1007/s11273-005-8827-z.

Laegdsgaard P, Johnson CR (2001) Why do juvenile fish utilise mangrove forests? *Journal of Experimental Marine Biology and Ecology* **257**, 229–253.

Manson F, Loneragan N, Phinn S (2003) Spatial and temporal variation in distribution of mangroves in Moreton Bay, subtropical Australia. *Estuarine, Coastal and Shelf Science* **57**, 657–670.

Manson FJ, Loneragan NR, Harch BD, Skilleter GA, Williams L (2005) A broad-scale analysis of links between coastal fisheries production and mangrove extent: a case-study for north-eastern Australia. *Fisheries Research* **74**(1–3), 69–85. doi:10.1016/j.fishres.2005.04.001.

Masel JM, Smallwood DG (2000) Habitat usage by postlarval and juvenile prawns in Moreton Bay, Queensland, Australia. *Proceedings of the Royal Society of Queensland* **109**, 107–117.

Maxted JR, Eskin RA, Weisberg SB, Chaillou JC, Kutz FW (1997) The ecological condition of dead-end canals of the Delaware and Maryland coastal bays. *Estuaries* **20**, 319–327. doi:10.2307/1352347.

McLennan M, Sumpton W (2005) The distribution of seagrass and the viability of seagrass transplanting in the Broadwater, Gold Coast, Queensland. *Proceedings of the Royal Society of Queensland* **112**, 31–38.

McPhee DP (1999) The biology and management of the surf zone carangid *Trachinotus botla* in Queensland, Australia. PhD thesis. University of Queensland.

McPhee DP, Sawynok W, Warburton K, Hobbs SJ (1999) The ranging movements of swallow-tail dart (*Trachinotus coppengeri*) in Queensland and northern NSW. *Proceedings of the Royal Society of Queensland* 108, 89–97.

Melville AJ, Connolly RM (2005) Food webs supporting fish over subtropical mudflats are based on transported organic matter not in situ microalgae. *Marine Biology* **148**, 363–371.

Morton RM (1989) Hydrology and fish fauna of canal developments in an intensively modified Australian estuary. *Estuarine, Coastal and Shelf Science* **28**, 43–58. doi:10.1016/0272-7714(89)90040-1.

Morton RM (1992) Fish assemblages in residential canal developments near the mouth of a subtropical Queensland estuary. *Australian Journal of Marine and Freshwater Research* **43**, 1359–1371. doi:10.1071/MF9921359.

Morton B (2008) Biology of the swash-riding moon snail *Polinices incei* (Gastropoda: Naticidae) predating the pipi, *Donax deltoides* (Bivalvia: Donacidae), on wave-exposed sandy beaches of North Stradbroke Island, Queensland, Australia. *Memoirs of the Queensland Museum – Nature* **54**, 303–322. doi:10.1071/MF9921359.

Morton RM, Pollock BR, Beumer JP (1988) Fishes of a subtropical Australian saltmarsh and their predation upon mosquitoes. *Environmental Biology of Fishes* **21**, 185–194. doi:10.1007/BF00004862.

Noriega R, Schlacher TA, Smeuninx B (2012) Reductions in ghost crab populations reflect urbanization of beaches and dunes. *Journal of Coastal Research* **28**(1), 123–131. doi:10.2112/JCOASTRES-D-09-00173.1.

Pittman SJ, McAlpine CA, Pittman KM (2004) Linking fish and prawns to their environment: a hierarchical landscape approach. *Marine Ecology Progress Series* **283** ,233–254. doi:10.3354/meps283233.

Pollock BR (1982) Movements and migrations of yellowfin bream, *Acanthopagrus australis* (Gunther), in Moreton Bay, Queensland as determined by tag recoveries. *Journal of Fish Biology* **20**(3), 245–252. doi:10.1111/j.1095-8649.1982.tb04705.x.

Saintilan N, Williams RJ (1999) Mangrove transgression into saltmarsh environments in southeastern Australia. *Global Ecology and Biogeography* **8**, 117–124. doi:10.1046/j.1365-2699.1999.00133.x.

Skilleter GA, Olds A, Loneragan N, Zharikov Y (2005) The value of patches of intertidal seagrass to prawns depends on their proximity to mangroves. *Marine Biology* **147**, 353–365. doi:10.1007/s00227-005-1580-2.

Thomas BE, Connolly RM (2001) Fish use of subtropical saltmarshes in Queensland, Australia: relationships with vegetation, water depth and distance onto the marsh. *Marine Ecology Progress Series* **209**, 275–288. doi:10.3354/meps209275.

Waltham NJ, Connolly RM (2006) Trophic strategies of garfish, *Arrhamphus sclerolepis*, in natural coastal wetlands and artificial urban waterways. *Marine Biology* **148**, 1135–1141. doi:10.1007/s00227-005-0154-7.

Waltham NJ, Connolly RM (2007) Artificial waterway design affects fish assemblages in urban estuaries. *Journal of Fish Biology* **71**, 1613–1629. doi:10.1111/j.1095-8649.2007.01629.x.

Waltham NJ, Connolly RM (2013) Artificial tidal lakes: built for humans, home for fish. *Ecological Engineering* **60**, 414–420. doi:10.1016/j.ecoleng.2013.09.035.

Waltham NJ, Teasdale PR, Connolly RM (2011) Contaminants in water, sediment and fish from natural and artificial residential waterways in southern Moreton Bay. *Journal of Environmental Monitoring* **13**, 3409–3419. doi:10.1039/c1em10664c.

Zigic S, King BA, Lemckert C (2005) Modelling the two-dimensional flow between an estuary and lake connected by a bi-directional hydraulic structure. *Estuarine, Coastal and Shelf Science* **63**, 33–41. doi:10.1016/j.ecss.2004.11.001.

Chapter 8

Wildlife of the Gold Coast wetlands

S. Burgin and D. McPhee

Local wetland types

Water in the landscape of the Gold Coast is dominated by marine and marine-influenced systems. The most obvious are the in-shore waters abutting the Gold Coast's world-famous beaches and estuaries. Little more than a glance at a map of the city also reveals the extensive canal estates built to take advantage of the marine waters, and indeed expand them. The waters of the rivers mix with the ocean's waters in the estuaries. These ecosystems are valuable nursery areas for marine wildlife, particularly, but not restricted to, fishes of commercial and recreational value.

Within the Gold Coast there are natural and man-made freshwater wetlands that support a variety of fauna. No matter what their origin, many wetlands have been constructed or modified as a direct result of the rush to satisfy an increasing Gold Coast urban population, underpinned by an upward trend in tourism. These wetland ecosystems show a gradation in salinity from seawater to fresh water, and from natural to man-made or man-modified systems. The previous chapter was confined to the marine systems of the Gold Coast. In this chapter we focus more generally on the 'freshwater' wetlands without discrimination based on origin. This is because all of these impoundments form important habitat for aquatic wildlife and the animals that depend on them.

Protection of the Gold Coast's wetlands

The most common image of the Gold Coast is that of sand, surf and to some extent sex and/or 'schoolies' week'. Very few residents and visitors consider the wetlands of the city a major attraction. However, many of these wetlands are important ecologically and culturally. For example, the indigenous people of the area view many of the Gold Coast's wetlands as culturally significant because they were important traditional sites for food and ceremonies.

Various aspects of Gold Coast biodiversity are protected under the Commonwealth *Environment Protection and Biodiversity Conservation Act 1999*. This legislation includes provisions for the protection and conservation of migratory species and gives effect to Australia's obligations under five international agreements:

- Ramsar Convention 1971;
- Convention of Migratory Species of Wild Animals 1979 (Bonn Convention);

- Japan–Australia Migratory Bird Agreement 1974 (JAMBA);
- China–Australia Migratory Bird Agreement 1986 (CAMBA);
- Republic of Korea–Australia Migratory Bird Agreement 2007 (ROKAMBA).

Wetland wildlife biodiversity: naturally occurring and introductions

Birds

The wetlands of the Gold Coast are not only important habitat for migratory birds, there is also a large number of endemic species including the Pacific black duck *Anus superciliosa*, grey teal *Anas gracilis*, Australian wood duck *Chenonetta jubata*, black swan *Cygnus atratus*, magpie goose *Anseranas semipalmata* and Australian pelican *Pelecanus conspicillatus*. The largest of these birds to breed on the Gold Coast is the black swan *Cygnus atratus*. Individuals arrive on the Coast's wetlands and await their mate's arrival. As do many humans, the young adults that have not already formed a pair bond come to the Gold Coast to seek a mate. When their reproductive activities are complete and the young are fledged, the swans typically move to inland waters.

Some species, such as the pelicans, tend to follow the 'good' seasons. For example, birds marked in Lake Eyre have been found visiting Papua New Guinea. While visiting the Gold Coast they are very happy to be presented with morsels provided by fishermen and/or local tourists, but also happily fish for themselves on the larger lakes and/or off-shore waters. Despite being typically considered a shore bird, the silver gull/seagull *Chroicocephalus novaehollandiae* will also move inland. On the Gold Coast, these gulls use wetlands away from the coast as part of their range. For example, on Lake Orr at Robina less than 2 km inland from Mermaid Beach there is a permanent colony on a small island which is often shared with visitors from out-of-town, including ducks, pelicans and swans. While these species move between coastal saline and freshwater wetlands, others, such as the dusky moorhen *Gallinula tenebrosa*, prefer the margins of freshwater wetlands with thick plant cover, including swamps, lakes and artificial and/or moist areas. With feet that appear out of proportion to their body size, they are well adapted to walking in very moist places and are able to access a wide diversity of food items including water plants (algae, seeds, fruits) and invertebrates including molluscs. Their omnivorous diet includes foraging at the margins of wetlands in the grassed areas of local suburban parks and on urban manicured lawns and, together with a range of other species that live in association with water, including the silver gull and the Australian white ibis *Threskiornis molucca*, visiting local refuse tips.

In contrast to the dusky moorhen which prefers the moist, boggy edges of wetlands, common species such as the white-faced heron *Egretta novaehollandiae* typically obtain their food by wading. The darter *Anhinga melanogaster*, little pied cormorant *Phalacrocorax melanoleucos* and great cormorant *Phalacrocorax carbo* tend to prefer overhanging branches or fallen tree trunks from which to launch their attack on aquatic prey.

However, not all bird species that visit the wetlands associate directly with them. Often small congregations of the welcome swallow *Hirundo nigricans* may be seen flying above the open water at dawn and dusk. These birds take advantage of the emergence of invertebrates that, as larval insects, contribute substantially to the biomass of 'bugs' (invertebrates) that inhabit the wetlands. Thus, while the birds are probably the most obvious visitors to the wetlands, they are not the most numerous.

Other species such as the rainbow bee-eater *Merops ornatus*, sacred kingfisher *Todiramphus sanctus* and laughing kookaburra *Dacelo novaeguineae* are often seen in association with wetlands with adjacent wooded areas, natural or planted. While they may drink from a convenient wetland, they do not otherwise depend directly on the aquatic ecosystem. However, they often hunt in the riparian environment, taking prey from the terrestrial environment.

'Bugs'

There is a diversity of invertebrate 'waterbugs'. Many of these species are familiar as adults. These species lay their eggs in the water where the larvae hatch and contribute to the diversity of bugs that inhabit the wetland. Ultimately these aquatic inhabitants metamorphose into adult form ready to mate and lay eggs, and thus perpetuate the species. Alternatively, they do not make it to metamorphosis but fall prey to predators that associate with these wetlands. Some bugs, even within the same species, may have larval stages of quite different lengths. For example, some Australian species may develop in shallow warm waters – the warmer the water, the faster the development. Under such conditions they may metamorphose within weeks rather than the months that it may take those of the same species that drop their eggs into more permanent, deeper waters (Watson *et al.* 1991).

Since many of the wetland bugs are the offspring of flying insects that typically simply deposit their eggs as they fly over the water, most of those that inhabit the Gold Coast wetlands belong to species that have a widespread range. Some have a reputation for being worrisome to humans, although sometimes they are simply much maligned. For example, there are some 190 species of non-biting midge (Chironomidae) recorded from the Moreton Bay region, which includes the Gold Coast (MBRC undated). On occasions there may be large emergence events of non-biting midges that may be confused with nuisance species. However, some chironomids of the Gold Coast, most commonly *Culicoides ornatus*, do bite humans. To minimise the impact of this species on humans, the Gold Coast City Council's Pest Control Unit runs ongoing surveillance programs across the waterways to watch for larval biting midge and, when appropriate, undertakes control at peak emergence times to reduce numbers to 'an acceptable level' (GCCC undated).

Fish

The fish fauna of natural waterways of the Gold Coast region is not well studied; however, available information and personal observations have identified that it consists of a wide range of common (mostly small) native fishes and a range of introduced pest species. In terms of larger native species, two species of eel, the long-finned eel *Anguilla reinhardtii* and short-finned eel *Anguilla australis*, occur on the Gold Coast and elsewhere on the east coast of Australia. Eels have an interesting lifecycle. Adults migrate from freshwater wetlands out to sea to breed before dying. A female may produce 5–10 million pelagic eggs, and the leptocephali hatch in two to 10 days. These are carried on the East Australian Current to the continental shelf and, somewhere between one and three years after hatching, having formed an eel-like shape, these 'glass eels' move into the estuaries. Ultimately the pigmented elvers move upstream into accessible waterbodies. While many stay in the rivers, under appropriate weather conditions, large numbers also move into wetlands. When the eels reach maturity, estimated to be eight to 12 years for males and 10–30 for females, they migrate back to the ocean to spawn. Occasionally, during particularly wet weather when water covers much of the landscape, they can be observed in large numbers moving towards the local river, leaving sinuous tracks in the grass. They are generally a maligned species, disliked by many people because of their snake-like appearance and slimy skin.

Another large fish that has a range that encompasses the Gold Coast is the catfish *Tandanus tandanus*. In Queensland, this species is one of the most common freshwater fishes living in coastal flowing streams and even moderate sized wetlands such as dams. Although considered a 'very good table fish' (Grant 1978), there is effectively no published research on the species.

Although considered to be restricted to the Mary and Burnett Rivers and possibly the Brisbane River, the threatened Queensland lungfish *Neoceratodus forsteri* has been translocated to several other locations in southern Queensland, including the Coomera River on the Gold Coast (Kemp 1995). Outside of south-east Queensland, the closest relatives of this lungfish species inhabit waters of South Africa and South America. Based in part on this information, scientists trace their ancestors to Gondwana – they are truly an 'ancient fish'.

Most other freshwater species found in wetlands on the Gold Coast are typically small in size (<200 mm). Based on the Brisbane region freshwater fish assemblages, we assume species would include hardyheads, for example, Marjorie's hardyhead *Craterocephalus marioriae*, Pacific blue-eye *Pseudomugil signifier*, crimson-spotted rainbow fish *Melanotaenia duboulayi*, bullrout *Notesthes robusta*, mouth almighty *Glossamia aprion gillii*, striped gudgeon *Gobiomorphus australis* and firetail gudgeon *Hypseleotris galii* (Leggett 2004). While the native fish of discrete wetlands would typically invade impoundments in times of flood, there are stories of fish falling from the sky in heavy storms as a result of eggs or small fry being drawn up with the water evaporating from the surface of wetlands, held in the moist clouds and released in rainfall events.

Introduced fish on the Gold Coast (and elsewhere in Australia) are politely referred to by ecologists as 'escaped pets'. While there are various circumstances whereby introduced fish species can colonise an area, the release of pet fish is the most common origin of feral fish in Australia (Lintermans 2004). When no longer interested in their pets, many people believe that the most humane disposal is to release them into the closest waterway so that they can 'return to the wild', despite the local creek not being within the species natural distribution. Some unknown proportion of these released fish survive. This probably would not be a major issue except that it takes only one pregnant female to be the basis of an aquatic invasion: judging by the distribution of aquarium fish across many wetlands and waterways of urban Brisbane (Arthington and Milton 1983; pers. obs.), there must have been a large number of pregnant fish that were released, survived and formed the basis of new feral populations. As a result of such releases occurring over many years, it is now possible to collect any species of aquarium fish commonly sold in Australia from the local wetlands and creeks. However, unless feral species become a negative economic and/or pest issue, typically they are ignored, especially when they are common aquarium fish. However, these species may introduce disease, outcompete local species or in other ways impact on the natural biodiversity associated with local wetlands.

In large wetlands such as the Gold Coast's Hinze Dam, native freshwater fish have been stocked to support recreational fishing. Indeed, the Hinze Dam Fish Management Committee was established for the purpose of stocking and managing the freshwater fishery within the dam. Species stocked include Australian bass *Macquaria novemaculeata*, golden perch *Macquaria ambigua*, silver perch *Bidyanus bidyanus*, saratoga *Scleropages leichardti* and Mary River cod *Maccullochella mariensis*. Populations of the banded grunter *Amniataba percoides* have also become well established in the Hinze Dam which is outside their natural range; they are considered a pest species locally. The dam also has large populations of red claw crayfish *Cherax quadricarinatus* which, while a species that is native to Australia, is not native to the Gold Coast. The dam's populations are likely to have originated from aquarium releases or aquaculture escapes. Red claw crayfish are not legally stocked in the dam, but it now supports a self-sustaining population which in turn supports recreational fishing (Ahyong and Yeo 2007).

The feral species that Arthington and Milton (1983) found in over 90 per cent of the creeks they sampled in the Brisbane urban area was the poecilid fish *Gambusia affinis*. This species is listed as one of the 100 of the world's most invasive alien species by the International Union for the Conservation of Nature (ISSG/IUCNSSC undated). As the common name hints, the mosquito fish was introduced to control the larvae of problem mosquitoes. Whether it has been successful is a moot point. Although the species certainly eats mosquito larvae, it also consumes native fish and frog eggs and larvae. The fish are able to cope with a wide range of water quality and wetland habitats and have become effectively ubiquitous in the Australian environment where, based on research in artificial ponds, they have reduced several wetland inhabitants including rotifer, crustacean and insect populations and changed the dynamics of wetlands (Hurlbert *et al.* 1972; Hurlbert and Mulla 1981). Another introduced poecilid fish found in the Gold Coast waterways is the swordtail *Xiphophorus helleri*.

The goldfish carp *Cyprinus carpio* is another species that has entered Gold Coast wetlands as an 'escaped pet'. This species is listed as one as of the 100 of the world's most invasive alien species (ISSG/IUCNSSC undated), and is widespread throughout Australian waterways. Much of the impact of these herbivores on local wetlands result from their mode of feeding. They uproot plants and 'work the sediments'. This modifies the in-stream habitat by removing the vegetation and increasing turbidity which, in turn, inhibits regrowth of plants and the associated fauna. As a result, there may be a significant impact on species abundance and the diversity of macrophytes and some macroinvertebrates (Miller and Crowl 2006).

Reptiles

Fish are not the only pets that have 'escaped' and colonised Gold Coast waterways to the detriment of native species. Now present in local wetlands is the pet terrapin (red-eared slider *Trachemys scripta elegans*). Endemic to large areas of North America, since the pet trade in this species was initiated in the 1930s the industry has continued to grow. By 2002, over 10 million slider hatchlings were exported annually from the US and they had become the ubiquitous turtle internationally (Burgin 2007). This species is also listed among the 100 of the world's most invasive alien species. It is listed as a Class 1 pest in Queensland under the Land Protection (Pest and Stock Route Management) Regulation 2003. Undoubtedly it has become resident on the Gold Coast as a consequence of the release of pets.

Three species of native freshwater turtles occur on the Gold Coast: the long-necked turtle *Chelodina longicollis*, Brisbane River turtle *Emydura macquarii signata* and saw-shelled turtle *Elseya latisternum* (Cann 1998). However, to be scientifically correct these 'turtles' should be referred to as 'terrapins'. This is because they have legs, not flippers as do marine turtles, and they are not fully terrestrial as are tortoises. Instead they are adept at both overland terrestrial and aquatic movement. One of the local species, the long-necked turtle, spends more time in terrestrial activity than any Australian turtle species (Ryan and Burgin 2007). Despite the semantics, the Australian freshwater species are colloquially widely known as 'freshwater turtles'. Apart from the freshwater turtles, Australia has few aquatic reptiles, and none of these occur on the Gold Coast (Cogger 2014).

Frogs

While turtles are largely aquatic with relatively limited time spent in terrestrial activity, native frogs spend most of their adult life in the terrestrial environment, moving to the water only to breed.

There are 25–32 species of frogs whose range may include the Gold Coast wetlands. Some endemics, such as the green tree frog *Litoria caerulea* and spotted grass frog *Limnodynastes tasmaniensis* occur over large expanses of Australia. For other species the Gold Coast is close to the extreme of their range (e.g. the green and golden bell frog *Litoria aurea*, Fletcher's frog *Lechriodus fletcheri*, green-thighed frog *Litoria brevipalmata*), and several with a restricted distribution that broadly encompasses the local region are likely to retain breeding populations locally if appropriate habitat is present (e.g. the wallum frog *Crinia tinnula*, giant barred frog *Mixophyes iterates* and laughing treefrog *Litoria tyleri* (Cogger 2014; Czechura 2004).

While each species has a preferred habitat, all need freshwater ecosystems. For example, the current distribution of the green and golden bell frog (classified 'vulnerable' because of the widespread contraction of its range) indicates that the species is able to persist in wetlands that are too saline for chytrid fungus, a disease-causing organism that is considered a major contributor to the decline of amphibians worldwide (Briggs and Burgin 2004). Species that may prosper where other frogs fail is *Limnodynastes peronii*. This species is often the only frog to breed in artificial 'frog ponds' in urban gardens (Hengl and Burgin 2002). However, in their natural environment in the presence of healthy assemblages they are typically a small component of the wetland assemblage, whereas in degraded wetlands with few to no other species they may became common (Ferraro and Burgin 1993; Schell and Burgin 2003). Another species that inhabits the Gold Coast, *Crinia signifera*, is common throughout most of its range and may be the last species to survive in a declining assemblage (Lane and Burgin 2008).

In Western Sydney we observed that the diversity of frogs is equivalent in farm dams and natural wetlands, although in urban areas the diversity was substantially lower. While there does not appear to have been an equivalent study on the Gold Coast, we expect that the more managed the wetlands are for aesthetics, the more likely it is that the diversity of frogs using the wetlands will have declined. This is because with the attempts to improve the aesthetics of the wetland, the habitat for animals becomes more homogenous. If the wetland environs are also 'manicured' there will be fewer appropriate terrestrial shelter sites – the very place adult frogs spend much of their time waiting for rain and the opportunity to breed.

One noticeable decline in urban frogs over recent decades has been the green tree frog which, from the downpipes or rainwater tanks of Gold Coast homes, once commonly heralded rain events. It has been a casualty of mosquito control. These frogs require shallow but persistent water for up to several months because of their relatively long larval stage compared with many of the more explosively breeding local native frogs (Anstis 2002). Their preferred habitat is also that of troublesome (for humans) mosquitoes. As a consequence, much of their wetland habitat has been filled in or subjected to mosquito control with insecticides.

The cane toad *Rhinella marina* is another species now in Australia that is on the 100 most invasive alien species (ISSG/IUCNSSC undated). It was introduced in 1935 into north

Queensland as a (failed) biological control effort that was meant to deal with pest species affecting sugarcane, including the cane beetle *Dermolepida albohirtum*. The range of cane toads has been expanding inland, particularly west and south, ever since (Natrass 2004). They have been resident at the Gold Coast for many decades. Hero (2005) reviewed the potential for controlling toads on the Gold Coast and concluded that hundreds of thousands of individuals would need to be harvested annually to even control the species. He considered this an unrealistic undertaking.

Although there has been relatively limited research on the risk that cane toads pose to native predators, they have a devastating effect on both aquatic and terrestrial species. Their toxin also kills domestic dogs (Natrass 2004). However, there is evidence that species may evolve responses to overcome the toxins. For example, Phillips and Shine (2006) found that the black snake *Pseudechis porphyriacus* exposed to cane toads showed increased resistance to toad toxin, and a decreased preference for them as prey in fewer than 23 generations.

Current status and future prospects for local wetland ecosystems

The Gold Coast has at least four species of introduced pests that are considered among the world's 100 most invasive alien species. These, and other, invasive non-native species have undoubtedly changed the ecosystem dynamics in wetlands of the Gold Coast. However, even without these alien invasive species, the water in the landscape has changed dramatically due to human intervention. In the transformation, there was, at most, limited consideration of the wetlands as habitat for aquatic species. Many wetlands now in existence have been retained due to serendipity, for example, to enhance urban aesthetics. Others, in flood-prone areas or within protected areas or wetlands used to absorb nutrients associated with sewage treatment, have remained. Only where there has been legislation for conservation of specific species/assemblages or ecosystems, do the wetlands remain at least largely unmodified. None have been specifically retained because of their in-stream fauna biodiversity conservation values. In general, therefore, the biodiversity of the remaining wetlands of the Gold Coast, whether natural or man-made, saline or freshwater, continue to be valued predominantly for their aesthetics. Limited attention is paid to the status of the native wildlife they contain.

Undoubtedly, the feral species that have entered these ecosystems (e.g. toads, fish, turtles) will continue to place pressure on the native fauna of the wetlands. Without recognition of their vulnerability, the ecosystems will continue to degrade. It is possible that species will be lost before it is noticed that the ecosystems were vulnerable.

References

Ahyong ST, Yeo DCJ (2007) Feral populations of the Australian red-claw crayfish (*Cherax quadricarinatus* von Martens). *Biological Invasions* **9**, 943–946. doi:10.1007/s10530-007-9094-0.

Anstis M (2002) *Tadpoles of South-eastern Australia*. Reed New Holland, Sydney.

Arthington A, Milton D (1983) Effects of urban development and habitat alterations on the distribution and abundance of native and exotic freshwater fish in the Brisbane region, Queensland. *Australian Journal of Ecology* **8**, 87–101. doi:10.1111/j.1442-9993.1983.tb01597.x.

Briggs C, Burgin S (2004) Congo red: an effective tool for revealing chytrid fungi in frogs. *Mycologist* **18**, 98–103.

Burgin S (2007) Status report on *Trachemys scripta elegans*: pet terrapin or Australia's pest turtles? In *Pest or Guest: The Zoology of Overabundance*. (Eds D Lunney, P Hutchings and S Burgin) pp. 1–7. Royal Zoological Society of NSW, Sydney.

Cann J (1998) *Australian Freshwater Turtles*. Beaumont Publishing, Singapore.

Cogger H (2014) *Reptiles and Amphibians of Australia*. 7th edn. CSIRO Publishing, Melbourne.

Czechura GV (2004) Frogs. In *Wildlife of Greater Brisbane*. (Ed. M Ryan) pp. 143–164. Queensland Museum, Brisbane.

Ferraro T, Burgin S (1993) Amphibian decline: a case study in western Sydney. In *Herpetology in Australia: A Diverse Discipline*. (Eds D Lunney and D Ayers) pp. 197–204. Royal Zoological Society of NSW, Sydney.

GCCC (undated) *Midges. City of GoldCoast*. Gold Coast City Council, Gold Coast. http://www.goldcoast.qld.gov.au/environment/wetlands-4098.html.

Grant EM (1978) *Guide to Fishers*. Queensland Government Printer, Brisbane.

Hengl T, Burgin S (2002) Reproduction and larval growth of the urban dwelling Brown striped marsh frog *Limnodynastes peronii*. *Australian Zoologist* **32**, 62–68. doi:10.7882/AZ.2002.006.

Hero J-M (2005) Evaluating public cane toad eradication programs. In *A Review of the Impact and Control of Cane Toads in Australia with Recommendations for Future Research and Management Approaches. A Report to the Vertebrate Pests Committee*. (Eds R Taylor and G Edwards) pp. 38–41. National Cane Toad Taskforce, Canberra.

Hurlbert SH, Mulla MS (1981) Impacts of mosquitofish (*Gambusia affinis*) predation on plankton communities. *Hydrobiologia* **83**, 125–151. doi:10.1007/BF02187157.

Hurlbert SH, Zedler J, Fairbanks D (1972) Ecosystem alteration by mosquitofish (*Gambusia affinis*) predation. *Science* **175**, 639–641. doi:10.1126/science.175.4022.639.

ISSG/IUCNSSC (undated) Global Invasive Species Database. Invasive Species Specialist Group/IUCN Species Survival Commission. http://www.issg.org/database/species/search.asp?st=100ss&fr=1&str=&lang=EN.

Kemp A (1995) Threatened fishes of the world: *Neoceratodus forsteri* (Krefft, 1870) (Neoceratodontidae). *Environmental Biology of Fishes* **43**, 310. doi:10.1007/BF00005863.

Lane A, Burgin S (2008) Comparison of frog assemblage structure between urban and non-urban habitats in the upper Blue Mountains (Australia). *Freshwater Biology* **53**, 2484–2493. doi:10.1111/j.1365-2427.2008.02068.x.

Leggett R (2004) Freshwater fish. In *Wildlife of Greater Brisbane*. (Ed. M Ryan) pp. 121–129. Queensland Museum, Brisbane.

Lintermans M (2004) Human-assisted dispersal of alien freshwater fish in Australia. *New Zealand Journal of Marine and Freshwater Research* **38**(3), 481–501. doi:10.1080/00288330.2004.9517255.

MBRC (undated) Non-biting midge *Larsia albiceps*. Moreton Bay Regional Council, Queensland. http://www.moretonbay.qld.gov.au/uploadedFiles/common/forms/environment/Non-biting-Midge.pdf.

Miller SA, Crowl TA (2006) Effects of common carp (*Cyprinus carpio*) on macrophytes and invertebrate communities in a shallow lake. *Freshwater Biology* **51**, 85–94. doi:10.1111/j.1365-2427.2005.01477.x.

Natrass R (2004) Cane toads. In *Wildlife of Greater Brisbane*. (Ed. M Ryan) pp. 165–166. Queensland Museum, Brisbane.

Phillips BL, Shine R (2006) An invasive species induces rapid adaptive change in a native predator: cane toads and black snakes in Australia. *Proceedings. Biological Sciences* **273**, 1545–1550. doi:10.1098/rspb.2006.3479.

Ryan M, Burgin S (2007) Gone walkabout? Movement of *Chelodina longicollis* from farm dams in northwest peri-urban Sydney. *Journal of Biological Research* **8**, 119–127.

Schell CB, Burgin S (2003) Swimming against the current: the *Lynmodynastes peronii* success story. *Australian Zoologist* **32**, 401–405. doi:10.7882/AZ.2002.017.

Watson JAL, Theischinger G, Abbey HM (1991) *The Australian Dragonflies: A Guide to the Identification and Habitats of Australian Odonata*. CSIRO Publishing, Melbourne.

Chapter 9

Rainbow lorikeets, possums and pythons: the wildlife of the Gold Coast

S. Burgin

With over half a million inhabitants, over 10 million visitors to the Gold Coast annually and decades of rapid infrastructure development to maintain pace with demand, wildlife is typically the forgotten victim of the Gold Coast's development. The wildlife theme parks allow tourists, school groups, researchers and the rest of the community to learn about and get close to many iconic Australian species, to observe the animals at close quarters. This is the subject of Chapter 10. However, urban wildlife of the Gold Coast involves much more than just a visit to the local theme park – wildlife is ubiquitous!

Because of Australia's separation from any other landmass over 40 million years ago, much of the wildlife on this the largest, and only, island continent has evolved in isolation. The result is an amazing and unique diversity of wildlife. To conserve this diversity, Australia has developed a large estate of protected lands and boasts more Natural World Heritage areas than any other nation. The majority of these are reserved, at least in part, for the protection of wildlife (Hardiman and Burgin 2012). Gold Coast wildlife is protected in reserves that range in size from the smallest national park in Australia, the Burleigh Head National Park, abutting the coast beside the mouth of Tallebudgera Creek and bounded on another two sides by one of the longest-established urban tourist areas on the Gold Coast – Burleigh. At the alternative end of the spectrum of park size is the Gondwana Rainforests of Australia (formally the Central Eastern Rainforest Reserves), part of which is in the south-west of the Gold Coast. Inscribed on the World Heritage List in 1986 (extended in 1994), the area was reserved, in large part, for its natural values. The Gondwana Rainforests of Australia includes the most expansive area of subtropical rainforest worldwide and encompasses the major remaining area of rainforest in south-eastern Queensland/northern New South Wales. Its biodiversity includes a wide range of animals, communities and habitats with their origins in Gondwana. Many of its species are restricted (entirely or largely) to the World Heritage area, and a substantial number that inhabit the area are threatened or endangered (DoE undated).

Gold Coast residents and tourists may experience the wildlife of these natural areas as private visitors (walking the Burleigh Head National Park trails) or with commercial tours such as a trip to the wonders of glowworms at night in Springbrook National Park (within Gondwana Rainforests of Australia). However, effectively everywhere on the Gold Coast, wildlife can be viewed from the windows of hotel rooms, on the streets, along the coastline or in suburban backyards. Depending on where you are, there will typically be a picture-perfect view of at least one bird species, most commonly 'seagulls' (silver gulls *Chroicocephalus novaehollandiae*) along the coast and rainbow lorikeets *Trichoglossus haematodus*, noisy miners *Manorina melanocephala* or magpies *Cracticus tibicen* in urban gardens and parks.

Wildlife in the suburbs

While many species have been badly affected by urbanisation, the magpie has prospered. Its preferred habitat includes scattered trees that provide perches, calling platforms and nesting sites at a secure level above-ground but not too high to survey the movement of prey in the lawn (or short grass) adjacent to the tree. There is, therefore, much urban landscape that mimics the magpie's preferred habitat. It is an example of what scientists refer to as pre-adapted[1] to urban landscapes and may often achieve higher density in urban areas than typically occurs in its natural habitat. Magpies live in groups and defend their territory, particularly in the breeding season (June–September). They are maligned for reputedly taking pleasure in swooping pets and humans, particularly the local posties! However, in reality, only around 10 per cent of magpies attack those who venture too close for their comfort.

In contrast, seagulls and ibis *Threskiornis moluccus* have no desire to attack humans. They seek to exploit residents and tourists alike, and happily loiter in their company when there is any sign of food about, scrounging the potato chips that appear to have become their staple diet. However, an excess of this diet is as detrimental to the birds' health as it is for tourists. Although such studies are rare on birds, tourist feeding of southern stingrays *Dasyatis americana* off the Cayman Islands revealed detrimental effects due to the food provided and the associated crowding of animals (Semeniuk *et al.* 2009). This was despite the offerings being much closer to the stingrays' natural diet than chips are for birds. Back to the seagulls and ibis – they are also not averse to picking over food scraps left lying around, or food that has temporarily been left unguarded. They also forage in rubbish bins, the local garbage tip, anywhere offal from fishermen's catches is to be found – any place that will provide food.

Not all common urban birds of the Gold Coast compete directly for human food (and leftovers). The honeyeaters, the most obvious of which is the rainbow lorikeet, and noisy miners have increased dramatically in number in recent decades with the rising popularity of native gardens filled with bird-attracting plants. The concept of incorporating native plants into urban gardens is not new. Australia's first landscape gardener/nurseryman, Thomas Shepard, advocated their use in 1830, although it was not until the mid 20th century that the botanists/authors Thistle Harris and Florence Sulman, and the architects Walter Burley Griffin and Marion Mahony, advocated the integration of indigenous plants into landscape design (Hambrett 2004). However, the concept did not gain momentum until decades later when native plants in gardens were linked with bird conservation, due largely to the convergence of the objectives of bird conservation in the Royal Australasian Ornithologists Union (more recently Birds Australia) and the Birds Observers Club (more recently Bird Observation and Conservation Australia). Indeed, it was the recognition of this convergence towards conservation that resulted in a merger of the two societies into BirdLife Australia in 2012. With over 10 000 members, a further 25 000 supporters (Birdlife Australia 2012) and the major program 'Birds in Backyards', there is no doubt that advocacy for growing bird-attracting plants in backyards has been substantial. The success is evident in plant nurseries: even the most conservative has a range of native cultivars – 'bird plants' – for sale. The plant nurseries in the Gold Coast hinterland provide these plants for their urban neighbours.

As a result of demand, there is continual development of new native plant cultivars. Especially popular are the *Grevillea* cultivars with their interesting leaf shapes and terminal, brightly coloured flowers on shrubs that flower prolifically for extended periods. Very different from the more conventional garden plants, they have become popular. Their ability to produce copious quantities of nectar fulfils the promise of 'bird plants'. While a diversity of native honeyeaters visit these plants (e.g. wattlebirds, noisy friarbird *Philemon corniculatus*, little friarbird *Philemon citreogularis*) rainbow lorikeets have effectively become synonymous with these garden plants. This lorikeet has been an iconic species of the Gold Coast for much longer than the popularity of 'bird plants'. This is because, as outlined in the following chapter, the Currumbin Wildlife Sanctuary has attracted crowds to view the lorikeet-feeding for decades. Because all birds fed at the sanctuary are free-living, the Gold Coast was the first city where lorikeets became synonymous with a city landscape, whereas it was the more recent advent of 'bird plants' that resulted in rainbow lorikeets becoming the most common bird species in most of Australia's capital cities (Burgin 2007).

Two marsupial species, the common brushtail possum *Trichosurus vulpecular* and common ringtail possum *Pseudocheirus peregrinus* have also prospered in urban areas, including on the Gold Coast. As implied by the inclusion of 'common' in the names of both species, they were historically abundant. Indeed, in the early 1900s, governments provided a bounty on their skins. Today, much of their habitat has been removed for agriculture, urbanisation and associated infrastructure. Although listed in the Red Data List of the International Union for the Conservation of Nature (IUCN) as of 'least concern', a leading Australian zoologist, Professor Dan Lunney, has suggested that they have declined throughout their range and that if they were not common in urban areas and a major feral pest in New Zealand, they would be candidates for listing as 'vulnerable'.

Due to their nocturnal habits, possums cohabiting with humans often initially remain unnoticed because they are out and about when the human inhabitants settle in for the evening. However, sooner or later, the possum's footsteps and scratching will come to home-owners' notice. Alternatively, if the possum chooses wisely or the owners are away for an extended period, the first indication that a possum has taken up residence in the ceiling cavity may be a strange (and smelly) stain on the ceiling.

Some hazards for urban wildlife

While possums may not be welcome houseguests, one animal group that is typically not tolerated at all is snakes. A surprising number of people hate them, and insist that 'the only good snake is a dead one'. People have an aversion to snakes because they are considered dangerous – and many are.

Australia does have some venomous snakes but not all of them can achieve purchase on anything larger than a finger or toe, and few attack unprovoked.[2] Other than attempting to kill or handle a snake, the most dangerous encounter a human can have with one is when the animal is sluggish, having recently emerged from its shelter site after a cool period to thermoregulate.[3] If startled while still sluggish, the snake may retaliate. Unfortunately for urban reptiles (including snakes), often the most efficient place to thermoregulate is in full sun on a tarred road surface. Consequently, many end up as roadkill, particularly in early spring when they emerge after spending the cooler months inactive.

However, it is not only snakes that become such victims. Two reptile species that occur on the Gold Coast, the bearded dragon *Pogona barbata* and jacky lizard *Amphibolurus muricatus*, suffer the same fate. The most frequent victims appear to be the largest adults. Size does matter in reptiles; larger animals tend to lay more and larger eggs than smaller individuals. Loss of the larger animals from the population can therefore significantly impact on the population's viability (Hitchen *et al.* 2011). While writing this in early spring when reptiles typically emerge after winter inactivity, I observed a large eastern water dragon *Physignathus lesueurii*, coloured to attract a discerning female, on the edge of the Gold Coast Highway (M1), oblivious to the vehicles screaming by at 100 km/hr. I sincerely hope that he did not attempt to cross the highway in the peak hour traffic.

The Australian freshwater turtle, the long-necked turtle *Chelodina longicollis*, prefers terrestrial environments more than other Australian turtle species (Ryan and Burgin 2007). The species is native to the Gold Coast. While they spend much of their time in water, some individuals move among wetlands and may also bruminate (often assumed to be estivation but with physiological differences) on land. When migrating, these animals move in effectively a straight line: when a 'new' obstacle (e.g. building, motorway) blocks their path, they proceed if possible. If the obstacle totally blocks their migration path they become confused. For example, I have intercepted the same turtle on three occasions over a period of five to six years; its migration path had been blocked by a building for ~30 years. This turtle was (presumably) using that migration route before the building was erected.

Because they are slow-moving, migrating turtles are common victims of vehicle collision. A new motorway is particularly deadly, but the number of animals killed by vehicles soon dwindles – presumably because the turtles that use the migration route that requires them to cross the new roadway have been decimated.

Frogs are another taxon that is particularly vulnerable to vehicle collision. The impact varies depending on the number of frogs, the traffic volume and how close the breeding wetland is to the road. Breeding in a wetland adjacent to a road with high-volume traffic is dangerous, particularly on a warm summer's rainy night. I have witnessed 'swarms' of frogs hopping erratically on the road on warm rainy nights. Many became victims of vehicle collisions. Short of the driver changing route, the huge number of frogs may make it impossible to drive through the crowd without collision.

Just as putting in 'bird plants' is popular, so is building 'frog ponds' in urban gardens. However, most frogs require specific wetland conditions for breeding although a few species (of those that occur on the Gold Coast, particularly the cane toad *Rhinella marinai*) are generalists (will breed in just about any puddle). These backyard ponds are therefore typically acceptable habitat for toads and one or two other species, although these taxa do not like sharing with toads. The most common native species that will breed in frog ponds in the area, the brown striped marsh frog *Limnodynastes peronii*, is a minor component of most natural assemblages (Ferraro and Burgin 1993). By providing backyard habitat this species has become more common in urban areas than in its natural habitat (Hengl and Burgin 2002).

Even small species of frogs can live much longer than the few years commonly assumed. For example, the brown striped marsh frog can live for at least 16 years. The green tree frog *Litoria caerulea*, which is happy to cohabit with humans and to generously alert them to imminent rain by croaking loudly, is not yet an adult at 18. These frogs have a long tadpole phase during which they require shallow wetlands that retain water for several months, giving them time to grow and metamorphose. Mosquitoes also like to breed in these wetlands. This is unfortunate for the green tree frog because Gold Coast residents (and others) do not like mosquito breeding wetlands, and prefer to have them removed in order to diminish the mosquito plagues of summer. As a consequence, the green tree frog numbers have also declined. Unfortunately, even if habitat were to be reintroduced for these frogs, rebuilding their population on the Gold Coast would be a slow process because they breed irregularly, not annually. This places the Gold Coast population of green tree frog in a precarious situation.

Just as many of the frog species struggle to maintain populations on the Gold Coast, other iconic species also struggle. The koala *Phascolarctos cinereus* does not sit in a single eucalypt tree; rather, it moves among trees within its home range. When trees become scattered in the process of urbanisation, koalas have to descend to the ground more frequently, cross roads and brave backyards that often contain dogs that could attack them.

There has been serious effort to maintain koalas on the Gold Coast with caveats placed on koala trees in new developments where a known colony exists. However, if retaining trees is based on the simplistic view that koalas only need eucalypts to survive, the efforts probably will not achieve the outcomes sought. Contrary to urban myth, koalas do not require only eucalypts, and indeed they have been recorded to use some 27 plant species, a substantial proportion not eucalypts (Pahl 1990). However, trees are important for more than food. For example, koalas released in a Brisbane reserve during heatwave conditions moved downhill to dense *Melaleuca* species on the bank of the adjacent waterway and stayed there until the weather conditions moderated. If that dense vegetation had not been available, some of the koalas probably would have died.

Although removal of trees from gardens on the Gold Coast can be an offence, a good excuse to do so is that they are 'widow-makers'. Unlike deciduous trees (that drop their leaves annually), eucalypts are evergreens (they do not shed all leaves at once), although they do shed approximately six canopies in eight years. They are more prone to dropping branches than deciduous trees, especially, but not only, in wild storms. Most eucalypts also tolerate drought and low nutrient levels. In gardens they tend to receive an abundance of water and nutrients. Some die as a result but those that survive often grow faster than in their natural habitat. However, their timber is less dense, which makes them brittle and more prone to dropping branches than occurs naturally. They may, therefore, be a risk in urban gardens.

Once a tree has been removed or heavily modified, the koala habitat and that of thousands of invertebrates, birds, reptiles, flying foxes and sundry other species that use the tree, however fleetingly, are affected. This reduces connectivity between habitat patches and thus forces koalas to spend more time on the ground where they are most vulnerable.

Lack of information

One issue with managing Gold Coast wildlife, or indeed Australian wildlife generally, is a lack of information. For example, small skinks (*Lampropholis* spp.) are common in urban gardens of Australia's east coast, including the Gold Coast. One species is sufficiently common for it to be known as the 'garden skink'. In many gardens there is a sister species that can be equally common. When I commenced my doctoral studies (mid 1980s), apart from taxonomic analyses, effectively nothing was known of these species. Indeed, research papers were few and relatively minor. For example, one was on the observation of communal egg-laying and another reported the winter shelter site of several individuals. While much more has been written of the taxon in subsequent years, for a common taxon it remains relatively unknown.

NIMBY (Not in My Back Yard) complex: an issue for urban wildlife

While some species are effectively ignored, flying foxes have gained notoriety and not because they are critical as pollinators of numerous rainforest species. In Queensland, one species, the grey-headed flying fox *Pteropus poliocephalus*, is a carrier of the lethal (to humans) Hendra virus. They act as vectors in the transmission of the virus to horses; in turn, horses pass it to humans. Fruit trees, such as mangoes and papaws, grown in urban gardens, do not escape the ravages of flying foxes. On a summer's night when mangoes are ripening on a Gold Coast tree, flying foxes will be heard dropping into the tree's foliage for a snack. Not surprisingly, with their reputation and habits, they are not favoured visitors.

A nocturnal species, the grey-headed flying fox spends much of its day in 'camps'. In large numbers, flying foxes trash roosting trees and are smelly, largely due to the faeces they deposit on the ground from their treetop roosts. However, despite generally being an unwelcome neighbour, a breath-taking vision at dusk is the spectacle of large numbers of flying foxes overhead at the commencement of their night's foraging. Some fly hundreds of kilometres a night. At the time of writing, the mangoes are ripe on the trees and the Gold Coast City Council is seeking public submissions to a flying fox management plan.

Some species, historically considered pests, have declined substantially on the Gold Coast. Two species, the sand goanna *Varanus gouldii* and lace monitor *Varanus varius* have a range that encompasses much of Australia. The larger of the two species, the lace monitor, is the more common on the Gold Coast. The sand goanna prefers drier areas and thus its local range is more restricted but it is common on South Stradbroke Island. Both commonly scavenge and are predators. They were more common when backyards typically provided vegetables, fruit and eggs to supplement the household diet. These reptiles, and to a lesser extent snakes, enjoyed the easy pickings of the chook pen (poultry enclosure) in the backyard (bottom of the garden).[4] Goannas can remove the eggs from a chook pen with ease in a single visit. As unwanted 'vermin', they were killed but with the demise of chook pens the attraction to urban backyards has diminished. They are still present in appropriate habitat in local bushland, however, from whence they may patrol picnic areas for food scraps. In such surroundings, kookaburras *Dacelo novaeguineae* also appreciate rations from the picnic basket and typically do not always wait until the visitors have left it unattended. They will swoop onto the picnic table and retreat to a nearby tree branch with a beak full of food, consuming it before seeking more.

On the Gold Coast, the snakes mentioned in relation to chook pens are carpet pythons *Morelia spilota variegata*. While these have typically been unwelcome guests in Gold Coast backyards, most local farmers welcome their residency in farm sheds. While the benefit of cohabiting with possums is one-sided, pythons form a symbiotic association with humans. They obtain food and a relatively safe, dry home. In return, farmers have the rats and mice kept in check. However, the relationship often turns sour if the python decides to switch diet from vermin to the chook pen for a meal on eggs and/or the odd chicken (the story of the 'Goose that laid the golden egg' has not been translated into snake language). They may also take family pets.[5] There is, however, no fear of a venomous python bite. Their fangs do not carry venom although a bite may transfer pathogens that could result in infection. These snakes immobilise their prey by coiling around it and constricting the victim until it suffocates.

With the demise of chook pens and most agriculture on the Gold Coast, the python's anthropogenic habitat with a surfeit of food has diminished and it could be assumed that pythons have declined significantly. However, while undertaking fieldwork for my doctorate in the Gondwana Rainforest of Australia (mid 1980s), pythons were strikingly common and, although confirmation would be required now it's 30 years later, there is no obvious reason to doubt that there are viable populations in this World Heritage forest.

More examples of 'losers'

An innocuous group that has been particularly impacted by urban development on the Gold Coast is the small birds that live in the shrub layer in local bushland. Although it is possible to create appropriate habitat in urban gardens for these birds, even by accident in 'unmanicured' gardens, there is no evidence of nursery operators advocating planting species for this bird group. On the Gold Coast these species typically occur only in unkempt gardens with dense shrubs. A range of small birds (e.g. superb fairy-wren *Malurus cyaneus*, striated pardalote *Pardalotus striatus*, eastern spinebill *Acanthorhynchus tenuirostris*) use these unkempt gardens.

Small birds are under pressure because gardens of the Gold Coast are typically designed as showcases with immaculate lawns and specimen plantings or as more typical Australian gardens that attract the large-bodied and/or showy birds (Catterall 2004) including magpies, kookaburras, butcherbirds (e.g. pied butcherbird *Cracticus nigrogularis*) and noisy miners. As indicated above, smaller, less obvious species are often overlooked in landscaping despite many gardeners buying 'food species' that provide berries and/or nectar. The pied currawong *Strepera graculina* has taken advantage of this greater food security. Historically the species migrated between the cooler mountainous hinterland and the warmer coastal clines. With reliable food supplies in urban areas, colonies have become resident year-around on the Gold Coast. Since currawongs are omnivorous, the pressure on small birds has increased.

The cane toad is probably the most universally despised animal in Australia. After numerous attempts, it was finally established in northern Queensland in 1935 to act as a biological control agent against pests of the canefields (Sabath *et al.* 1981). It is beyond comprehension that a government would introduce the species. It was already known, or should have been, that the toads' preferred habitat was open savannah (e.g. areas of short grass) not canefields, hence their penchant for open parklands and gardens of the Gold Coast where they were early colonisers. However, while their overall range continues to expand, interestingly, over recent decades populations have declined in areas of north Queensland where they were previously well established and incredibly abundant for decades (Freeland *et al.* 1986). However, it is undoubtedly too early to celebrate their demise. It has been estimated that to simply manage cane toads at their current levels on the Gold Coast, hundreds of thousands would have to be removed annually, a target that was concluded to be unrealistic (Hero 2005). Hopefully nature will take its course.

Examples of some 'winners'

The noisy miner is a species that has vastly increased its numbers in recent decades. A honeyeater, it is greatly advantaged by the popular 'bird plants' (e.g. *Grevillea* cultivars). The species also appreciates the opportunity to nest within roof cavities and other appropriate urban sites. Such sites enable birds to successfully hatch and fledge more chicks annually than they could without such warm, safe, dry nesting sites.

Noisy miners are aggressive and intolerant of encroachment into their space. A miner will chase and even attack much larger birds (e.g. kookaburras, magpies). It is not uncommon to see several miners attacking hawks, cockatoos and family pets. The attack most often appears to be designed to chase the animal away although sometimes the birds do appear to attack to kill – they then consume the victim. These aggressive birds appear to seldom lose the battle.

The common myna *Acridotheres tristis*, which has been introduced to numerous countries as a caged bird because of its ability to 'talk', is also prone to making aggressive attacks on other species. The species also has a penchant for nesting in roof cavities or other urban nooks, and enjoys the chance to consume ripe fruit and attack the family pet. It is interesting that although noisy miners (native) and Indian mynas (introduced) are not closely related and do not even look particularly alike, they are often mistaken.

House sparrows *Passer domesticus* could also be conceived as a native species although they are less common on the Gold Coast, and in many other urban areas worldwide, than in the past (Shaw *et al.* 2008). They are often fed by well-meaning residents and tell-tale cubes of bread indicate that someone nearby is 'looking after' them. With the advent of urban shopping centres (e.g. Robina Town Centre, Pacific Fair), as opposed to discrete streetfront shops, that concentrate shopping opportunities into large complexes under the same roof, large undercover parking areas have been erected. These car parks may be inhabited by sparrows, which may become increasingly dependent for sustenance on the discards of visitors to the car parks.

Sparrows are not unique in scrounging from humans to supplement their diet. On the Gold Coast, seagulls, ibis, kookaburras and crows *Corvus orru* all tend to seek food where humans congregate to eat. Cane toads also learn to obtain food from pet bowls.

Provisioning occurs, even among law-abiding citizens who would not otherwise consciously break the law. These people may ignore notices that warn them not to feed animals. Some humans just do not seem to be able to help themselves. For example, despite more than 1.5 million collisions between deer and vehicles annually in the US, one of the issues in managing urban deer is that people feed them. Supplementary feeding of deer also occurs in Australia, and one person on the Gold Coast admitted that they feed the deer 'to encourage them to stay in the area'. Supplementary feeding only encourages deer not to be wary of humans and thus to become less shy of urban areas.

When winning can also mean losing

When generations of a species rely on human handouts, animals may never learn to forage. Their ability to survive under natural conditions may therefore be lost or at least diminished. If a significant proportion of a local population of one (or multiple) species has been subjected to supplementary feeding, when food is withdrawn it may cause a substantial impact on the population and, potentially, on the urban wildlife dynamics of the area. For example, the urban community now 'manages' noisy miners with *ad hoc*[6] feeding, both hand-feeding and by providing 'bird plants' that produce prodigious amounts of nectar. Those who provide the provisioning may not intentionally target a specific species; for example, the person who supplementary feeds may primarily be interested in attracting rainbow lorikeets and not even want noisy miners in their garden because they are aggressive towards other species. However, the diets of the species overlap. A reason for withholding food from noisy miners is that they are often confused with the Indian myna, an introduced species. Thus miners may be seen as 'bad' and mynas as 'good'; however, the species compete for the same food types. By planting native *Grevillea* cultivars or other prolific flowering species with abundant nectar, the gardeners are inadvertently advertising to all nectar-seeking species in the area and not just to their target species. The outcome has been that several species have been advantaged, particularly rainbow lorikeets and noisy miners, and thus their numbers have increased greatly in recent decades. This has undoubtedly impacted on other species that have not had an equivalent advantage.

There is a range of issues associated with supplementary feeding, and it would not be appropriate to leave the subject without returning to the need to recognise that supplementary provisioning has implications beyond the act of one person. The action has far-reaching effects for the dynamics of the urban wildlife ecosystem. For example, provisioning noisy miners does not lead to a physiologically detrimental outcome for the birds – they produce more and larger eggs, more frequently. With all else being equal, birds that receive food will fledge more chicks, earlier, that are stronger and healthier (because their parents were well- fed and able to maximise nutrition to the eggs). This will provide more offspring from individuals that access the food, and thus those birds leave a greater proportion of individuals with their genes to subsequent generations. If the situation continues over subsequent generations, the birds most adapted to obtaining supplementary food will increase in number in the population. However, if the supplementary food is stopped a large proportion of the population will be disadvantaged, and may be unable to survive without provisioning. On the Gold Coast this could occur with a continued downsizing of urban blocks and the increasing numbers of units and/or with a change in garden fashion. If the Currumbin Wildlife Sanctuary for some reason ceased feeding the rainbow lorikeets it would be a disaster for the lorikeets of the Gold Coast. In such a scenario, it is realistic to expect a major crash in the lorikeet population.

Disease due to supplementary feeding is one issue of concern. For example, beak and feather disease may be lethal, and is particularly an issue if birds leave infected saliva that another individual collects on their visit to the food source. This disease is found in the wild, but the artificial crowding of birds at supplementary feeding sites exacerbates the chances of spreading disease. In a situation where increasing numbers of people are offering seed and increasing numbers of birds are seeking it, the risk of a serious epidemic within the wild population is enhanced. While there is the potential for this to occur among honeyeaters, seedeaters are most at risk. The spread of any contagious disease in any animal species is most likely to affect a greater proportion of the population when individuals congregate, especially when they congregate in unnatural numbers. Although this scenario has been restricted to birds, the same issue has the potential to arise in effectively any species given the appropriate conditions.

Provisioning is not necessarily deliberate. For example, one species that is not observed frequently on the Gold Coast but nevertheless is present, the red fox *Vulpes vulpes*, enjoys a meal from the urban garden, often from the rubbish bin. Unlike domestic dogs that typically overturn a bin and scatter food scraps around, much to the pleasure of the seagulls and ibis, foxes approach the bin differently. They tend to jump into the bin and collect the food without making a mess. They also enjoy eggs from the backyard chook pen and will kill the chickens. Unless disturbed, they will kill more than they can carry off to their den.

On the Gold Coast, domestic cats are much more likely than dogs to have an impact on wildlife, particularly birds and small reptiles. They can be particularly effective predators of small birds, even those as large as rainbow lorikeets. Provisioning birds, by providing seed or nectar-bearing plants, encourages birds and other species to be attracted to the blossoms (or the cover provided by garden shrubs) and thus enhances the chance of pet cats successfully capturing them. However, it is not just the well loved domestic cat that preys on native wildlife. Feral cats can grow to be much larger than domestic cats when prey is plentiful, and are now ubiquitous in the Australian environment.

'New' wildlife settlers on the Gold Coast

One of Australia's foremost pests, the rabbit, is widespread. Introduced with the First Fleet (1788), the first feral population was recorded in Tasmania in 1827. Although there were unpublicised releases of rabbits on the mainland that contributed to the feral population, Thomas Austin is typically credited with providing the basis of the extensive feral populations on mainland Australia. He imported 24 wild rabbits from England in 1859 and released them onto his property in southern Victoria. Only seven years later over 14 000 rabbits were shot for sport on his property alone. By 1910 they had arrived on the Gold Coast. Despite this relatively early establishment, because of the climatic conditions (rabbits prefer more temperate conditions), they have been less successful on the Gold Coast than in southern climes (Coman 1999).

Although it is illegal to keep rabbits as pets in Queensland, it is legal to keep them across the border in New South Wales. It seems that some Gold Coast residents ignore the Queensland rules. For example, recently there was a rabbit population boom on the Gold Coast, originating from a pet that escaped at Bilinga, the suburb where Coolangatta Airport is situated. More recently, three additional colonies were located further north in the city; however, the Gold Coast City Council acted quickly to remove the infestations (Lewis and Cane 2013).

Less likely to remain an intermittent issue and clearly an emerging pest in south-east Queensland, including the Gold Coast, is feral deer. Six species have formed feral herds in Australia. They were originally released by acclimatisation societies in the late 18th and early 19th centuries to enhance the Australian landscape with English animals and to provide prized hunting experiences. In the 1970s, deer farming became popular. Some releases from farms were accidental, but many deer were released in the 1990s when promised profits did not materialise. Others were translocated to improve hunting opportunities. Consequently, in the last two decades substantial numbers of additional herds have developed from released animals. Deer are now present on the Gold Coast and predicted to become increasingly common. Deer will become an expensive feral species due to vehicle collisions and the associated increases in insurance premiums.

On the Gold Coast there are at least two species of macropod (red-necked wallaby *Macropus rufogriseus*, swamp wallaby *Wallabia bicolor*) which have the potential to be involved in traffic collisions, particularly during drought. The problem is exacerbated during drought because when roadsides are slashed and moisture from road runoff and percolation from under the tarred surface provides moisture for 'green pick', these areas maintain vegetation longer than much of the adjacent landscape. Collisions occur more often on medium traffic level roads than on highways or local roads, and there is a particular issue where there is a barrier on only one side of the road. An animal feeding on the roadside and spooked towards the barrier by an oncoming vehicle may turn back into the path of the vehicle. Often the encounter is lethal for the animal (Burgin and Brainwood 2008).

One species that has taken up residence on the Gold Coast in recent years, rather than being a seasonal migrant from Indonesia, is the channel-beaked cuckoo *Scythrops novaehollandiae*. This species does not brood its offspring: it discards the eggs of a nesting bird, lays its eggs in that nest and leaves the nest's owner to brood the interloper's eggs and raise its fledglings. Although the direct impact on bird populations that have been duped into rearing cuckoo young is unknown, there is undoubtedly a strong negative correlation as the numbers of reproductively active channel-beaked cuckoos increase.

Is this really all there is to Gold Coast wildlife?

The answer to that question is a resounding 'NO!' In this chapter, invertebrates which comprise 'the other 99%' (Ponder and Lunney 1999) of animals have barely been mentioned, nor have aquatic or marine species, or the habitat that the species live within which ecologists, at least, acknowledge as part of the definition of wildlife. Mammals have also received scant coverage and while this may be appropriate given the proportion of mammals compared to the other groups that make up the wildlife of the Gold Coast, they are the group, other than birds, that many humans identify with most closely and thus are typically of greatest interest.

At this point I scanned a book on urban wildlife with chapters contributed by various authors, that I co-edited some years ago (Lunney and Burgin 2004), and while I've referenced a single chapter of my own from that volume (White and Burgin 2004) I have made no mention of the other chapters and, therefore, their wildlife subject.

I have written this chapter with a view to providing not an overview, but rather vignettes of Gold Coast wildlife in the hope that it will be informative and provide 'food for thought' so that the next time you look out your window or venture outside, your consciousness will have been raised. More of the wildlife will be noticed, together with knowledge of the issues that we need to grapple with to even begin to manage the wildlife of the Gold Coast for a future that will include an increasingly larger urban population. I say 'will include' with certainty – the population of the world is becoming increasingly urban and that trend is the same for Australia and for the Gold Coast. The future management of wildlife will, therefore, be within the context of further habitat loss, biodiversity loss and climate change, to name just a few of the issues. To slow the loss of biodiversity it is not sufficient to protect natural areas. We need to better understand wildlife in the suburbs. This is because wildlife will increasingly be relegated to urban areas, simply because the world is becoming more urbanised and cities, including the Gold Coast, are expanding.

Once a string of discrete villages scattered along the coast with the odd inland village that predominantly serviced the local agricultural community, over the last century the space between those villages has diminished until the whole has become the Gold Coast, and still the area continues to expand to fill the spaces of vacant land left unurbanised. Within this context, the backyards, parks and remnant bushland of the Gold Coast will become increasingly critical for wildlife habitat if we are to minimise the biodiversity loss of the associated wildlife. That has been the subject of this chapter. The first step is to raise awareness. If that has happened then we are one step closer to effectively managing our urban wildlife on the Gold Coast and beyond.

Notes

1. Often people speak of animals adapting to an area. In science this implies evolutionary change which does not occur within a lifetime of an individual, rather the species (or at least some genetic lineages) have a genetic predisposition to be able to cope with conditions that may appear to the human observer to be very different from those of

the species' natural range. In reality, the human-modified area has characteristics that can be exploited by the species or lineage and so they appear to become adapted when they have not – they are pre-adapted.

2. As a child in country Central Queensland ('taipan country'), my Dad's sage advice for when we encountered a snake was to stand perfectly still and enjoy its beauty. Although I always followed these instructions, I did find it difficult to hold my ground when a very large taipan *Oxyuranus scutellatus* decided to take a shortcut over my foot.
3. Unlike humans, who are warm-blooded, snakes are cold-blooded and need the warmth of their surroundings (e.g. sun, warm rock, tarred road) to heat their bodies.
4. Australians are notorious for the use of slang, and while there are increasingly regional differences some words become so entrenched that they are typically used in place of formal English. Australians, if they have one, have a 'chook pen' in their 'backyard' rather than, for example, a chicken coop at the bottom of their garden. Hence my use of the words 'chook' and 'backyard'.
5. The consumption of pets by pythons made the news in Lismore (northern New South Wales: e.g. <http://www.abc.net.au/news/2014-03-14/family-dog-swallowed-by-python-inside-its-kennel/5321744>) and I have observed a very contented snake with the appropriate number of tummy bulges, curled up in the basket where previously a litter of kittens had slept contentedly. In the Gondwana Rainforests of Australia, I observed a python with a full-sized wallaby still struggling within its stomach. With opportunity, the snake could readily consume a cat or small dog.
6. In this sense *ad hoc* refers to individual householders independently determining strategies to attract birds to their garden without considering (or even being able to) what others are doing to supplementary feed the same species or even the same birds. They may be inadvertently providing the food, for example the garden may have been planted purely for the aesthetics or because of the current garden fashion without thought that nectar from the plants may be a food source for a local wildlife species.

References

Birdlife Australia (2012) History. http://www.birdsaustralia.com.au/who-we-are/our-organisation/history.

Burgin S (2007) Status report on *Trachemys scripta elegans*: pet terrapin or Australia's pest turtles? In *Pest or Guest: The Zoology of Overabundance*. (Eds D Lunney, P Hutchings and S Burgin) pp. 1–7. Royal Zoological Society of NSW, Sydney.

Burgin S, Brainwood M (2008) Comparison of road kills in peri-urban and regional areas of New South Wales (Australia) and factors influencing deaths. In *Too Close for Comfort*. (Eds D. Lunney, A Munn and W Meikle) pp. 137–144. Royal Zoological Society of NSW, Sydney.

Catterall C (2004) Birds, garden plants and suburban bushlots: where good intentions meet unexpected outcomes. In *Urban Wildlife: More than Meets the Eye*. (Eds D Lunney and S Burgin) pp. 21–31. Royal Zoological Society of New South Wales, Sydney.

Coman B (1999) *Tooth and Nail: The Story of the Rabbit in Australia*. Text Publishing, Melbourne.

Ferraro T, Burgin S (1993) Amphibian decline: a case study in western Sydney. In *Herpetology in Australia: A Diverse Discipline*. (Eds D Lunney and D Ayers) pp. 197–204. Royal Zoological Society of NSW, Sydney.

Freeland WJ, Delvinquier BLJ, Bonnin B (1986) Decline of cane toad, *Bufo marinus*, populations – status of urban toads. *Wildlife Research* **134**(4), 597–601.

Hambrett (2004) *Rise of the Australian Plant Garden.* http://anpsa.org.au/design/rise.html.

Hardiman N, Burgin S (2012) Extreme sports in natural areas: looming disaster or a catalyst for a paradigm shift in land use planning? *Journal of Environmental Planning and Management* **55**(7), 921–940.

Hengl T, Burgin S (2002) Reproduction and larval growth of the urban dwelling Brown striped marsh frog *Limnodynastes peronii. Australian Zoologist* **32**, 62–68. doi:10.7882/AZ.2002.006.

Hero J-M (2005) Evaluating public cane toad eradication programs. In *A Review of the Impact and Control of Cane Toads in Australia with Recommendations for Future Research and Management Approaches. A Report to the Vertebrate Pests Committee.* (Eds R Taylor and G Edwards) pp. 38–41. National Cane Toad Taskforce, Canberra.

Hitchen D, Burgin S, Wotherspoon D (2011) Notes on the population structure of the jacky dragon Amphibolurus muricatus in a small urban remnant. *Pacific Conservation Biology* **16**(4), 237–243.

Lewis D, Cane C (2013) Escaped pet blamed for Gold Coast rabbit infestation. *ABC News*, Brisbane. http://www.abc.net.au/news/2013-07-11/gold-coast-rabbit-plague/4813128.

Lunney D, Burgin S (2004) *Urban Wildlife: More than Meets the Eye.* Royal Zoological Society of NSW, Sydney.

Pahl L (1990) Koala and bushlands survey of West and Central Logan City. Report prepared for the Logan City Council.

Ponder W, Lunney D (1999) *The Other 99%: The Conservation and Biodiversity of Invertebrates.* Royal Zoological Society of NSW, Sydney.

Ryan M, Burgin S (2007) Gone walkabout? Movement of *Chelodina longicollis* from farm dams in northwest peri-urban Sydney. *Journal of Biological Research* **8**, 119–127.

Sabath M, Boughton WC, Easteal S (1981) Expansion of the range of the introduced toad Bufo marinus in Australia from 1935–1974. *Copeia* **1981**(3), 676–680.

Semeniuk CAD, Bourgeon S, Smith SL, Rothley KD (2009) Hematological differences between stingrays at tourist and non-tourist sites suggest physiological costs of wildlife tourism. *Biological Conservation* **142**(8), 1818–1829.

Shaw LM, Chamberlain D, Evans M (2008) The house sparrow *Passer domesticus* in urban areas: reviewing a possible link between post-decline distribution and human socioeconomic status. *Journal of Ornithology* **149**, 293–299.

White A, Burgin S (2004) Current status and future prospects of reptiles and frogs in Sydney's urban-impacted bushland reserves. In *Urban Wildlife: More Than Meets the Eye.* (Eds D Lunney and S Burgin) pp. 109–123. Royal Zoological Society of NSW, Sydney.

Chapter 10

'Getting up close and personal': wildlife of the Gold Coast theme parks

S. Burgin

Who's who in the zoo? Definition of the Gold Coast's wildlife attractions

With the greatest concentration of theme parks in the southern hemisphere, Gold Coast residents and tourists alike are spoilt for choice. With two exceptions, these theme parks provide visitors with an opportunity to get 'up close and personal' with wildlife.

In discussing theme parks I immediately run into a problem associated with defining the term since my interest is in the wildlife exhibits rather than the theme parks *per se*. The familiar theme parks of today, the large multi-purpose entertainment/education facilities (e.g. Dreamworld) include wildlife exhibits. What of the much smaller, single-purpose wildlife attractions? In some sense they were the catalyst for the wildlife exhibitions in larger parks that have a diversity of attractions. In this chapter I wish to discuss the wildlife attractions, no matter whether they are associated with the large multi-dimensional theme parks of today, or whether they focus purely on wildlife. For the purposes of this chapter I have, therefore, defined any attraction that allows patrons to view wildlife as a 'theme park'.

The first wildlife attraction

The history of the wildlife exhibits in the Gold Coast's theme parks dates from the early days of the coast's development as a mass tourist destination. Jim Cavill's first tourist hotel on the Gold Coast was built in 1925 at Elston (later renamed Surfers Paradise), on the northern end of what subsequently became known as the Gold Coast. After the hotel burnt down in 1936 it was rebuilt in a grander art deco style, complete with the 'Surfers Paradise Zoo'. Its major attraction was a kangaroo exhibit.

The Porpoise Pool

At the other end of the Gold Coast, at Snapper Rocks on the Queensland/New South Wales border, the 'Jack Evans Pet Porpoise Pool' opened in 1961. The animals that gave this attraction its name were not, however, porpoises. They were dolphins, a close relative of the porpoise (Harding 2005).

The concept for the exhibit began as a joke. Friends of Jack Evans who were fishermen (the Boyd brothers) released two dolphins into his swimming baths. The resulting publicity prompted him to expand the 'porpoise pool' attraction by adding a whale pool but this resulted in substantial financial loss due to a failed lawsuit associated with the building of the structure. Over time the dolphin exhibit outgrew the original site and Jack Evans moved his Pet Porpoise Pool to the mouth of the Tweed River at Snapper Point. At its peak of popularity, the Porpoise Pool was the 'centre of the universe for top divers'. For many others associated with the place, the Porpoise Pool provided a background for their career. For example, Hec Goodall went on to establish the Pet Porpoise Pool at Coffs Harbour (Harding 2005).

Changes in environmental legislation and complaints about the conditions for capturing and displaying marine animals threatened the closure of such exhibits, and some closed when leases expired. Today, only the remnants of the once-popular Jack Evans Porpoise Pool remain (Harding 2005).

Sea World

Working for the Jack Evans Porpoise Pool in the early 1960s, Ronald Harvey Cox dreamed of opening his own beachfront attraction at The Spit with trained dolphins, sea lions and a variety of fish. On the land that is now occupied by the Sheraton Hotel, he opened Marineland in 1966. A decade later (1976) the theme park was sold to Keith Williams, reportedly for $1.2 million. Dolphins, owned by Keith Williams, were moved into Sea World, Marineland was transformed into a bird attraction and, subsequently, the major attraction of the theme park was Spanish horses. The land was ultimately sold for the construction of the Sheraton Mirage which opened on the site in 1986. While Marineland was not the most famous of the Gold Coast's theme parks, it was a pioneer in marine mammal rescue and research methods which Sea World adopted, adapted and improved, ultimately becoming a world leader in marine research and rescue (GoldCoast.com.au undated a).

Founded in the late 1950s by Keith Williams and originally known as the Surfers Paradise Ski Gardens, in 1971 after major dredging works to build a water ski lake the attraction was moved to The Spit. With the addition of dolphins, a marine display and other infrastructure, a year later the Surfers Paradise Ski Gardens were renamed Sea World. While this theme park has broadened its exhibits to include the more traditional rides and other activities, it has also continued to upgrade its wildlife exhibits (GoldCoast.com.au undated b). For example, in 2000, Polar Bear Shores was billed as the 'most technologically advanced exhibit for Polar Bears' – the bears could be viewed from above-ground and at ground level, and their underwater activities could be viewed via perspex windows below the water's surface. In 2013 the exhibit had four polar bears *Ursus maritimus*, including a cub born at Sea World.

In 2004 Shark Bay was opened at Sea World. It consisted of a collection of artificial lagoons that allowed the activities of sharks to be viewed from above and underwater. This exhibition included large and potentially dangerous bull and tiger sharks. In 2008 Ray Reef was introduced with more than 100 stingrays whose underwater activities can be viewed (GoldCoast.com.au undated a). Upgrade of exhibits in 2010 saw some wildlife experiences closed (e.g. Sea World Aquarium) and new features introduced (e.g. Penguin Encounter and Sea Harbour). An African jungle exhibit, now being built, will include gorillas, hippopotamus and crocodiles. In addition to Sea World's substantial efforts in conservation and rescue of marine animals, it promotes marine environmental education.

While Sea World has retained its name since the 1960s, it is now linked commercially with other theme parks on the Gold Coast including Warner Bros Movie World, and Wet'n'Wild Water World, through the theme park division of Village Roadshow. Those two theme parks do not have wildlife exhibits although 'wild' experiences are the order of the day.

Currumbin Wildlife Sanctuary

A particularly unusual theme park on the Gold Coast is best known for its flocks of colourful, screechy, free-flying rainbow lorikeets *Trichoglossus haematodus*. This iconic attraction grew from a trial in 1947 by flower-grower and bee-keeper Alex Griffiths to stop lorikeets from destroying his flower plantations, taking the pollen intended for his bees. Initially known as the Currumbin Bird Sanctuary and now as Currumbin Wildlife Sanctuary, Griffiths' feeding of the birds was a curiosity but it soon developed into a popular tourist attraction and, for decades, thousands of birds and hundreds of tourists have flocked there for the twice-daily feedings (National Trust of Queensland 2013).

Alex Griffiths was probably considered crazy for trying to protect his flowers from birds by feeding them. The concept could be considered counter-intuitive. A current method of excluding birds (and other species) from high-yield, high-value crops grown in a small space (e.g. flower plantations) is to net the crop. However, this approach is costly and only realistic with modern materials, rather than in 1947 when Alex Griffiths was seeking a remedy to the birds' impact on his livelihood. At the other end of the cost spectrum and much more aesthetically pleasing, a quaint method of deterring birds is using scarecrows which, urban myth holds, does work – although there are as many images of a scarecrow with birds sitting on its shoulders as of scarecrows without such adornment. Another method used for deterring birds from a crop is to use sound, typically a 'scare gun', programmed to make a loud noise at intervals. This approach has some issues in an urban area, not the least of them annoying neighbours with the constant noise. Other methods such as poisoning, trapping and shooting do result in dead and dying animals. But in urban and peri-urban areas these animals are likely to be highly visible and the sight of them could be expected to upset the neighbours, especially when the target of destruction is a colourful species such as the rainbow lorikeet.

So from an innovative mechanism for reducing the impact of this particular 'pest' of Alex Griffiths' crop, an iconic tourist attraction was born on the Gold Coast – the Currumbin Bird Sanctuary. It would not have been long before holiday photographs of tourists to the Gold Coast feeding the lorikeets began to find their way into photo albums. The idea took hold. With the major surge in amateur photography due to the advent of social media and quality cameras in mobile phones, photos can be sent to friends and families anywhere in the world in a second. As a consequence the number of photos of lorikeets hand-fed on the Gold Coast must have risen exponentially in recent years.

Over time the Currumbin Bird Sanctuary morphed into the Currumbin Wildlife Sanctuary. While the rainbow lorikeets remain the hallmark attraction (see Plate 9), visitors may now view, be informed about and in some instances interact with a range of additional Australian endemic species as diverse as koalas *Phascolarctos cinereus*, crocodiles *Crocodylus porosus*, eels *Anguilla reinhardtii*, dingoes *Canis lupus* and emus *Dromaius novaehollandiae*, making the experience of a visit to the Currumbin Wildlife Sanctuary even more diverse, informative and memorable than in the past. An innovative approach to deterring a nuisance species from a floriculturist crop has gone through multiple morphs to become home to one of the largest collections of Australian native wildlife in the world. As with Sea World, Currumbin Wildlife Sanctuary has active programs of conservation-based research and public education, and cares for injured and sick wildlife. Since 1976, these activities have been funded from the Sanctuary's profits. This is because at that time the property was handed to the National Trust of Queensland, a not-for-profit organisation dedicated to preserving natural and cultural heritage.

David Fleay Wildlife Park

Another attraction that has been on the Gold Coast for almost as long as the Currumbin Wildlife Sanctuary, Fleay's Fauna Reserve was established in 1952 (renamed David Fleay's Wildlife Park in 1997). At an early age, David Fleay developed an interest in Australian native wildlife, no doubt fostered by his mother who studied art under Frederick McCubbin, a prominent Australian painter of the late 18th and early 19th centuries who specialised in painting landscapes and scientifically accurate flora and fauna. A mature-aged student at university, David Fleay taught at a private school while studying for his Bachelor of Science degree and Diploma of Education at Melbourne University. In 1931, the year he graduated in zoology, botany and education, he married a fellow science student, Mary Sigrid Collie. While teaching, he continued to privately study native animals. One of his many claims to fame was that he was bitten by the last surviving Tasmanian tiger *Thylacinus cynocephalus* while photographing and filming it. The scar was worn with pride for the rest of his life.

Fleay published much on native wildlife and was widely recognised for his expertise. Despite his acknowledged expertise, however, and in the face of a public outcry, he was dismissed from Healesville Sanctuary in Melbourne (he had been previously dismissed from Melbourne Zoo) due to disagreement with its management over the appropriate husbandry of the native animals in his care.

Fleay's greatest achievement was considered to be breeding the first platypus in captivity, a feat that was only repeated – also at Healesville – some 55 years later. After leaving Healesville, David Fleay maintained and exhibited a private wildlife collection until 1951 when legislation was enacted in Victoria that banned private individuals from accepting money from visitors to view private wildlife collections. As a consequence, David Fleay moved to the Gold Coast to continue his native wildlife research and public education.

Dreamworld

The most recently introduced wildlife experience on the Gold Coast occurred in 1974 when John Longhurst, chasing his personal dream, opened Dreamworld. However, it was not until 1987 that the theme park's first Australian wildlife exhibit, Koala Country, opened. When it was launched in 1995, Tiger Island exhibited Bengal tigers and was billed as being only the second interactive tiger exhibit in the world. After financial hardship resulted in negotiations to trade out of receivership, Dreamworld was acquired by P.L. Kua, a Singaporean businessman, in 1996. The following year, as part of an expansion of exhibits, Wildlife for Kids was introduced, together with a wildlife education program. Dreamworld again changed hands in 1998, when it was acquired by the Macquarie Leisure

Trust and was managed by Macquarie Leisure Operations Ltd (a subsidiary of Macquarie Bank). In the same year, the first litter of Sumatran tigers were born at the theme park. More recently (2001), the Koala Country exhibit was expanded to include other Australian wildlife (Ardent Leisure Group 2013).

Conclusion

There is no doubt that the variety of theme parks, in particular those with wildlife, attractions and conservation programs, have played a significant role in instilling pro-environmental attitudes and otherwise influenced the lives of countless numbers of individuals.

References

Ardent Leisure Group (2013) *Dreamworld Wildlife Foundation.* http://www.dreamworld.com.au/Wildlife/Dreamworld-Wildlife-Foundation/.

GoldCoast.com.au (undated a) *Gold Coast History: 1981–2000.* http://prelive.goldcoast.com.au/article/2007/07/17/689_gold-coast-history.html.

GoldCoast.com.au (undated b) *Gold Coast History: 1961–1980.* http://prelive.goldcoast.com.au/article/2007/07/17/686_gold-coast-history.html.

Harding JH (2005) *Pet Porpoise Pool ...Tweed Heads, NSW.* http://www.thejohnharding.com/archives/00000520.htm.

National Trust of Queensland (2013) *National Trust of Queensland: Registered Places: City of Gold Coast, Gold Coast.* National Trust of Queensland, Brisbane.

Chapter 11

The legacy of David Fleay, a pioneering Gold Coast conservationist

B. McDougall

David Fleay is known today as an Australian pioneer of conservation. His life work was to educate the public about Australia's unique fauna and the importance of preservation of endangered species and their habitat. As mentioned in Chapter 10, Fleay showed early signs of his passion for wildlife. From a young age he began a personal collection of Australian native fauna, starting with snakes and lizards and gradually acquiring large marsupials and birds such as wombats and owls (see Fig. 11.1). The unique collection grew over several years through trips to the bush for particular species, as well as the rehabilitation of injured wildlife. This stage of Fleay's life was the beginning of a fascinating journey that would inspire many and continue long after his passing.

Below is a list of animals that Fleay recorded as part of his personal collection of fauna, all of which were kept in his backyard in Melbourne in the 1930s (Fleay-Thomson 2007, p. 41):

F Phalangeridae
- 1 Mountain Possum
- 5 Silvergrey Possums (one in pouch)
- 5 Ringtailed Possums
- 1 Dormouse Possum
- 5 Greater Flying Phalangers
- 1 Yellow-bellied Phalanger
- 6 Lesser Flying Phalangers
- 1 Pygmy Flying Phalanger

Dasyuridae
- 1 Tiger Cat
- 6 Native Cats (one black)
- 4 Brush-tailed Phascogales
- 2 Yellow-footed Phascogales
- Swinsons Phascogales

F Peramelidae
- 2 Short-nosed Bandicoots
- 2 Water Rats

Reptiles

3 Northern Blue-tongued Lizards
1 Southern Blue-tongued Lizard
1 Western Blue-tongued Lizard
2 Gippsland Water Lizards
1 Tiger Snake

Birds

1 Wedge-tailed Eagle
1 Powerful Owl
2 Tawny Frogmouths

Fig. 11.1 David Fleay with two powerful owl chicks, 1942.

2 Diamond Doves
1 Chestnut-eared Finch
2 Canaries

Fleay's journey began in Ballarat in Victoria and through his years of teaching and studying his personal collection of animals continued to grow. They were a crucial part of his life, even joining him in college at the University of Melbourne. Strange at first, but people who knew him got used to the collection of reptiles, marsupials, mammals and birds. It was a highlight for school students to go and visit 'Mr Fleay's' wildlife. Years later, this is still the experience of school-age children who have the opportunity to visit Fleay's Fauna Reserve at West Burleigh on the Gold Coast.

Life on the Gold Coast

David Fleay was a naturalist of the old school. He understood very well the importance of native fauna, and it was his passion for the bush and all that it holds that pushed him through university and out the other side to take a rollercoaster ride that finally brought him and his family to West Burleigh on the Gold Coast in 1952. They had a piece of paradise, which Fleay sought to preserve for the benefit of his much-loved wildlife and the education of future generations.

David Fleay found prime land, a hill behind Tallebudgera Creek, on which to build his reserve and establish his home. In his eyes it was natural habitat, not a recreated zoo-like environment, where his collection of wildlife could flourish and which native wild animals could enjoy without much disruption. Many of the animals could come and go as they pleased. Only some were fenced in, for practical reasons; cassowaries were an obvious example. The reserve was prime real estate, land that could have made Fleay and his family very wealthy if they had decided to sell it. That was not a consideration; it was the place for a sanctuary. The David Fleay Wildlife Park continues to exhibit threatened and vulnerable unique native fauna of Queensland and of Australia.

However, it was not as simple to acquire the land as it was to find it. The area that Fleay wished to build his wildlife sanctuary on covered three separate properties and was owned by three different people. In two separate negotiations, Fleay purchased the two main sections of the property in July and October 1952 and the final piece, land that would be used as a buffer and car park, in 1965.

At capacity the wildlife park had 450 animals in its care. The animals were sick or injured, recovering before release back into the wild or remaining at the park for study and exhibits. Fleay did not want the park to be a zoo. His main priority was study and observation of Australian native fauna; his second objective was to use that knowledge and educate the public to ensure that fellow humans understood native wildlife and would, hence, care for it. This was best done through displays not zoo-like shows, through exhibits of animals in their natural environment.

The handover

David and Sigrid Fleay wished their work to continue even when they could no longer perform their wildlife duties. They wanted the sanctuary to remain fully functioning, so reached an agreement to transfer the reserve to the Queensland government bit by bit, first 37 acres, next 20 acres and finally the remaining 7.5 acres. The transfer was not a straight-out gift, nor was it a commercial real estate sale.

Rosemary Fleay-Thompson reports that in October 1983 the reserve was handed over to the Queensland government, to be run by the Queensland National Parks and Wildlife Service. David Fleay wished to provide ongoing help to the new owners based on his expertise. He wanted to continue to build the collection of wildlife and improve the state of the enclosures. Upon handing over the sanctuary David and Sigrid Fleay outlined their aims for its future. These were to be the basis of a binding agreement between the Fleays and the state of Queensland, the latter acting on behalf of the people of the state. Fleay's requirements were:

> *The preservation of the unique environment.*
>
> *The preservation of the Tallebudgera Creek and banks from commercial development.*
>
> *The protection of the vital fish breeding habitats, mangroves, wetlands, scenic environment and all features of the waterway.*
>
> *A continuing natural home for captive fauna which has lived on site for many years including the maintenance and welfare of same and the continuance of my study of the life histories of native fauna.*
>
> *Protection of Aboriginal Middens in a unique environment.*
>
> *The status quo to be sacrosanct.*
>
> (Fleay-Thomson 2007, p. 296)

David Fleay also requested that he be consulted in regard to anything to do with the 'housing, feeding and general welfare of fauna' (Fleay-Thomson 2007, p. 296).

Rosemary Fleay-Thompson, David Fleay's daughter, has written that the government did not value the agreement nor follow it to the degree which the Fleay family hoped. An assessment was undertaken by the government and many suggestions were made. Little of this list of recommendations tied in with David and Sigrid's wishes for the future of the park. Rosemary Fleay-Thompson mentions one 'absurd' idea in the assessment – to eliminate the entire property fence, i.e. the fence that protected the fauna within the park by keeping predators out. Several animals were lost during the takeover (including the male and female cassowaries), many due to mistakes that could have been avoided if Fleay had been consulted (Fleay-Thomson 2007).

David Fleay passed away in 1993. The reserve remains open with wildlife displays that include kangaroos, wallabies, crocodiles, cassowaries, dingoes, various birds, a nocturnal house that includes a platypus, reptiles and possums, to name a few. Fleay was an excellent teacher. He used his collection of animals to engage students and to explain each creature, its biology and its role in the fragile ecosystem in which it belongs. Today this aspect of Fleay's life work continues. There is a very strong educational focus with daily 'shows' which aim to educate visitors about different animals and enable them to get up 'close and personal' to learn about Queensland's unique biodiversity.

The educational programs and demonstrations involve all aspects of the reserve with programs for both summer/spring and winter/autumn. Their focus is varied but they are likely to include several nocturnal species, the feeding of the crocodiles, and particular attention to the platypus, the tree kangaroo and cassowaries. A special presentation, called Fur, Feathers and Scales, includes surprise guest animals from each category. Online reviews claim it is a wonderful experience for the whole family, and that whether you are a local or a visitor to the Gold Coast, you will find something at Fleay Wildlife Park that interests you. And this is true.

> *This is my life, I would hate to think it could be lost after I've gone. I'm guessing most of the developers have got the message now – or at least for the meantime – that I won't sell. Anyway I've got nowhere else to go, this is my home (David Fleay).*

Educational programs

Park Ranger for a Day is a program run throughout school holidays. This activity gives visiting children an idea of what it is like to be a wildlife ranger and the duties undertaken on a daily basis to ensure that animals are well looked after and that their enclosures resemble their natural environment as closely as possible. After gathering for a brief introduction, the ranger and the group of children head out for a 'behind the scenes' tour of the reserve. This involves going into the food preparation areas, then out to distribute food to the selection of animals. I was fortunate enough to join a tour and that particular day the pademelons were being fed. As soon as the group entered the enclosure the animals scattered but we could see that they were watching, waiting for us to leave so that they could come and enjoy their breakfast. That day the student group also went 'fishing' to catch yabbies, food for the platypus. Hollow pipes and nets were used by the children to gather up enough yabbies to put into the platypus enclosure to entice the female out of her burrow. The children were successful on this occasion; she was out and swimming around in no time. The enthusiasm shown by the children, aged between six and 12, was something to experience.

This isn't the only program run by David Fleay Wildlife Park. There are several others, based on wildlife experiences, to encourage adults and children into nature and educate them at the same time.

Mangrove Mania is a program run to exhibit the natural mangrove habitat surrounding David Fleay Wildlife Park. It is run by a park ranger and takes groups on a tour to discover what can be found in the mangrove environment. The unique environment is crucial as it provides habitat for a large range of marine species.

Creature Feature is another program run at David Fleay Wildlife Park to exhibit native animals to family groups during holiday periods. It provides detailed information and up close and personal encounters with various animals that call the park home. Bush Detectives allows families to enjoy the native wildlife while learning skills that enable them to detect what wildlife may be living in their backyard, local park or school grounds. The group tours the sanctuary in search of clues such as markings on trees and droppings, to identify which animals may have been in the area. Pouched Pals is a program that takes a detailed look at Australia's native marsupials. A ranger takes the group around the park to discuss what makes these animals unique. One marsupial that the program focuses on has become known by children as the 'Easter Bilby'.

Today, David Fleay Wildlife Park hosts a range of different school programs tailored to specific age groups. Programs target the school curriculum and engage students, in contrast to 'book learning'. Each program provides an introduction and overview of the importance of maintaining biodiversity, and the benefits that this provides for nature as well as human beings. Students actively participate in the program. They have access to a professional guide to answer any questions about the animal's behaviour, eating habits, native habitat, predators and biology. Students are encouraged to ask questions so as to get the most out of their visit. From first-hand experience of the work and observation of the rangers, they certainly do.

The programs for school groups are generally targeted at particular age brackets, but there are two programs – Queensland Natives and Get Active with Nature – that accommodate all age groups. The remaining programs focus on a whole range of aspects of nature, and generally run for four hours. The program offered for the youngest schoolchildren (Prep kids) is called Needs of Living Things. It considers the needs of living organisms and how their senses help them to know what their body is in need of and how all animals can do the same thing as humans do in this regard; for example, babies turn to their mothers (not exclusively) for food, they turn to their siblings to 'play' (exercise for their growing muscles).

Year 1 students are offered a program called Australia Plants and Animals, focusing on the large variety of plants and animals that are native to Australia and where in particular they may be found. There are two programs for Year 2 classes, Watch me Grow that considers an animal's life-cycle and The Past in the Present: David Fleay, that examines the life of David Fleay and how he built up the wildlife park over decades. Year 3 children get to take a closer look at Fur, Feathers or Leaves, where emphasis is on the differences between living and non-living organisms.

Life Cycles and Food Chains are the learning experiences offered for Year 4 students. Life Cycles examines the cycles of several different categories of animals including birds and reptiles. Food Chains looks into the ways in which predators and prey interact, including animals and plants in the food-chain cycle. Year 5 students get to assess Habitats and Adaptations to see which habitat caters to specific species' needs and how these habitat areas differ. Extreme Environments is the program specifically designed for Year 6 children, focusing on the mangroves surrounding the wildlife park, and how native species survive in what can appear to be a harsh environment.

The two learning experiences offered for Year 7 children are Classifications and Food Webs and Habitat Interactions. Year 7 students get to learn about the classification system and the reasoning that scientists use to place each animal in a specific category. The introduction of food webs, one of the building blocks of biology, allows students to examine a variety of habitats and the function of animals in these habitats. Human influence is also analysed to create an understanding of how easily an ecosystem can be impacted.

Students in Year 9 are also offered two programs. Ecology and Ecosystems focuses on several habitats, the ecosystems that form them and the species which are an important part of them. Planning for Parks enables students to learn about the importance of wildlife park management to maintain biodiversity and reduce human impacts at the same time as allowing people to enjoy nature. Year 11 and 12 students get to focus on Biodiversity in Our Ecosystems. The description of biodiversity is analysed and the ways in which scientists measure it is discussed. The classification system is considered in some detail. Loss of biodiversity due to human impacts is also examined.

Park staff continue the campaign

The staff are extremely important in continuing the legacy of David Fleay. In an interview with Jessica Rosewell, the Visitor Management Ranger, we discussed the roles held by park staff. She gave an informed breakdown of particular responsibilities.

Fleay Wildlife Park employs Customer Service Officers, the staff who welcome visitors as they walk through the door. They handle customer enquiries and work in the on-site café. Wildlife Rangers are in charge of the fauna within the park. This includes ensuring that the animals are happy and healthy. They also take care of the enclosures, make sure that they are maintained to resemble the animals' natural environments as closely as possible and feed the animals their correct daily diet. Maintenance Rangers ensure that the park and all enclosures are well maintained for the benefit of the public, employees and animals. Park Managers oversee the reserve and manage all the staff that keep it running. As well as these employees, there are Park Volunteers. Volunteers assist the staff where necessary and in general provide support for the functioning of the park by donating their time to various activities. As of the time of writing, a new Park Management Plan is in preparation.

Jessica Rosewell, the Visitor Management Ranger, has a vital role as she is the coordinator of all the educational programs. David Fleay's legacy is evident in the enthusiasm and knowledge of the generations of wildlife carers who are following him.

Reference

Fleay-Thomson R (2007) *Animals First*. Petaurus Publishing, Natural Bridge, Numinbah Valley.

Chapter 12

The Pink Poodle, swimming pavilions and Miami Ice

L. Armitage and S. Burgin

Introduction

The 3 km of golden beach that lap the shores of Surfers Paradise have become synonymous with urban beaches worldwide. Its name was invented, in a stroke of marketing genius, by Jim Cavill who proposed the name 'Surfers Paradise' and pipped the previous preferred title of 'Sea Glint' for this beachside hideaway. Jim Cavill also built the first hotel in Surfers Paradise, in 1933, and subsequently his Surfers Paradise Zoo. However, it was not until the late 1950s and through the 1960s that the ribbon development of the Gold Coast increased rapidly. Many motels, guesthouses and holiday homes were built during this period, an era of expansion that substantially shaped today's Gold Coast. While some of the original buildings remain (e.g. bathing pavilions, original motels and the high-rise building, Kinkabool), many have been demolished. For example, many of the post-war Gold Coast motels (motor-hotels) have been demolished. The best known of these, the Pink Poodle, became synonymous with the Gold Coast's racy and colourful image and was especially popular with honeymooners. It even inspired a novel by Matthew Condon, *A Night at the Pink Poodle*. Its publisher, Random House Books, promoted it as: 'Glitz and glamour, greed and sleaze, fall and redemption. It's all happening on the Gold Coast'. In 2002, Tor Hundloe published *What was the Commissioner doing at the Pink Pussycat*? Hundloe, in his role as the Commissioner of the Industry Commission, was holding public hearings into the future of the Australian tourism industry when he inadvertently referred to the Pink Poodle as the Pink Pussycat. It did not go unnoticed by the media – the hearings were being held in Kings Cross, a well-known Sydney suburb (Hundloe 2002).

The Pink Poodle Motel was opened in 1967 and demolished in 2004. In its place stands the 15-storey Mantra Wings Hotel with the original neon sign from the Pink Poodle attached to the building. The hotel's bar and restaurant carry the name 'Pink Poodle'. In 2010, the Gold Coast City Council moved to have the neon sign listed on its Heritage Register as a celebration of what made the Gold Coast unique (Stolz 2010). A modern motel in the area also incorporates the historic name – the Best Western Pink Poodle Motel.

Another iconic building of the Gold Coast, Miami Ice, was never placed on the local Heritage Register because the owner declined the offer. It was constructed by joining two Australian Army sheds together in 1944 to provide ice during the Second World War (1939–1945) when large numbers of troops, both Australian and American, were stationed on the Gold Coast or visited for rest and recreation (R and R). It became a cultural landmark. Although not the most glamorous of buildings from the outside, it became immortalised in John Farnham's video clip for the song, 'Two strong hearts' (Larkins 2013).

After the death of its owner, Miami Ice was put up for sale with zoning for 'tourist and residential purposes' (Larkins 2013). Within a few days of its listing for sale, a Facebook page aimed at saving the building attracted over 3000 followers. However, despite being considered one of the last remaining landmarks within the postcode and with a great deal of community objection to its loss, the property was demolished (Ardern 2013; Stolz 2013).

Such losses do not occur because of a lack of heritage legislation or because the National Trust is silent; the problem is that those who shape the Gold Coast urban and tourist areas are devoted to the 'ever new'. In the words of Stolz (2013), the issue is 'the Coast's slash-and-burn development style, landmarks such as the Pink Poodle Motel, Birdwatchers Bar, Chevron Hotel, Magic Mountain and Tallebudgera Playroom have not so much been consumed by the sands of time as sandblasted out of existence.' The Gold Coast is not the only city where this occurs. Television broadcaster, archaeologist and historian Neil Oliver (2012) has seen this value system worldwide. In his words, 'we seem to do no more than construct taller and taller rectangles of glass and steel identikit cathedrals raised only for the worship of [money]'.

This focus on the 'new' at the expense of the established infrastructure is incongruent with the rhetoric of Australian governments. For example, Australia has more designated World Heritage areas than any other country (Hardiman and Burgin 2013), including the Gondwana Rainforests of Australia, a segment of which is within the Gold Coast hinterland. The rainforest is the largest reserve of temperate rainforest on Earth. More importantly, Australia and Queensland are signatories to the Burra Charter 1999. This Charter and its accompanying guidelines are considered 'best practice' for cultural heritage management in Australia (ICOMOS 1999). As the fight for the Miami Ice building shows, it is not that the community is apathetic. Maybe it is the legislation that is deficient. In this chapter we outline the heritage laws and non-government approaches as they apply on the Gold Coast. We seek to contribute to the discussion of heritage by providing details of the current heritage management system at the three levels of government as they relate to the Gold Coast.

Context

In Australia, the community has played a significant and enduring role in the conservation of natural and built heritage sites – one which predates formal government participation in the conservation arena by more than two decades. This coordinated, large-scale community involvement in the conservation of heritage places dates from the mid 1940s when the National Trust of Australia, a non-government organisation, was founded in Sydney (AGPC 2006). In contrast, formal government recognition of the role and importance of heritage sites is a relatively recent phenomenon. The 1970s heralded the birth of conservation-focused legislation that served as both a manifesto and then a mandate for the introduction of a framework of statutory control mechanisms for the identification and protection of Australia's rich stock of heritage places (Irons 2008).

In 2011, the key findings on heritage of the quinquennial State of the Environment Report, an independent report to the federal Minister for Sustainability, Environment, Water, Population and Communities, concluded that there remained a need for 'thorough assessments that lead to comprehensive natural and cultural heritage inventories' combined with 'improved resourcing and more flexible heritage management approaches and practices' (DSEWPC 2011).

Tools for the identification and management of heritage places take many different forms, which tend to vary with the profession primarily responsible for the listing of the heritage site. For example, an archaeologist would have a different perspective from that of an architect, a town planner may hold different views from an historian, and different segments of the community will have different views about what is worth conserving and what they are prepared to forgo.

Within Australia, listing is the primary mechanism for specifying heritage conservation objectives. The various registers and their Gold Coast listings are given in appendices to this book. Heritage listing, which can also be called 'designation' and 'registration', refers to a process whereby a place or item, having been recognised as of heritage value, is entered on a list, inventory or register.

The listing of heritage sites carries a raft of implications for land owners. The impact on value, which often varies with the character of the listing, is frequently at the forefront of concern. In the case of statutory listing, legal obligations are created. Such is not the case, however, with non-statutory listings. For example, the National Trust is a non-government, community-based organisation that has no statutory basis for its listing. Its role is confined to informing and recognising heritage significance. In contrast, statutory listing provides statutory protection that imposes control over the nature and extent of changes that may be made to a listed site, for the purpose of safeguarding the heritage significance. While the nature (restrictiveness) of the controls imposed is subject to jurisdictional variation, such controls invariably have some bearing on private property rights which may, in turn, affect property value.

A synopsis of the current listing system follows; the hierarchical three-tier (Commonwealth/federal, state, local) government structure of the Australian legislative system is adopted. Places listed by the National Trust of Queensland are noted in Appendix 3.

Issues affecting statutory listing in Australia

The Australian heritage listing system draws on both international and historic circumstances. The forces that have shaped this system are many and varied, and include the influence of international conventions, such as the Athens Charter and Venice Charter. The Burra Charter prepared by the Australia ICOMOS (International Council on Monuments and Sites) has a critical role (ICOMOS 1999). In addition, the advocacy work of various non-government community-based bodies including the National Trust is influential. These contextual stimuli are acknowledged as important because they have played a dominant role in shaping contemporary heritage conservation policy and practice.

The formalisation of government-based heritage conservation practice in Australia has its statutory roots in the *Australian Heritage Council Act 1975* which, among other things, established Australia's first official national heritage list, the Register of the National Estate. Following this inaugural legislation at federal government level, heritage legislation has been introduced by all state and territory governments. Local governments may also have registers of heritage listings. The Gold Coast City Council maintains such a register, as do all local governments in Queensland. As a consequence, recognition and protection, associated legislation and heritage registers and lists now exist at Commonwealth, state and local government level. This three-tier structure was implemented in response to the

1997 Council of Australian Governments (COAG) Heads of Agreement on Commonwealth and States Roles and Responsibilities for the Environment. The Agreement places responsibility for environmental and heritage matters of national and world significance in the hands of the Commonwealth government, while the responsibility for matters of state significance rests with state governments. In turn, most state governments have delegated responsibility for matters of local heritage significance to local government level with heritage conservation managed according to established 'level of significance' thresholds reflecting the national, state or local significance of a place or entity.

Similar legislative arrangements govern the identification and conservation of heritage places at Commonwealth and state government levels. These include a statutory register of heritage places and the establishment of a Heritage Council to manage the register and to advise government (DEWHA 2007). At local government level, all states require, or make provision for, their local governments to establish and maintain a register of places of local significance (AGPC 2006; DPIPWE Tas 2013). The protection and conservation of places listed at local government level is customarily given effect through the incorporation of heritage-focused provisions governing land use and development within local town planning schemes, as occurs within the jurisdiction of the Gold Coast City Council.

Statutory listing at the national level

The Commonwealth and National Heritage lists were established in early 2004 under an amendment to the *Environment Protection and Biodiversity Conservation Act 1999*. The Commonwealth Heritage List inscribes places of heritage importance that occur on Commonwealth-owned or controlled lands. For example, within the Gold Coast hinterland the World Heritage area, Gondwana Rainforests of Australia, is inscribed on the Commonwealth Heritage List. Indeed, all World Heritage areas within Australia are inscribed on the Commonwealth Heritage List. Places on this list are afforded statutory protection under the EPBC Act which requires that approval be obtained from the federal Minister for the Environment before any action that could impact the national heritage value of a listed site. The EPBC Act (s. 523) defines an 'action' to include a project, development, undertaking, activity or series of activities. Substantial civil and criminal penalties apply under s. 15B of the Act if an action is taken without approval. There are 31 Queensland places on the Commonwealth list, 13 in south-east Queensland including the Canungra Land Warfare Centre Training Area (part), Boonah Post Office, Enoggera Barracks, Brisbane General Post Office, Naval Offices [Edward Street] and Victoria Barracks in Petrie Terrace.

The different levels of legislation are nested such that there is a requirement for sites listed on the Commonwealth Heritage List to be protected to the same degree on the National Heritage List and by local government. However, the reverse does not necessarily occur; for example, a site listed on the Gold Coast as of local significance is not automatically considered for listing on the Commonwealth and National Heritage Lists. The Commonwealth Heritage List is, therefore, in most material respects strongly comparable to the National Heritage List in terms of its compilation, administration and management, and the assessment procedures and criteria applied for inclusion. The key difference arises with regard to the level of significance. This must be demonstrated for a place to be listed. To reach the threshold for entry on the National Heritage List, the Australian Heritage Council must assess a site as having 'outstanding' heritage value to the nation. To be entered on the Commonwealth list, a place must be deemed to possess 'significant' heritage value. Responsibility for administering both the Commonwealth and the National Heritage Lists rests with the Commonwealth Department of the Environment.

The National Heritage List provides for the identification and protection of places that possess outstanding heritage value to Australia. It includes places of outstanding indigenous, historic and/or natural heritage value within state jurisdictions. For example, the Burleigh Head National Park on the Gold Coast, on state-owned land, is listed on the National Register. The criteria against which heritage places are evaluated for inclusion in the list flow naturally from the definition of heritage value established under the EPBC Act and may incorporate a place's aesthetic, historic, scientific or social significance. The National Heritage listing assessment criteria include outstanding heritage value to the nation derived from a place's possession of uncommon, rare or endangered features; association with significant people; aesthetic qualities; research potential; social, cultural or spiritual associations; representativeness; creative and/or technical importance; and importance as part of indigenous tradition. There are nine National Heritage List criteria; a site is considered to possess National Heritage value if it meets one or more of those criteria.

Australian Heritage database

Commonwealth legislation requires that all sites listed under the Commonwealth Heritage List also be on the National Heritage List. The Australian Heritage Council, under the auspices of the *Australian Heritage Council Act 2003* which was amended in 2006, is responsible for assessing nominations for the National Heritage List. Anyone can nominate a place to be considered for inclusion. When a place is nominated, the Heritage Council evaluates its heritage value against criteria and significance thresholds established under the EPBC Act and provides a recommendation to the Minister for the Environment (AHC 2009).

The Australian Heritage Database contains information about more than 20 000 natural, historic and indigenous places, including places on the World Heritage List, National Heritage List, Commonwealth Heritage List, Register of the National Estate, List of Overseas Places of Historic Significance to Australia and places under consideration or that may have been considered for any one of those lists (DoE 2013).

When introduced on 19 February 2012, references to the Register of the National Estate were removed from the EPBC Act. This is because those parts of the Register have been superseded by stronger ongoing heritage protection provisions under national environment law and have been incorporated in the Australian Heritage Database. The information now used to describe each place includes values, legal status, significance, physical condition, history, location and boundaries, physical description and a bibliography. Photographs are included if available although information on many indigenous places in the Register of the National Estate are not included on the internet out of respect for Aboriginal cultural preferences.

Statutory listing at the state level

In Queensland, the protection of heritage operates under legislation, policy and guidelines. The principal Act, administered by the Department of Environment and Heritage Protection, is the *Queensland Heritage Act 1992*. The Act established the Queensland Heritage Council as an independent statutory authority to provide advice on strategic and high-priority heritage matters to the Queensland government (DEHP Qld 2013). The Heritage Council decides on entries to and removal of places from the Queensland Heritage Register, a list of Queensland's significant heritage places. It also advises on the development of state-owned heritage sites. Best practice is assured for the management of cultural heritage by the government's adherence to the Burra Charter (ICOMOS 1999).

Queensland's Heritage Act provides for every local government to establish a process to determine and record local heritage places, either on a managed local heritage register or via an overlay in its planning scheme. Places of local heritage significance are identified in the local heritage register with guidelines available to councils and fact sheets and other information available to the public. For example, the Gold Coast City Council has a heritage team within the Office of the city's Architect and Heritage Department and they maintain a popular website (GCCC 2013). Local governments may employ heritage advisers to provide conservation advice to owners of local heritage places; the Gold Coast City Council has a Heritage Branch which is responsible for such advice to local property owners.

Under the *Queensland Heritage Act 1992*, the development of heritage sites is through the *Sustainable Planning Act 2009*. There is a provision in the former Act that requires a heritage agreement between property owners and the relevant department when a property is listed. The purpose of these agreements is to give certainty to owners and to ensure the conservation of the cultural heritage significance of a site. A range of activities is specified including use, development work, conservation work standards, public access and maintenance. The agreement is normally listed on the property's certificate of title and is binding on the owner or occupiers.

Under Part 1, s. 3, the *Queensland Heritage Act 1992* does not apply to:

(a) a place that is of cultural heritage significance solely through its association with Aboriginal tradition or Island custom; or

(b) a place situated on Aboriginal or Torres Strait Islander land unless the place is of cultural heritage significance because of its association with Aboriginal tradition or Island custom and with European or other culture, in which case this Act applies to the place if the trustees of the land consent.

Some relics of the past are automatically heritage-listed. For example, all shipwrecks and associated artefacts over 75 years old within Queensland jurisdiction are protected by the *Historic Shipwrecks Act 1976* which the Department of Environment and Heritage Protection administers on behalf of the Commonwealth government. Details are held in the Australian National Shipwrecks database. There are two shipwrecks listed for the Gold Coast – the site of the wreck of the *Cambus Wallace* (in Canaipa Passage, Jumpinpin, South Stradbroke Island) and the site of the wreck of the *Coolangatta*, near the mouth of the Coolangatta Creek, Kirra Beach (Curtis and Banks 2010).

Statutory listing at the local government level: Gold Coast City Council heritage register

The Gold Coast City Council website has links to the local heritage register, which was established in 2010, and provides an introduction. This register includes a list of 55 local heritage places (GCCC 2013, 2014). The Council's heritage website also provides access to newsletters, videos and other resources which offer details of the city's history, walks, museums, funding opportunities, education resources and publications, and contacts with local history groups. Publications range from brochures on particular localities such as Miami and Coolangatta to a more thematic coverage of tall buildings, highway heritage and sugarcane relics in the context of local heritage. The listings are varied and as diverse as, for example, a shipwreck, a surf life-saving club pavilion or a tree.

The statement of significance for the shipwreck is as follows:

> *The Maid of Sker, built in 1884, is historically significant for its role in the early economic use of inland waterways on the Gold Coast. From 1893 to the early 1930s the Maid of Sker made a weekly trip carrying cargo from Brisbane to Southport and Nerang. It is a characteristic example of an iron hulled, general cargo vessel of the late 19th century that evolved over time to meet the changing needs of water transport.*

The second is a more iconic reference to life-saving, with the following statement of significance:

> *The Main Beach Bathing Pavilion and Southport Surf Life Saving Club, built 1934–36, is historically important as evidence of the historical development of the Gold Coast as a holiday resort, in particular the growth of the Southport area as a tourist destination. It demonstrates the evolution of sea bathing from a curative activity to a recreational pursuit. The buildings and associated grounds are now rare examples of the beach setting and built environment of the 1930s Gold Coast. The area has an association with the Surf Life Saving Association of Queensland and in particular with the Southport Branch. The buildings are examples of the influence of the Spanish Mission style of architecture and of the public work of the prominent architectural firm, Hall and Phillips, at Southport.*

Probably considered by many to be the most esoteric is a listing in the hinterland of the Gold Coast – a macadamia tree (H2 Hinde tree at Colliston, Gilston). Its significance is described as follows:

> *The H2 Hinde Tree (Macadamia integrifolia) at Colliston, planted around 1920, is rare as the parent tree of one of two Australian-grown, officially endorsed, macadamia cultivars. The H2 Hinde Tree is historically significant to the commercial development of the Australian macadamia nut industry, particularly its establishment phase from the 1960s to the 1980s. The H2 Hinde tree has played a key role in the success of Australia's macadamia industry, first as scion wood, and in the last twenty years, as the parent of most rootstock used to propagate the large majority of commercial orchard macadamia trees in Australia. An orange metal tag, attached in 1948 by the Department of Agriculture and Stock, identifies the tree as a parent tree.*

In addition to listing sites of cultural value, the Council's website provides brochures for walking tours of historic sites.

National Trust of Queensland

The most influential non-government organisation in Australia that is associated with the listing and protection of heritage is the National Trust. As with all other states, there is one in Queensland devoted to heritage conservation, the National Heritage Trust of Queensland. The organisation describes itself as 'a membership-based community organisation that works to promote the natural, Indigenous and cultural heritage of our state' (National Trust of Queensland 2013). It was established under the *National Trust of Queensland Act 1963* with objectives that address preservation and maintenance, restoration or completion (in some cases where the building does not express its original design or intent), protection, augmentation, access and enjoyment by the public. Appendix 3 shows the 29 places on the Gold Coast that were listed by the National Trust as at October 2013. The list includes places which may be natural or constructed. While some are also inscribed on government lists at national, state and local levels, others are not. This reflects the different criteria of the individual listing bodies. One of the more unusual listings on the Gold Coast is the Currumbin Wildlife Sanctuary, which the National Trust runs as a commercial operation.

Conclusion

Despite the many places that may have been considered significant but that have been lost or changed beyond recognition, some important landmarks and places of significance have been maintained. With the introduction of formal legislation (*Environment Protection and Biodiversity Conservation Act 1999*) specifically to protect sites of heritage significance and the associated increased community awareness (e.g. over 3000 'friends' on Facebook within a few days of the Miami Ice being released for sale; Stolz 2013), future features of heritage value are more likely be retained than have been conserved in the past. As in all communities, the different groups represent the full range of social, economic and political perspectives whose preferences are variously identified in the changing nature of the protections afforded to listed places over time. Therefore, it is unlikely that in the near future all sites that, with hindsight, should have been listed, will be. There is no doubt that while we sincerely hope that sites of extreme cultural and heritage importance will be retained, it is probably more realistic to wish that fewer sites of significance will be lost in the future than have been in the past.

References

AGPC (2006) *Conservation of Australia's Historic Heritage Places*. Australian Government Productivity Commission, Melbourne.

AHC (2009) *Guidelines for the Assessment of Places for the National Heritage List*. Australian Heritage Council, Department of Heritage Environment, Water, Heritage and the Arts, Canberra.

Ardern L (2013) Historic Miami Ice demolished despite community action to save the building. *Gold Coast Bulletin*, 13 November 2013.

Curtis P, Banks I (2010) Ships and shipwrecks of the Gold Coast. *Sportdiving Magazine*, April/May, 91–92.

DEHP Qld (2013) *Protecting Queensland Heritage*. Department of Environment and Heritage Protection Qld, Brisbane. http://www.ehp.qld.gov.au/heritage/heritage-in-qld/protecting-heritage.html.

DEWHA (2007) *Heritage List Criteria and Thresholds*. Department of the Environment, Water, Heritage and the Arts, Canberra. http://www.environment.gov.au/heritage/publications/about/pubs/criteria.pdf.

DoE (2013) *Australian Natural Heritage Assessment Tool (ANHAT)*. Department of the Environment, Canberra. http://www.environment.gov.au/heritage/anhat/index.html.

DPIPWE Tas (2013) *Tasmanian Heritage Register*. Department of Primary Industries, Parks, Water and Environment Tasmania. http://www.heritage.tas.gov.au/thr.html.

DSEWPC (2011) *Australia State of the Environment 2011. Independent Report to the Australian Government Minister for Sustainability, Environment, Water, Population and Communities*. State of the Environment Committee, Department of Sustainability, Environment, Water, Population and Communities, Canberra.

GCCC (2013) *Gold Coast Local Heritage Register - Introduction*. Gold Coast City Council, Gold Coast. http://heritage.goldcoast.qld.gov.au/uploads/heritage-register-pdf/GOLD%20COAST%20LOCAL%20HERITAGE%20REGISTER%20INTRODUCTION%20AND%20INDEX_NEW_.pdf.

GCCC (2014) *Welcome to Gold Coast Heritage*. Gold Coast City Council, Gold Coast. http://heritage.goldcoast.qld.gov.au/.

Hardiman S, Burgin S (2013) World Heritage Area listing on the Greater Blue Mountains: did it make a difference to visitation? *Tourism Management Perspectives* **9** 63–64.

Hundloe T (2002) *What was the Commissioner doing at the Pink Pussycat?* Boolarong Press, Brisbane.

ICOMOS (1999) *The Burra Charter: The Australia ICOMOS Charter for Places of Cultural Significance 1999*. Australia ICOMOS, Sydney.

Irons J (2008) *Heritage Listing and Property Value*. MPropEcon. Queensland University of Technology, Brisbane.

Larkins D (2013) *Save Miami Ice Campaign Heats Up*. ABC Gold Coast. http://www.abc.net.au/local/stories/2013/08/06/3819056.htm.

National Trust of Queensland (2013) *National Trust of Queensland: Registered Places: City of Gold Coast, Gold Coast*. National Trust of Queensland, Brisbane.

Oliver N (2012) *Vikings: A History*. George Weidenfeld and Nicholson, London.

Stolz G (2010) Pink Poodle Motel sign proposed for heritage listing. *Courier Mail*, 30 March 2010.

Stolz G (2013) Gold Coast icons such as Miami Ice the focus of social media campaigns to halt development. *Courier Mail*, 17 August 2013.

Chapter 13

Reducing the ecological footprint: the prospect for green energy

S. Telfer and T. Hundloe

In this chapter we ask the question: what scope is there for Gold Coast citizens, businesses and government agencies to play a proportionally appropriate role in replacing greenhouse gas-producing fossil fuels (in the generation of electricity and for transport) by environmentally friendly energy sources? We could expect that a sunny coastal city caressed by waves, subject to diurnal tidal flows and noted for its sea breezes would have more than average potential to play a leading role in this cause. This we will explore after putting the question into perspective.

The peaks and climate change combine

The need to seek alternatives to conventional fossil-fuel energy sources is two-fold. First, there is the build-up of greenhouse gases in the atmosphere and the global warming that results. The Gold Coast has enough extreme weather events carrying sand away and threatening dwellings perched on the foredunes to not need any increase in these due to climate change. Second, there is the fact that fossil fuels (e.g. coal and petrol, respectively the sources of electricity and transport on the Gold Coast) are finite resources. Take, for example, the concept of 'peak oil'. This represents the point in time when the maximum rate of oil extraction has been reached. From then on the production of oil is in decline. In other words, for each barrel of oil used in drilling for and extracting oil, less and less is produced. The day will come when one barrel of oil used in producing oil will produce less than one barrel! Despite ongoing debate to determine this point, most optimistic predictions suggest a decline commencing in 2020. Similar 'peak' concepts apply to all non-renewable resources, indicating a highly challenging reality for the future if we continue to rely so heavily on these declining resources. We face two challenges: the negative effects of global warming and the depletion of fossil fuels.

Economic and technological limitations as well as underfunding of renewable energy research have significantly restricted the uptake of environmentally friendly energy sources in Australia. Renewable energy policies, especially targets, can play a driving role in the community's switch to renewables. The price a household receives from the sale of excess energy (generated by solar panels) to the network (the grid) is another factor. Finally, there is the most important consideration of all – the pricing to consumers of fossil fuel-produced energy. At the time of writing, there is little certainty on any of these variables.

Traditional energy suppliers are asserting that consumers who do not have solar panels are subsidising those who do. The carbon tax that was put in place by a previous government has been rescinded.

Unless the externalities (the cost of carbon pollution) are included in what we pay for fossil fuel-derived energy, there are serious difficulties in assessing the actual benefits of alternate energy sources. There is not an 'apples to apples' comparison. Governments, as shown recently in Germany, can have a significant effect on the economics of green power. The introduction of a carbon tax (making fossil fuels more expensive) and the use of feed-in tariffs to encourage the installation of solar panels are the conventional approach. The future of a carbon tax and feed-in tariffs in Australia is not at all clear.

Solar energy

The common alternative and environmentally friendly energy source is direct solar for heating water and in photovoltaic panels. The Gold Coast has about 300 days when the sun shines. This does not mean there is sunlight throughout the day, but that there is a period of sunshine for 300 days. Data from the Clean Energy Regulator, a Commonwealth government agency, indicate that as of early 2014 there were ~40 000 'small generation units' (solar panel installations) and 30 000 solar hot water systems installed at residences on the Gold Coast. As there were 195 850 households on the Gold Coast when the 2011 census was taken, this indicates that about one in five households has photovoltaic panels and between one in six or seven has solar hot water systems. This level of solar energy use compares favourably with the national average, which is that one in nine households has photovoltaic panels. A more realistic comparison is to other similar sunny locations, but we do not have that data. It can be argued that Gold Coast householders are pulling their weight in reducing greenhouse gases and slowing the inevitable exhaustion of fossil fuels by the installation of solar panels.

Wind energy

Wind power is an obvious consideration. A relatively detailed study was done on this and other green energy sources in 2009.[1] The consultants drew on existing assessments of the potential of green energy on the Gold Coast: Griffith University's 2003 study of in-shore Gold Coast tidal energy, a 2007 assessment also by Griffith University, the study of Gold Coast wave energy, a wind energy study of the Gold Coast by ARIA in 2004 and the Draft South East Queensland Regional Study of Renewable Energy. These studies are somewhat dated as there have been technological advances and as more solar panels, windmill blades or whatever are manufactured, economies of scale are reducing their price. Nevertheless, we will use the findings of the 2009 study as a starting point, particularly in terms of the technical attributes required for a viable energy source; for example, unless there are strong and constant winds, we can forget about wind power. The 2007 study analysed critical thresholds for wind, tidal and wave energy pertaining to the 'physical conditions at which commercial scale projects are currently able to achieve economic feasibility'.

Wind is clean. Using it to generate energy causes zero greenhouse gases or pollution. Yet some believe it causes noise pollution. This was not a problem, it seems, when the windmills of old dotted the countryside of Holland, and even Australia has its share of farm windmills without complaints. The downside is that wind is temperamental and unreliable. Erratic wind, no wind and too much wind are all problems. Finding a site where wind blows continually and at the appropriate rate is the problem, one not easy to solve on the Gold Coast. Ridgelines are popular sites for wind farms as they are high (with greater wind speed than at ground level), and wind increases in speed as it flows over these topographical features.

A minimum annual average wind speed of 8 m per second (m/s) was established as appropriate by the analysts who studied the Gold Coast, then reduced to 7 m/s. There is a Bureau of Meteorology off-shore weather station near the Gold Coast Seaway, that records meteorological conditions. Data from 1991 to 2010 show that the average 9am wind (wind readings are taken twice per day) exceeded 30 km/hr for 9.5 per cent of the time, and at 3pm it exceeded 30 km/hr for 17.5 per cent of the time. The measure of 30 km/hr equates to 8.3 m/s. The readings indicate that for considerable amounts of time on an average day the wind speed is below the threshold. As a result, it was decided that the average wind speed was not sufficient to justify wind generation at the Seaway. We should not expect significant differences in wind speed at Surfers Paradise, Burleigh Heads or Coolangatta. Hence, coastal locations for wind farms were ruled out.

The 2009 assessment considered other sites, particularly in the mountainous areas of the Gold Coast. There was a suggestion that a wind farm could be viable in the Upper Beechmont area. An advantage of wind 'farms' is that conventional farming can take place in association with wind generation. Upper Beechmont is outside the boundaries of the Gold Coast (the city's boundary is between Lower and Upper Beechmont) and, more importantly, there is a considerable distance to the nearest feed-in opportunity. However, it was suggested that the site warranted further investigation.

When assessing the viability of wind farms on Beechmont there is a need to be aware of potential public objections, as have occurred in parts of Australia. We cannot go into the pros and cons here, but simply note that objections tend to focus on the impacts on human health (noise) and bird strikes. These matters aside, the manufacturing of wind turbines and blades are costly. So is their installation. Maintenance costs are also high due to wear and tear. The cost of wind generation in Australia is influenced by the cost of importing the turbines, which is affected by the exchange rate. The manufacture and delivery of the turbines account for ~70 per cent of the total cost of wind farms. Notwithstanding a gradual reduction in price due to economies of scale (resulting from their drastic increase in Europe, China and the US), only a significant carbon tax will promote wide-scale wind farms in Australia.

Wave and tidal energy

Mainly due to lack of data, the analysis of the potential of wave power was not positive. This suggests the need to revisit this issue and, in particular, obtain the necessary information on wave periods, wave heights and water depths. One of the frustrations with wave energy is that the higher the wave energy, the greater the construction costs as the apparatus needs to be built stronger to guarantee its survival.

We could expect considerable concern, probably opposition, to the construction and placement of devices to harvest wave power. As with wave energy, the consultants' report suggested there were insufficient data to allow a rigorous examination of tidal power. It should be noted that the preferred sites for tidal power are in the north of the country; in Queensland that means the Bowen, Mackay and Whitsunday area where the difference in height between high and low tide is significant. The rule of thumb is a difference of 5 m. Another factor that limits the potential for tidal power on the Gold Coast is that the tides need to be channelled into small areas rather than run up and down long beaches.

Other options

Geothermal energy and hydro-power generation are in the mix in most assessments of green energy. Geothermal can be ruled out for the Gold Coast. So can hydro, although there is a micro-hydro generator below the Hinze Dam. There is cogeneration at the Rocky Point sugar mill and at Elanora wastewater treatment plant, plus gas generation at landfill sites. That is it for the present.

Conclusion

The residents of the Gold Coast have limited ability to modify their energy footprint. While there is considerable scope to make more use of solar power, the only other medium-term possibility is energy from wind farms in the Beechmont area.

Note

1. This study was commissioned by the Gold Coast City Council and undertaken by the consulting firm ARUP.

Chapter 14

The Gold Coast business sector: meeting the environmental challenge

M. Waters

If the Gold Coast is to be the epitome of 21st-century sustainable development, the business sector will need to do its share of heavy lifting. As we shall elaborate in this chapter, considerable effort is already being made by the larger Gold Coast-based businesses. It is these businesses, such as the theme parks, integrated resorts, hospitals, universities, major shopping centres, sporting stadiums and large construction companies that are best placed to take social responsibility for their level of environmental and social impact. As noted earlier, most of the city's businesses are small-scale – highway motels, restaurants, coffee shops and a vast array of retail traders. These small businesses have neither the human nor the monetary resources for full-scale corporate social responsibility (CSR) policies. This does not mean that small businesses cannot, and should not, work to reduce their environmental impacts.

What is corporate social responsibility?

> *The time is not far off when companies will have to justify their worth to society with greater emphasis being placed on environmental and social impact than straight economics.*
>
> Founder of Lend Lease, Dick Dusseldorp, 1973 (Lend Lease Corporation 2011).

The above quote is poignant. It introduces the idea of the triple bottom line (discussed below) and illustrates that the idea of CSR is far from new: it was over 40 years ago that Dusseldorp said 'the time is not far off'.

With the growing concern for our natural environment and the social aversion to the downside of the invisible hand of powerful corporations, CSR, in its various forms, is gaining momentum as a way for companies to promote the positive impacts of their business activities. Corporate social responsibility is the notion that companies, who traditionally have had little accountability for the third-party effects of their business operations, have an ethical responsibility to mitigate their direct impacts on the environment and the community. A corporation's CSR policy is, or should be, an integrated part of its business model and is a form of self-regulation to ensure that stakeholders and customers are aware of a business' ethical standards and that the business can be held accountable (ethically if not legally). Corporate social responsibility is a move beyond legal compliance to environmental and other third-party matters.

Traditionally, profit maximisation has been the objective of business and, consequently, decisions have been based purely on economic factors. However, there has been a shift in thinking towards achieving triple bottom line outcomes. The triple bottom line refers to broadening a company's cost–benefit analysis to encompass social and environmental factors as well as economic. Social and environmental costs can negatively impact a company's profitability, therefore compromising fiscal success and becoming a significant consideration to shareholders. Perceptions of a business as a 'good' or 'bad' corporate citizen can affect patronage, advocacy and sales. In this situation, there are benefits to adopting a CSR policy. Acknowledging and showing commitment towards the local community and environment improves a business' branding and reputation, and can create a point of differentiation. There are also internal benefits to the firm. Operational costs can be cut through the reduction of energy and water consumption and the reduction of waste. Future costs can be anticipated and therefore avoided or reduced, such as costs of having to alter processes to comply with new legislation. Corporate social responsibility can assist in attracting and retaining staff as it tends to create a positive work culture.

This chapter will explore how some of the major industries on the Gold Coast are responding to the increasing regard for CSR and selected environmental protection schemes (e.g. EMS) and how their efforts can benefit the companies as well as the city.

Theme parks

Given the large number of visitors to Gold Coast theme parks, second only to the beaches in visitation, a large ecological footprint attaches to the parks. Energy and water use (and wastewater disposal) are key concerns. As the theme parks have been located on land with lesser biodiversity value and adjacent to the highway, there has been little loss of natural attributes. How the major theme parks deal with their environmental and (to the extent necessary) social challenges is discussed next.

Village Roadshow is responsible for several tourist attractions and recreational activities on the Gold Coast, including Sea World and its integrated resort, Wet'n'Wild, Movie World, Paradise Country and Australian Outback Spectacular. In 2010, sustainability committees were established at these parks. With the goal of integrating and implementing an environmental policy across the businesses, the committees consist of senior management representatives as well as staff from other operational areas (Village Roadshow 2010).

All Village Roadshow theme parks comply with the Queensland Water Commission's Water Efficiency Management Plans (WEMPS) and water usage has been significantly reduced, by 45% at Sea World sites and 32% at the Oxenford site (which houses all parks excluding Sea World) (Village Roadshow 2010). Recycling procedures are in place for solid waste, e-waste and oils. A public beverage recycling initiative at Movie World, Wet'n'Wild and Paradise Country saves ~20 t of beverage containers from landfill annually. Waste audits were completed in 2010 in the search for further improvement.

The business' environmental policy aims to reduce electricity use, which is the biggest contributor to its carbon footprint. Considerable energy is required to operate mechanical attractions such as rollercoasters, stunt shows and climate-controlled animal enclosures.

Sea World and Sea World Resort had an independent firm audit their energy usage in 2010. This led to optimising the use of water filtration and chilling plants in animal pools and at the resort through upgrading equipment. The Oxenford site, which encompasses Movie World, Wet'n'Wild, Village Roadshow Studios, Paradise Country and Australian Outback Spectacular, has energy efficiency initiatives which entailed replacing hot water systems with gas or solar and managing air compressors associated with the rides to match use patterns.

Established in 1991, the Sea World Research and Rescue Foundation Inc. (SWRRFI) has made significant contributions to marine research and conservation. Medical and protective care has been provided to marine animals, with rescue staff and resources at the ready for emergencies such as the beaching of a whale. The SWRRFI has attended to hundreds of stranded dolphins and whales and has rescued and released thousands of birds and turtles throughout its years in operation. Another environmental feature is that many of the Sea World attractions involve educating visitors about marine life and how to protect it – an example of a business making money while providing a public good. In addition to these environmental initiatives, Village Roadshow makes donations to charities that help sick children, including the Starlight and Make a Wish Foundations.

Dreamworld is a significant tourist attraction on the Gold Coast, owned and operated by Ardent Leisure. Ardent Leisure does not currently have a CSR policy or an equivalent, such as a sustainability strategy or environmental management plan; however, the company's board has requested that a Safety, Sustainability and Environment Committee be formed. The committee is in the early stages of coordinating sustainability efforts, with a focus on reducing energy, water and waste (Ardent Leisure Group 2013a).

The Dreamworld Wildlife Foundation was established in 2012, supporting wildlife conservation and research (Ardent Leisure Group 2013b). A current project is a partnership with Griffith University to study the reproductive biology of the critically endangered Kroombit tinkerfrog and fund field conservation work in the species' natural habitat. Dreamworld also has partnerships with various community charities, such as the Starlight and Make a Wish Foundations, and Camp Quality.

Sporting venues

The Gold Coast prides itself on its state-of-the-art sporting venues and its status as host for the 2018 Commonwealth Games. Stadiums (on the Gold Coast this means football grounds) bring large numbers of spectators together for a few hours on the days matches are played. Water and energy use are the major impacts. Golf courses are very different in their environmental impacts; once built, water for irrigation is the prime matter. Metricon Stadium and Cbus Super Stadium are the two large sporting stadiums on the Gold Coast, for the AFL and NRL codes respectively.

Cbus Super Stadium is the NRL sporting venue in Robina, and has a total capacity of 27 400 seats. The stadium has numerous initiatives in place to avoid or mitigate potential adverse environmental impacts. Post construction, the building achieved the equivalent of a 4-star 'Green Star' building rating. Green Star is a rating system devised by the Green Building Council of Australia; it assesses buildings in categories including indoor environmental quality, energy use, water management, materials used, land use impacts and pollution emissions.

Individually zoned lighting controls have been installed in enclosed spaces such as corporate suites, allowing electricity to be reduced in areas that are not in use. General use of energy-efficient lightbulbs throughout the stadium has contributed to the reduction of electricity use. Electricity consumption is further reduced by the use of gas for instantaneous water heating for bathrooms, kitchens and showers, as well as energy-efficient air-conditioning which is achieved by using variable speed drives on chilled water pumps, air supply fans and exhausts.

Water consumption has been reduced at Cbus Super Stadium by installing water-saving fittings on taps and showers. In regards to irrigation, native plants that require minimal water were incorporated into the landscape design and stormwater capture tanks with a capacity of 1 million L are located on-site and used for irrigation of the playing field. In order to monitor overall water use, meters have been installed to measure potable water, non-potable water and trade waste. All recyclable waste is collected on-site. In order to avoid atmospheric pollution, all refrigerants at Cbus Super Stadium have an 'ozone depletion potential' of zero (Harding 2013).

In addition to the design techniques at Cbus Super Stadium, its location and transport facilities support alternative travel methods rather than car use. The venue has no on-site parking facilities and the nearby Robina Town Shopping Centre does not allow sports patrons to use its parking facilities, thus discouraging car travel. The Robina train station is located within 400 m of the venue, with joint ticketing agreements to encourage public transport use. Cyclist facilities are installed to further support alternative modes of travel. An Environmental Management Plan has been developed and used as a means to manage waste, energy and water (Harding 2013).

International best practice case study: the Gold Coast Convention and Exhibition Centre

With international accreditation and recognised global initiatives, the Gold Coast Convention and Exhibition Centre is a best practice case study for CSR. In 2013, the Centre became the first convention centre in the world to achieve EarthCheck Gold certification. EarthCheck is an international environmental management and tourism program. The Gold status recognises the Convention Centre's continuous commitment to the highest environmental and business performance standards over the past five years.

The Convention Centre has integrated environmental practice into its operations since its opening in 2004, including comprehensive energy, water and waste management plans. The general manager and the management team have worked to embed environmental consciousness and values into the workplace culture, realising this is the key to ongoing commitment and success. 'Over the years, we have been perfecting a greener way of living in our own homes and it's phenomenal that this eco-consciousness has evolved and weaved its way into the Centre's operational cultural fabric' (GCCEC 2011).

The Convention Centre's efforts are driven by a green committee, Project Green, made up of 10 key staff members representative of every department, ensuring that efforts comprehensively cover the Centre's various operations. With quarterly meetings, the committee is continually reviewing sustainable practices and searching for further improvements. Constant communication between the Project Green Committee and staff is imperative, with the intranet, noticeboards and staff newsletters used as channels for communication and education. 'Staff are trained on the Centre's green procedures as related to their roles upon employment at the GCCEC' (GCCEC 2013). This embeds sustainability into the culture of the workplace. In addition to the Project Green Committee, a Power Committee was recently established to focus on improving the Centre's carbon footprint.

Energy

In regards to energy management, the Centre has implemented many strategies to reduce overall consumption. Lighting controls, such as sensors in all public amenities and meeting rooms, and a central Dyna Lite System ensure electricity consumption is minimised. The Centre has retrofitted many areas with LED lighting which reduces overall energy use and costs. Daily recordings of water for air-conditioning and evaporative cooling towers are logged and monitored, with the results employed to modify use.

Due to the variability of electricity needs for each client and event, programmed changes to air-conditioning and lighting are inefficient. As a result, manual control is best and the air-conditioning system is operated only on demand. 'This year the Centre introduced policy changes that require exhibitors to power down and turn off all non-essential lighting in booths when not in use. The Centre is also working closely with exhibitor equipment suppliers to implement power saving devices including automated power boards that are time sensitive' (GCCEC 2013).

Water

The Centre receives Class A recycled water from Gold Coast City Council treatment plants in Elanora and Merrimac, which then undergoes on-site treatment, ultraviolet disinfection and chlorination. This water is used for irrigation and for external taps. Mains water at the Centre is managed through the use of water-saving devices in accordance with Queensland Water Commission guidelines. Examples include flow restriction, which reduces water use by up to 25.5 L per minute, dual-flush toilets and zip-master time-delay flush systems in urinals.

Waste

Extensive recycling activities occur at the Centre, including everyday materials such as plastics and general building materials such as metal and wood. Unopened food packages are donated to local food banks, while off-site recycling occurs for objects such as fluorescent light globes and cooking oil. Recycling is encouraged during events by making bins easily accessible and clearly marked. Recycled paper is used in all printers and faxes. Waste avoidance, reuse, minimisation, recycling, energy recovery, segregation, treatment and disposal strategies are in place. Waste reduction methods are promoted through signs, posters and noticeboards throughout the venue and by providing bins and waste storage areas.

The food menus at the Centre consist of 85% locally sourced and Australian-grown ingredients. Agreements with suppliers have been made to improve packaging and delivery. Most suppliers now use cardboard boxes which are then recycled on-site.

Collaboration with clients

The Project Green Committee 'believes in a partnership with clients to ensure environmental and social sustainability' and works closely with clients, local and state governments and industry bodies to develop and implement new initiatives (GCCEC 2013). This collaborative approach ensures commitment, which is further proven through annual third-party audits and the external commitment to EarthCheck.

The Centre publishes a Green Event Guide to assist clients in achieving greener events. This guide focuses on small changes, similar to many the Centre has made, such as

Box 14.1: How the Convention Centre promotes greener events

1. Choose from local accommodation houses within walking distance to the event.
   500 delegates each cutting back on 5 km of car travel over a three-day conference is 857 kg CO_2e (carbon dioxide emissions) in savings, the equivalent of a car driving from Melbourne to Townsville.
2. Use online registration as an alternative to paper.
   The use of online registration by 500 delegates, saving 500 sheets of paper, is the equivalent of 3.8 kg CO_2e, or a 20 W lightbulb running for over 200 hours.
3. Reduce conference materials distributed at the event.
   Conference packs containing promotional materials, pens, pads and brochures often have a short life-span and are not wanted by all event participants. Cutting back on conference packs typically containing a satchel, pad, brochure and CD by 50 per cent for 500 delegates is the equivalent of 232 kg CO_2e, or a fully laden articulated truck travelling for 125 km.

recycling efforts and ensuring the provision of locally grown food. A succinct list of Three Easy Steps shows how to simplify greening an event (see Box 14.1).

Benefits and results of following the guidelines are also outlined. As you can see in Box 14.1, the potential impact of each step is specified. Moreover, several overall benefits of greening an event are acknowledged. These include saving resources and reducing costs, reducing waste, boosting the morale of delegates, enhancing brand reputation, setting a benchmark, encouraging market transformation and, essentially, protecting the environment.

Results

Operational costs and the Centre's carbon footprint have been reduced, benefits in addition to the community and industry recognition of the various initiatives. The Centre's 2008 commitment to EarthCheck was an astute response to the growing demand and attractiveness of sustainability, and the opportunity to become a leader in global best practice.

Stewart Moore, Chief Executive Officer of EC3 Global, responsible for EarthCheck benchmarking, recognised the Centre's achievements: 'the Australian and global tourism and travel industry can look to the GCCEC for inspiration on how to successfully integrate sustainability practices into their own planning and ongoing business operations.'

Social initiatives

In addition to these extensive green efforts which help preserve the Gold Coast's natural environment, the Centre has many social initiatives within its CSR policies. For example, donating unopened food packages to local food banks provides assistance to those unable to afford meals, and the local food supply agreement has provided employment for local producers.

The Centre undertakes fundraising activities and donates items to various organisations and charities. The Centre donated 500 backpacks on behalf of a client to a Gold Coast primary school for students to utilise on camps; 300 backpacks were also donated to three primary schools in the Lockyer Valley region, which were affected by flooding in early 2013 (GCCEC 2013). The Centre provides funding to ACT for Kids from its annual corporate Christmas cards, and internally supports Earth Hour, Ride to Work Day, the RSPCA Cupcake Day and the Smith Family Christmas appeal.

The GCCEC is home to one of the 20 koala sculptures created for the Animals with Attitude Sculpture Trail by the Currumbin Wildlife Hospital Foundation. The sculpture trail aims to increase awareness of the endangered and nationally iconic koala, and raise funds for the wildlife hospital to continue its conservation work. The hospital receives no government funding and the majority of its financial aid is from the Currumbin Wildlife Sanctuary. Consequently, the foundation is in constant need of funding assistance: by showcasing the artwork, the Centre is helping raise awareness of the local and national protection of a natural symbol of Australia.

CSR in Gold Coast accommodation services

With the large number of tourists visiting the Gold Coast, the accommodation and hospitality industry is a crucial part of the economic fabric of the city. While there are countless small motels and units, many of the larger ones, especially the international brands, have integrated CSR into operations.

Marriott

Marriott International Inc. was the first major Gold Coast hotel company to calculate its carbon footprint and it has received awards for its environmental efforts. The Surfers Paradise Marriott Resort and Spa is operated under the Marriott International's Environmentally Conscious Hospitality Operations (ECHO) program. Established in 2007, this involves water and energy conservation through the introduction of fluorescent lighting and water-saving taps and appliances, and reduce–reuse–recycle waste management. Supply chain management is another key aspect of the ECHO program, achieved through the purchasing of 'green' items such as pens and keycards made from recyclable material, Eco-Smart pillows filled with polyester microfibre, and coreless toilet paper.

In order to comply with this international program, management of the Surfers Paradise Marriott established an in-house Environmental Committee. A considerable challenge for Marriott was to meet guests' wishes while reducing its environmental impacts. As the guests' requirements are paramount, sustainability improvements and processes must be conducted after hours or during off-peak seasons. Nevertheless, the Marriott's Environmental Committee has successfully integrated many sustainability processes throughout the company's operations. Since the ECHO program began in 2007, the Surfers Paradise Marriott Resort and Spa has received more than 10 environmental awards and it aims to implement new initiatives, such as on-site water harvesting and treatment by installing rainwater tanks, borewater pumps and a treatment plant. The Gold Coast of old, where every residence had a rainwater tank, is reappearing in the Gold Coast of the 21st century.

Hilton

Another major international hotel company that has taken a strong environmental stance on the Gold Coast is the Hilton Surfers Paradise. Establishing a Global Sustainability Policy in 2009, Hilton Worldwide has ISO 140001 certification and extensive CSR initiatives and reporting, covering energy, carbon footprinting, waste generation and disposal, water use and supply chain management. It endeavours to purchase eco-friendly and locally sourced products such as food and beverages, linens and pillows. Engagement and awareness initiatives and community outreach programs are part of Hilton's sustainability policy. It has various community projects, mainly focusing on sustainability education programs such as Teaching Kids to Care. This program includes tree planting, public clean-ups and garden growing activities.

Sheraton

The Sheraton Mirage Resort and Spa Gold Coast is an iconic Gold Coast hotel. Its management has implemented many environmental practices throughout its operations. Starwood Hotels and Resorts, owner and operator of Sheraton, has an Environmental Sustainability Policy and a Sustainable Food and Beverage Policy which support the vision of the Fair Trade Foundation and local and organic food producers. A key CSR initiative of the Sheraton worth highlighting is the Make a Green Choice program, which rewards guests with monetary vouchers when they choose to conserve resources by declining housekeeping services in their rooms (Starwood Hotels and Resorts Worldwide 2013). Not only does this reduce the hotel's resource consumption, it engages and rewards guests in making environmentally conscious decisions. Energy and water conservation efforts are in place, including efficiency lighting and sensors, water-smart fixtures and irrigation using underground water for gardening. Waste management processes include recycling and composting. Socially and environmentally responsible products and suppliers are preferred. Indoor environmental quality is considered important, with the use of green cleaning products and paints made of low chemical-emitting materials.

Mantra

Hotel and resort operator Mantra has three Gold Coast hotels, in Surfers Paradise, Broadbeach and Coolangatta. Mantra has introduced numerous environmental initiatives similar to those of the other hotels, including staff engagement, energy, water and waste management and biodiversity conservation, all coordinated by a Sustainability Committee (Mantra Group 2013). Furthermore, there are community initiatives such as partnerships with the Red Cross and a blood donor program called Mantra Group Lifesavers.

Jupiters Hotel and Casino

Another significant player in the Gold Coast tourist accommodation industry is Jupiters Hotel and Casino. Jupiters has various environmental practices including recycling green waste, energy-efficient lighting, using phosphate-free cleaning products, and providing public transport options including Translink buses from the hotel door. Its key CSR leadership stems from its water conservation. Jupiters management has established a Water Committee to monitor its Water Efficiency Management Plan. There is an on-site water treatment facility where Class C recycled water supplied from Merrimac and Elanora undergoes chlorination, sand filtration and ultraviolet light disinfection to produce Class A+ recycled water. This water is used in toilets and urinals and for ground irrigation, saving 96 ML of potable water each year. Efficient tap and shower fittings are installed, as are dual-flush toilets. An on-site reverse osmosis treatment plant is planned, as well as the installation of rainwater harvesting systems and the introduction of grey water for laundry processes. Since 2003, Jupiters Casino and Hotel has reduced its water consumption by

40 per cent, and has been dubbed a 'conservation champion' by the Queensland Water Commission.

CSR in the Gold Coast construction industry

Hutchinson Builders

Queensland-based building and construction company, Hutchinson Builders, is one of the most prominent players in the Gold Coast construction industry and has displayed a high level of leadership in CSR from 2007. The business has a Green Team consisting of Green Star accredited professionals, energy assessment experts and engineers. Their task is to develop ecologically sustainable design (ESD) approaches and techniques and maintain various high-level environmental standards. The Green Building Council of Australia has awarded only six projects a 'Round 1' certified rating; Hutchinson Builders designed and constructed three of them. Hutchinson's also has 19 Green Building projects in the design phase or under construction. Lyndon Christian, Team Leader of Services Engineering and ESD, says, 'our advantage within this market is experience, having delivered more accredited Green Building ratings than any other builder in Australia. Often we can provide cost advantages at reduced risk to our clients based on our performance rating and delivery knowledge' (Christian 2013).

Many ESD initiatives have been implemented in various projects, including the Bundall Corporate Centre Tower 2 which became the first 5-star As-Built Green Star-rated building on the Gold Coast, 'setting a new benchmark for environmental design on the coast' (Christian 2013). To achieve this rating, the firm focuses on indoor environment quality, water- and energy-efficient design, and recycling materials as elements of an Environmental Management System (EMS). Significant to the Bundall project was the use of shading and glazing to improve internal space and energy efficiency.

The business was the first construction company in Queensland to implement the following four sustainability techniques:

- a large-scale photovoltaic solar system for a commercial office building;
- a micro gas turbine on-site generation system for a data/operations centre;
- a tri-generation on-site cooling, heat and power generation system for a commercial office building;
- a large-scale 'chilled beam' air-conditioning system (Christian 2013).

Recently, Hutchinson Builders reached the A$1 billion milestone for the design and construction of Green Building projects for its contracts throughout Australia. It has achieved an estimated energy saving of 13.2 million kW hours, equal to 13.5 million kg of annual carbon emissions (Christian 2013).

What motivated Hutchinson's to incorporate such comprehensive CSR initiatives? The initial incentive stemmed from a paradigm shift as sustainability rating systems such as Green Star and NABERS became quality benchmarks of the Property Council of Australia.

Sustainability has been absolutely necessary for our business to achieve this longevity to date and to continue as an industry leader in all aspect of construction. We remain a family-owned and run business and our Board shares this vision to ensure our impact is positive on a social, economic and environmental front (Christian 2013).

ADCO Constructions

ADCO Constructions is another leading Australian construction company with a commitment to sustainability. As a member of the Green Building Council of Australia, ADCO has delivered many buildings with 4-, 5- and 6-star Green Star ratings. Commitment to ongoing sustainability efforts between the company and its clients has been shown by the firm's employment of environmental professionals and its ISO 14001 certified environmental management.

ADCO has built many iconic Gold Coast buildings, notably Bond University's School of Sustainable Development which was opened in 2008. The building received a 6-star Green Star rating, utilising the sustainable features as shown in Table 14.1. It was the first

Table 14.1. Sustainable development building, bond university

Feature	Information
Photovoltaic cells	An 18 kW solar photovoltaic power supply on the rooftop generates ~27 000 kW hours per year.
Sustainable use of materials	Reinforcement steel and concrete contain 60% and 30% recycled content respectively. All timber is post-consumer reused or Forest Stewardship Council certified.
Lift – regenerative drive	The lift has a regenerative drive unit which saves energy and feeds excess back into the building's electrical utility.
Water management	On-site rainwater tanks are used to collect water for toilets and irrigation of the landscape. Grey water from showers and sinks is treated and used for irrigation.
Water-efficient fixtures and fittings	Dual-flush toilets and 4-star fittings reduce water consumption in the building.
Building management system	The computer-based control system manages building operations and monitors outdoor conditions. With motion-activated lighting and air-conditioning, the BMS reduces energy consumption.
Weather station	The weather station on the roof monitors and records outdoor conditions for the BMS to regulate ventilation.
Ecological finishes	Glazed acoustic screens reduce the impact of traffic noise while the mineral fibre ceiling tiles and acoustic partitions minimise interior noise. Paints, sealants, carpets and furniture contain low VOC (volatile organic compounds).
Sun, glass and light	Utilising carefully designed window shading structures, specific window glass and the circulation spine, the need for artificial lighting and air-conditioning is reduced.
Cyclist facilities	Short- and long-term bicycle storage is offered, as well as showers and storage lockers. This encourages staff and students to ride, promoting low-cost and low-impact modes of transport.
Landscaping	Plants are native and drought-resistant species. Trees have a cooling effect on the microclimate, provide shade, maximise natural light and act as a wind barrier.
Bio-retention basin	The bio-retention basin is a vegetated device that filters stormwater runoff through surface vegetation then a specified layer of filter media.

Box 14.2: Awards won by the sustainable development building, bond university

2009 Gold Coast City Council Award of Excellence in Urban Design
2009 Gold Coast City Council People's Choice Award at the Urban Design Awards
2009 Gold Coast City Council Sue Robbins Award for Excellence in Urban Design
2009 Queensland Government Sustainable Industries Award for Sustainability in the Built Environment
2009 Australia Institute of Architects State Award for Sustainable Architecture
2009 Royal Institute of Chartered Surveyors Award for Sustainability
2010 United Nations Association of Australia Szencorp Green Building Award

6-star Green Star educational building in Australia, setting the standard for future educational projects.

The building provides offices and lecture theatres for staff and students of a variety of environmental, planning and green building, construction and real estate courses. The building's awards are listed in Box 14.2.

McConnell Dowell

Engineering, construction, building and maintenance contractor McConnell Dowell won the contract to build the Gold Coast Light Rail (tram lines and associated facilities). This public transport system consists of 16 stations along a 13 km route from Southport to Broadbeach. It may be extended north and south in the future.

Sustainability is embedded into McConnell Dowell's core values with a Sustainability Strategic Plan that incorporates six key themes: economics, health and safety, environmental impact, governance and risks, its people and community and social investment (McConnell Dowell 2013).

CSR on the Gold Coast

It is apparent that, although industry professionals like Lend Lease founder Dick Dusseldorp acknowledged the need for a triple bottom line approach in the 1970s, some Gold Coast companies have started to incorporate CSR into their business models only as recently as the first decade of the 21st century. A few acted earlier. However, many large-scale Gold Coast companies still have no sustainability initiatives in place. That stated, several high-profile companies have come a long way in a short time and it is evident that the take-up of CSR is gaining momentum.

The incorporation of CSR policy and practice into their business models and cultures not only provides benefits to the companies themselves, but brings positive improvements to the entire Gold Coast. Showing industry leadership in sustainability attracts attention and fits with the Gold Coast City Council's objective of making the city a world leader in sustainability. When the initiatives of these large businesses are promoted, this helps put the city on the global stage. This should result in an increase in tourism. Many companies' CSR policies include providing local employment, such as the GCCEC's food supply agreement with local farmers, further contributing to the local economy. Moreover, the Gold Coast's major industries are implementing CSR to ensure their sustainability as a business.

As a result, the local economy can anticipate, to an extent, long-term prosperity knowing that these industries and companies will continue to contribute economically into the future.

Local job creation is a significant benefit of most CSR policies. Also, community initiatives, such as the Suns Horizons programs, foster awareness and aim to promote social equality. Contributing to the well-being not only of direct shareholders and employees but of the wider community is key to successful CSR efforts. By firms taking responsibility for negative economic externalities, industries can reduce or completely remove third-party costs of production on society. This leads to an increased sense of belonging and trust between a company and the community. As many of the charitable foundations on the Gold Coast are supported by local businesses, such as the Currumbin Wildlife Hospital, community and environmental groups are assisted in achieving their goals.

In addition to the many economic and social improvements of CSR values, a range of environmental benefits results from corporate initiatives. A reduction in water and energy consumption lessens the pressure on natural resources and protects ecosystems. Resource extraction and allocation is improved by waste management systems and recycling initiatives, as is the pressure on waste disposal such as landfill and incineration. By encouraging and improving access to alternative modes of transport, Gold Coast residents and visitors can reduce their travel times and distances, and reliance on the motor vehicle. By promoting their policies and practices, industries can improve the general awareness of environmental issues and improve the treatment of the natural environment throughout the entire city.

Overall, by implementing and promoting strong CSR, Gold Coast companies can significantly contribute to the economic, social and environmental well-being of the city. However, there is a long way to go to ensure all industries are sustainable and committed to the city. There are many challenges in trying to balance triple bottom line outcomes. Nevertheless, with major players such as those discussed in this chapter leading the way, the future for CSR within major Gold Coast industries is bright.

References

Ardent Leisure Group (2013a) *Sustainability.* http://www.ardentleisure.com.au/Sustainability/.

Ardent Leisure Group (2013b) *Dreamworld Wildlife Foundation.* http://www.dreamworld.com.au/Wildlife/Dreamworld-Wildlife-Foundation/.

Christian L (2013) *CSR Publication Inquiry* [interview]. 24 November 2013.

GCCEC (2011) *Gold Coast Convention and Exhibition Centre Eyes Gold After Reachieving EarthCheck Silver Certification.* Gold Coast Convention and Exhibition Centre, Gold Coast. http://www.earthcheck.org/news/gold-coast-convention-and-exhibition-centre-eyes-gold-after-re-achieving-earthcheck-silver-certification.aspx.

GCCEC (2013) *Our Green Initiative.* Gold Coast Convention and Exhibition Centre, Gold Coast. http://www.gccec.com.au/our-green-initiative.html.

Harding K (2013) *CSR Publication Inquiry* [interview]. 22 November 2013.

Lend Lease Corporation (2011) *Our Approach.* Lend Lease Corporation. http://www.lendlease.com/en/worldwide/sustainability/our-approach.

Mantra Group (2013) *Corporate Social Responsibility.* Mantra Group. http://www.mantragroup.com.au/AboutUs/CorporateSocialResponsibility.aspx.

McConnell Dowell (2013) *Sustainability.* McConnell Dowell. http://www.macdow.com.au/assets/download/publications/sustainability/document.pdf.

Starwood Hotels and Resorts Worldwide (2013) *Sheraton Mirage Resort & Spa Gold Coast – Environmental Practices.* http://www.starwoodhotels.com/sheraton/property/features/environmental_details.html?propertyID=372.

Village Roadshow (2010) *Corporate Social Responsibility and Sustainability: Village Roadshow Theme Parks – Gold Coast.* http://villageroadshow.com.au/Additional-Investor-Information/Sustainability-and-Community-Engagement/VRTP.htm.

Chapter 15

Planning for the Gold Coast: processes, challenges and opportunities

B. Bajracharya, L. Too, D. O'Hare and I. Khanjanasthiti

Introduction

This chapter provides a broad overview of the Gold Coast from an urban planning perspective. What are the social and physical structures of the city? How has the city developed over time? What are some of the key planning challenges and opportunities the Gold Coast is facing? To answer these questions, the chapter provides a brief social profile of the city and examines its current land use patterns and urban form. It then discusses the planning processes and the role of key stakeholders in development of the city. Next, key current planning initiatives for the Gold Coast are outlined. The chapter concludes with discussion of planning challenges and opportunities for future development of the city.

People and employment

In terms of population, the Gold Coast is the sixth-largest city and one of the fastest-growing cities in Australia, as identified and documented in previous chapters. The Gold Coast has a significant overseas-born population, with 35 per cent of the city's population born outside Australia (ABS 2013). The majority of the city's immigrants are from New Zealand and the UK. The five most populous suburbs of the Gold Coast are Broadbeach–Mermaid Beach, Surfers Paradise, Labrador, Coolangatta and Varsity Lakes. These suburbs, with the exception of Varsity Lakes, are in beachside locations. This illustrates the popularity of the beach suburbs and the prevalence of high-density, high-rise apartments within those suburbs.

The primary economic sectors in the Gold Coast are retail, tourism and construction which employ 12.4 per cent, 11.7 per cent and 11.3 per cent of the city's workforce, respectively (ABS 2011a, b). Creative and information and communication technology (ICT) industries are emerging on the Gold Coast, adding diversity to a traditionally narrow economic base. These two emerging industries will be discussed later in the chapter.

The shape of the city: land use and urban form

The Gold Coast has a linear pattern of development which closely aligns with the coastline and its major transport corridors. The city has two major north–south transport routes for motor traffic, namely the Pacific Motorway and the Gold Coast Highway, which are located inland and along the coastline, respectively. A light rail (tram) system opened in 2014, with the first stage connecting Southport to Broadbeach. The city is currently serviced by a heavy rail (train) corridor which runs from Brisbane to Varsity Lakes, with plans for southerly extension to Gold Coast Airport. The Gold Coast Airport connects the city both domestically and internationally and is located at the southern end of the city in Coolangatta.

The Gold Coast's urban development is concentrated on the eastern side of the Pacific Motorway, primarily along the coastal corridor between Southport and Coolangatta. Land uses in the city's coastal suburbs consist primarily of residential and resort-style accommodation. High-rise residential towers have been established in several coastal suburbs, particularly Surfers Paradise, Broadbeach and Coolangatta. The majority of the city's permanent population resides close to the beaches although suburban growth is occurring in inland residential suburbs such as Coomera and Helensvale, near the Pacific Motorway and the main railway line. Another land use feature of the Gold Coast is the canal estates developed in the coastal areas. These waterways – so central to the Gold Coast image and spatial structure – offer the potential to develop new water-based transport options.

As shown in Plate 3, Southport and Robina, categorised as Key Regional Centres, are the major activity centres of the Gold Coast where commercial, retail, residential and recreational land uses aggregate. The two centres were ranked equally as Key Regional Activity Centres in the South-East Queensland Regional Plan from 2005 to 2013 (Queensland Government 2009), and both were arguably held back by having to share the primary regional role for the city. Consequently, in 2013 Southport was again declared the official Central Business District (CBD) by the Gold Coast City Council and Queensland state government. Robina remains important as a new master-planned community adjacent to Robina railway station. It comprises a major shopping complex, a sports stadium, Robina Hospital (the Gold Coast's second-largest hospital) and other major facilities still under development. Several other Regional Centres are located in coastal locations, reflecting the fact that urban development and economic activities are primarily concentrated along the city's shore. Meanwhile, Coomera is developing as a Regional Centre, with a new town centre to commence development adjacent to the rail station in 2014.

Governing the city

Gold Coast City, currently the second-largest Local Government Area (LGA) in Australia, has been assembled through historical amalgamation of smaller councils over more than a century. In 1879, six Divisional Boards, renamed Shires in 1903, were proclaimed south of Brisbane. In the early 20th century, Southport and Coolangatta had a strong development focus on tourism whereas the inland towns, namely Nerang, Beenleigh, Coomera and Waterford, developed as rural service centres. In 1948, the first major amalgamation occurred with the proclamation of two separate councils on the South Coast and its hinterland. The town of South Coast comprised the narrow coastal strip of Southport, Surfers Paradise, Burleigh Heads and Coolangatta. The second council, Albert Shire, covered the large area from the Brisbane City Council boundary through the rural hinterland to the border of Queensland and New South Wales.

After the Second World War, 'Gold Coast' was first used in a Brisbane daily newspaper, some would argue to describe the real estate opportunities available on the Gold Coast at the time. The initiative appealed to several local businesses and civic leaders, and South Coast Town Council adopted the name Gold Coast Town Council in 1958. The Logan City Council was proclaimed in 1979, removing the area between the Logan River and Brisbane City from the Albert Shire. The present Gold Coast City Council was formed in 1995 through the amalgamation of Gold Coast City and Albert Shire Councils.

Changing planning philosophy

The Gold Coast experienced rapid urban development during Australia's baby boom after the Second World War. The majority of the development took place along the beachfront to capitalise on growing tourist demand based on beach activities (Mullins 1991). Some local residents began to express concerns about the increasing dominance of high-rise residential towers which mainly cater for tourists and obstruct the ocean views which had previously been easily accessible. As a consequence of these complaints and what appeared to some residents to be a *laissez-faire* attitude, there has been a movement towards more prescriptive development regulations through the Council's planning scheme, particularly since the implementation of the Gold Coast Planning Scheme 2003. However, at the time of writing this chapter, there is a move towards relaxation of development regulations and streamlining development as a result of major state planning policy changes and the development of a new Gold Coast planning scheme, City Plan 2015.

Behind the red tape, white shoes and green groups: stakeholders in planning for the Gold Coast

To understand the processes of planning for the Gold Coast, it is important to recognise the roles of the three levels of government in Australia. In addition, there is a requirement to comprehend the status, power and influence of the development industry and local community groups.

The Queensland government has played a key role in shaping major developments on the Gold Coast, providing a guiding framework via an overarching planning legislation (the most recent being the *Sustainable Planning Act 2009*). Some of the major projects currently underway or recently completed, such as planning for the 2018 Commonwealth Games and the Health and Knowledge Precinct around Griffith University, are primarily driven by the state government, albeit with strong Gold Coast City Council leadership as well. A partnership between all three levels of government, together with the private sector, developed the first stage of the Gold Coast light rail. Similarly, the state and local governments have collaborated to attract private sector development of the Broadwater Marine Project described later in this chapter.

The 'development industry' has been instrumental in shaping the Gold Coast city, with projects such as major tourist infrastructure, shopping centres, master-planned communities and canal estates. For instance, throughout the 1970s and 1980s, there was considerable investment by Japanese investors in resort development. Well-known entrepreneurs and private developers have played a major role in the development of new master-planned communities such as Sanctuary Cove, Emerald Lakes, Varsity Lakes and the Observatory, while Queensland government legislation such as the *Robina Town Centre Act* facilitated the development of the major shopping centre and associated master-planned development of Robina. The private sector has also been instrumental in building major theme parks.

Community pressure groups such as Gecko have arisen to counteract the strong development lobby and to protect the natural environment. Recently, community groups such as Save Our Spit Alliance have been vocal in protesting against the proposed development at the Broadwater. This is a continuation of a significant history of strong community campaigns against significant planning and development proposals that would affect The Spit's natural state (Griffin 1998).

There has been limited involvement by the Commonwealth government in planning for the Gold Coast, with the exception of partly funding major projects such as the Gold Coast light rail. However, as discussed in previous chapters, the Commonwealth government has complete control over the World Heritage listed rainforests on the Gold Coast. Figure 15.1 summarises the main responsibilities and initiatives of major stakeholders in planning for the Gold Coast. The current planning framework and planning initiatives for the Gold Coast will be discussed in detail next.

Planning framework

The Gold Coast is currently governed by the Gold Coast Planning Scheme 2003, which was developed in accordance with the Queensland government's *Integrated Planning Act 1997*, since superseded by the *Sustainable Planning Act 2009*. All developments must comply with applicable planning law under the planning scheme. Thus, all developments throughout the Gold Coast are managed by the planning scheme which aims to ensure a desirable outcome for the city. The planning scheme, as a living document, is periodically reviewed and revised to reflect changing circumstances on the Gold Coast as well as any alterations to state government laws.

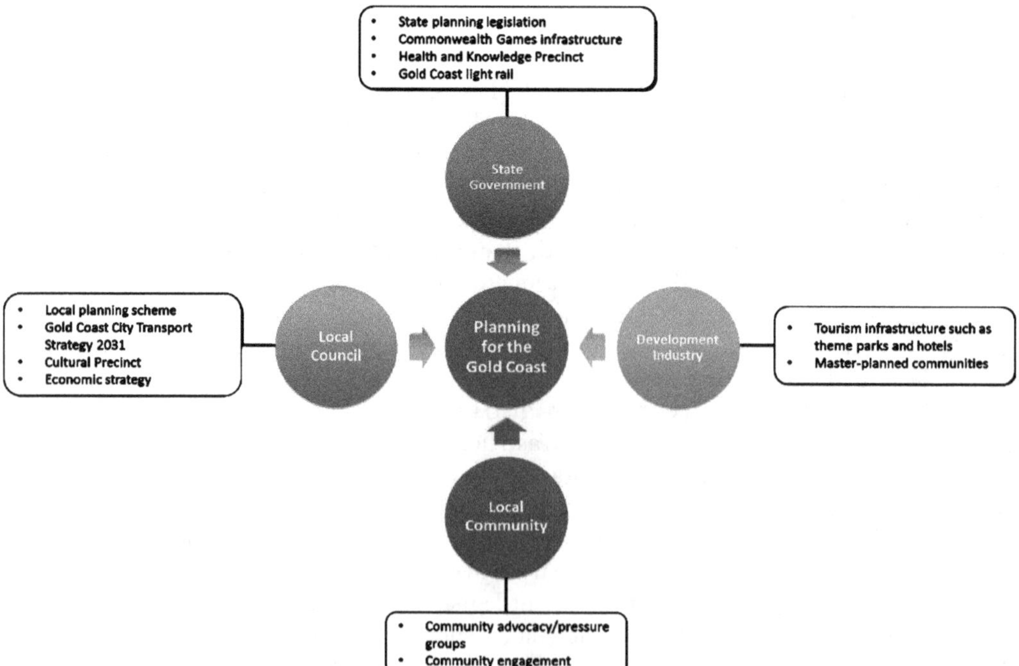

Fig. 15.1 The key stakeholders in planning on the Gold Coast.

While both the Queensland government's *Integrated Planning Act* and *Sustainable Planning Act* have an emphasis on balancing social, economic and environmental sustainability, as we write, the government is in the process of altering the state planning and development system. The change is expected to prioritise economic development, simplify the hierarchy of planning instruments and reduce regulatory red tape for the development industry. Accordingly, the current government is working on new planning legislation called the *Planning and Development Act*, which aims to replace the current *Sustainable Planning Act 2009* with a stronger focus on economic development.

The Gold Coast City Council is preparing City Plan 2015, which will supersede the Gold Coast Planning Scheme 2003 by early 2015. Like the current plan, the new planning scheme will be a living document. Key features include removal of building height restrictions in selected areas, promotion of small lot development and removal of Local Area Plans. These proposed changes intend to reduce planning red tape as well as deal with shortage of land for future development.

Having outlined the planning processes and framework for the Gold Coast, the chapter now provides a brief overview of current planning initiatives which provide the context for discussion of challenges and opportunities for the future of the city. The current planning initiatives include a range of projects, programs and strategies under the themes of health, transport and economy.

Active and healthy living program

Recognising the importance of promoting public health, the Gold Coast City Council has established an Active and Healthy Program. The program provides over 170 free or low-cost physical and well-being activities throughout the city. It has been highly successful, with thousands of citizens participating on a weekly basis. However, recent research has revealed that many local residents are not fully aware of the range of activities offered by the program (GCCC 2013b). Therefore, there may be a need to promote the program through various contemporary communication platforms including social media and smart-phone applications.

Gold Coast Health and Knowledge Precinct

A Gold Coast Health and Knowledge Precinct, embracing Griffith University, Gold Coast University Hospital and Griffith Health Centre has been established in Southport to provide a range of health and medical services for residents and to achieve the synergies available from knowledge-based urban development. The co-location of the hospital and Griffith University facilities is envisaged to create an 'ideal hands-on environment for the clinical training of doctors, nurses and future health professionals' (Griffith University undated). With the Health and Knowledge Precinct, along with Technical and Further Education (TAFE) campuses, Southport is emerging as the primary health and knowledge hub of the Gold Coast. Development of the business and residential core of the Gold Coast Health and Knowledge Precinct has been expedited through the construction of the 2018 Commonwealth Games Village on the Parklands site adjacent to the university and hospital.

Gold Coast City Transport Strategy 2031

In 2013, the Gold Coast City Council began implementing its Gold Coast City Transport Strategy 2031. The strategy aims to significantly improve the city's active transport network to promote the viability of walking, cycling and using public transport. Although the strategy lacks funding and time commitments, it represents a balanced approach towards reorienting the car-based structure of the city. Some of the key strategies articulated in the plan include (GCCC 2013a):

- an extension of the light rail network across the city;
- introduction of a rapid bus network on key transport routes;
- 'green bridges' across the many canals and waterways to provide safe walking and cycling connections, in key locations;
- dedication of community boulevards and pedestrian priority zones.

Gold Coast light rail

Light rail infrastructure, officially called the G:link, has been established on the Gold Coast and is now operational. The initial stage of the G:link system operates from Gold Coast University Hospital in Parkwood to Broadbeach with 16 stations along the 13 km corridor. G:link is intended to mitigate traffic congestion and improve the efficiency of public transport services on the Gold Coast.

Gold Coast City Transport Strategy 2031 supports 'significant extension' of the tram network with support and involvement from the private sector (GCCC 2013c, p. 18). However, funding could be a potential barrier to extending the light rail network. It is expected that Stage 2 of G:link, which provides a connection to the heavy rail line, will be in place before the 2018 Commonwealth Games. There have been strong public requests to extend the train corridor to Gold Coast Airport; the existing heavy rail system terminates in Varsity Lakes and is not connected to the airport.

Broadwater Marine Project

The Broadwater Marine Project is being canvassed on the Gold Coast as we write. The concept proposes 'the largest piece of integrated tourism infrastructure developed in Queensland's history' (Queensland Government 2013). It is proposed to be located on Wavebreak Island near The Spit. Wavebreak Island is a man-made island formed through the dredging of the Broadwater. The proposal is envisaged to comprise a mix of facilities primarily with a tourism focus, including a cruise ship terminal, hotel, casino, marina facilities, retail outlets, restaurants and residential apartments. There has been considerable debate about this project due to the economic and ecological value of the site. There are strongly held community concerns about environmental impacts, the technical and engineering feasibility of building a cruise ship terminal in this location, and the long-term costs to state and local taxpayers from the extensive ongoing dredging required.

Southport CBD: a priority development area

Southport will host several sporting events during the 2018 Commonwealth Games, as well as accommodating 6500 athletes. In light of these opportunities, the Gold Coast City Council has declared Southport a Priority Development Area under Queensland's *Economic Development Act 2012*. That status is expected to facilitate new economic development in Southport by removing town planning statutory barriers. The Gold Coast City Council is also planning to establish a Chinatown on Young and Davenport Streets in Southport to recognise and celebrate the culturally diverse nature of the area.

An innovation corridor and research triangle

The Pacific Innovation Corridor is one of the major economic development programs promoted by the Gold Coast City Council to transform the Gold Coast into a technology 'hot spot'. The program has designated 13 key locations as major areas for future economic focus and growth. The precincts are situated along the Pacific Motorway and Gold Coast Highway and are classified according to their existing economic activities. Oxenford, for example, is categorised as a Film and Interactive Media Precinct given the availability of studio and film facilities in the suburb. With the mix of hospital, university, government and legal services in the area, Southport is designated a Medical, Education and Technology and Business Centre. The Gold Coast Economic Development Strategy 2013–2023 supports further innovation by highlighting the development of 'an active research triangle between the three city universities and business' (GCCC 2013d, p. 15).

Theme park marketing campaign

The Gold Coast has recently been branded 'Famous For Fun' by Gold Coast Tourism and Events Queensland (Tourism and Events Qld 2013). The brand is reflective of the city's many theme parks, including Dreamworld, Sea World, WhiteWater World, Warner Bros Movie World and Wet'n'Wild, all of which are highly popular destinations for visitors and residents alike. Village Roadshow and Ardent Leisure, which own the five biggest theme parks on the Gold Coast, have formed a partnership with the Queensland government to promote the Gold Coast as one of the world's leading theme park destinations. The marketing campaign is expected to attract a higher number of visitors to the Gold Coast.

Having outlined the planning processes and current planning initiatives for the Gold Coast, the chapter now discusses key ***planning challenges and opportunities*** for the city.

Population growth pressure

Although in recent years annual population growth rates have slowed to ~2.3 per cent, the Gold Coast has a history of rapid population growth over more than half a century. With an expected population figure of more than 730 000 by 2026 (GCCC undated a), the city's infrastructure is currently experiencing pressure not only from population growth but from the increasing number of visitors it accommodates annually (GCCC 2013c). With limited land available for accommodating the increasing population, much of the new growth will have to be located in infill development. Transit nodes, which include major train and tram stations, are potential locations for future population growth. Continued population growth will put further pressure on housing affordability on the Gold Coast.

Urban sprawl

Like many Australian cities, historical growth and development patterns of the Gold Coast have created urban sprawl, which is the spreading of urban development, particularly low-density housing, into what was once the edge of a city. Urban sprawl is generally undesirable because as additional low-density housing is constructed on the outskirts, more residents need to commute by car to work and schools which are mostly located in the inner city or – in the case of the Gold Coast – in dispersed locations that are often not even located in centres or near public transport nodes. This form of settlement can lead to a car-dependent lifestyle which is associated with a range of negative environmental impacts and can contribute to an increased level of stress among the population.

On the Gold Coast, there is a considerable amount of low-density housing located adjacent to the Pacific Motorway in inland suburbs such as Helensvale, Coomera and Nerang. Although these population centres are located in close proximity to the train line, the development pattern of these suburbs has not been well related to the rail stations. The majority of employment on the Gold Coast is located in coastal suburbs such as Surfers Paradise and Southport. These distinct and separate locations of housing and employment have led to a car-dependent culture on the Gold Coast.

Car-dependent culture

Although the existing public transport system provides well connected, frequent services along the north–south coastal corridor, it does not provide sufficient east–west connections between coastal suburbs and inland suburbs. The existence of canal estates and waterways throughout the city has resulted in complex curvilinear road networks as well as disconnections between suburbs. These factors, together with the city's urban sprawl, have created a car-dependent culture among residents. Over 39 per cent of Gold Coast households own two cars and more than 74 per cent of employed persons aged at least 15 years commute to work by car. Eighty-eight per cent of all trips on the Gold Coast are made by car (GCCC 2013b).

Planning priority: residents or tourists?

A fundamental challenge the Gold Coast is facing is whether to plan primarily for residents, for tourists or for both. As an international and domestic destination where tourism is the major economic base, the Gold Coast has arguably been planned and developed with tourism as the main priority. Surfers Paradise is a prime example where many holiday apartment towers have been, and more will be, established. The new City Plan 2015 proposes to remove height restrictions for buildings from Broadbeach through Surfers Paradise to Southport. The repeal of height regulations is intended to stimulate the establishment of additional high-rise residential towers in these locations to reduce future urban sprawl and help accommodate the projected 320 000 additional residents by 2035 (Stephens 2013).

The initial stage of the light rail system could be argued to target tourism and residents with equal balance. On the one hand, its corridor runs through major tourist suburbs, namely Surfers Paradise and Broadbeach. On the other, it links Griffith University and the Gold Coast University Hospital with the CBD in Southport and major destinations at Broadbeach (the Convention and Exhibition Centre, Pacific Fair shopping centre and the city's major bus interchange).

Safety issues

Many of the post-1990 suburbs in the Gold Coast were designed primarily for cars, not for pedestrians or cyclists. As such, safety in many suburbs, particularly at night, is limited due to the lack of adequate lighting and active frontages on streets. Active frontages, which could be facilitated by having cafés, restaurants and other retail uses at ground level – or simply having habitable rooms, instead of cars and garages, facing the street – can provide passive surveillance and therefore improve safety for pedestrians and cyclists. There are active frontages in certain parts of the coastal suburbs, such as Nobby Beach and Broadbeach, but very few in the inland suburbs.

There have been several crime incidents in the recent past on the Gold Coast, including unarmed and armed robberies, shooting incidents and gang-related activities. The Gold Coast City Council had established over 150 safety cameras as at November 2013 to monitor and discourage crime activities in key areas (GCCC undated b). Improving the city's safety further through planning and design solutions could also be an important strategy.

Barriers to walking and cycling

Walking and cycling, which are major transport modes for many cities around the world, could be better encouraged on the Gold Coast. In addition to the low safety factors for pedestrians and cyclists discussed above, several suburbs lack dedicated, connected pedestrian footpaths. Cycling is an unsafe transport mode given the limited number of cycling lanes which are separated from main roads. Cyclists are required to share a lane with cars in many circumstances. They made only 1.9 per cent of all daily trips across the city in 2011 (GCCC 2013b).

Funding and resources for beach restoration

Beach erosion has been a long-term problem on the Gold Coast, most notably in the cycle of storms and cyclones that occurred from the mid 1950s to the mid 1970s. The Council's $30 million plan to restore the severely eroded beaches from the storms in early 2013 is facing funding challenges. Although the Council requested the Queensland government to fund half the project the state government did not agree, on the basis that beach restoration is a local council's responsibility. The Queensland Beach Protection Authority, a state agency providing advice to local councils in coastal management initiatives, was dissolved under the *Coastal Protection and Management Act 1995*. Due to absence of direct involvement from the state government in coastal management, councils across Queensland now lack resources to fully address coastal management issues.

While the Gold Coast faces many planning challenges, there are several new ***planning opportunities*** which can provide future directions for the city. These are briefly discussed next.

Commonwealth Games legacy

The Gold Coast will host the Commonwealth Games in 2018, which represents a major opportunity for the city to benefit from the event's potential economic, social and cultural legacy. Key outcomes could include an increase in economic development and employment before, during and after the event; stimulation of tourism as sports fans also experience the city's beaches, rainforests and other tourism attractions; an increase in physical activity among residents, as they become inspired by the sports; and strengthened partnerships between all organisations involved in hosting the event. To ensure these outcomes are realised and sustainable, a degree of strategic planning and collaboration between all relevant stakeholders is required before the commencement of the Commonwealth Games.

As part of its initiatives to gain a legacy from the Commonwealth Games, the Gold Coast City Council is planning to develop a new cultural precinct at Evandale, Bundall, with the establishment of an arts museum. It is envisaged that the cultural precinct, connected to Chevron Island via a green bridge, will celebrate and showcase the Gold Coast's culture and creativity to visitors as well as television viewers, during the Commonwealth Games. After the conclusion of the Games, it is anticipated that the cultural precinct will become a significant component of the city's attractions. The Games Village at Southport will become a major element in the Health and Knowledge Precinct.

Co-location of health and knowledge facilities

Three university campuses and five TAFE campuses, along with several private and public hospitals, are located on the Gold Coast. Given the co-location of hospitals and tertiary education campuses, there is a strong case of potential collaborative linkages. Hospitals can provide practical training facilities for medical and para-medical university students; universities can allocate health course graduates to hospitals as interns and future professionals. This opportunity is already being pursued on the Gold Coast, but there is great scope for recognising and developing the network of health hubs and knowledge nodes throughout the city.

Attractive environment for walking and cycling

The city's extensive beach environment and walking tracks in the hinterland provide attractive settings for walking and cycling. The Council has established the Gold Coast Oceanway, a 36 km pathway along the coastline from Main Beach to Coolangatta. It is popular with local residents. However, due to the inadequate east–west public transport connectivity between the foreshore and inland suburbs, most residents are required to drive to the foreshore. Consequently, parking space is often fully occupied along the coastal pathway during peak periods, limiting the level of physical activity that could otherwise be achieved among local residents. Recreational alternatives will be enhanced by the development of the 1000 ha Green Heart located on the floodplain in the inland suburbs, with good access from Robina rail station.

Transit-oriented development opportunity

There are currently seven train stations and 16 tram stations established throughout the Gold Coast. There is an opportunity to facilitate transit-oriented development, which consists of high-density, mixed-use development around a transit station. Transit-oriented development promotes walkability and public transport usage and improves the quality of life of those who take advantage of it. The Gold Coast City Council has announced an intention to facilitate transit-oriented development around light rail stations (Davies and Lodge 2011). It remains to be seen whether the impetus, contained in the South-East Queensland Regional Plan and other state government documents such as the Next Generation Planning Guideline (Queensland Government 2011), will be maintained under the new approaches to planning that commenced with the election of a new Queensland government and Gold Coast City Council (with a new mayor in 2013).

Economic diversification

The creative industries on the Gold Coast, with film and television production the most significant activity, contribute substantial income and employment to the economy of

Queensland. Several universities, TAFE institutions and schools offer specialised training in aspects of film and television. As a result, the Gold Coast is producing skilled workers for the creative industries. The city's rich natural assets offer several potential production sites for movie-making. There is a film studio and production studio at Village Roadshow Studios in Oxenford.

Several ICT businesses are located on the Gold Coast. Silicon Lakes acts as an incubator for ICT start-ups and seeks to promote the Gold Coast as a desirable location for high-tech businesses. Gold Coast TechSpace has been organising workshops for local communities to learn about latest technologies. Thus, a skilled workforce and businesses in the ICT industries are continually being nurtured on the Gold Coast. There are offices in Robina which cater for and are currently home to ICT businesses. They all contribute to developing the Gold Coast as a potential knowledge-based economy.

As such, there is an opportunity to further diversify the city's economy with stronger focus on the creative and high-tech industries. By doing so it could be less reliant on tourism and construction, and thereby more resilient in economic recessions. The Gold Coast City Council is pursuing this opportunity through several approaches such as forming partnerships with local creative and high-tech businesses and organising conferences under the themes of these industries. Innovation and knowledge-based urban development will be supported if the Council's 'research triangle' concept is developed around the Gold Coast's three universities.

Conclusion

The Gold Coast is a relatively young and fast-growing city with a strong focus on tourism. It is rich in natural assets, which encompass not only the ocean and the beach but also the hinterland and its rainforests. The city is, given the north–south beach orientation, linear in its urban settlement and development patterns. In recent times, urban development has been forced westward into the Nerang area and north to the Coomera area. Like many cities around the world, the Gold Coast's major challenge is the widespread urban sprawl, leading to a car-dependent culture among local residents. Ever-increasing attention will need to be given to this and the other challenges identified in this chapter if the city's population continues to grow as projected.

The planning legislation for the Gold Coast is becoming less prescriptive under the new planning scheme and the state planning amendments. While such changes are positive for stimulating the local development industry, the needs of local communities and other stakeholders should not be neglected in the move towards a more streamlined and flexible planning system.

Looking forward to the future of the Gold Coast, there are significant opportunities for the city with the 2018 Commonwealth Games, the proposed development of a cultural precinct and the establishment of collaborative networks between the three universities and local businesses. Lastly, given the local availability of businesses and workforce in the creative and knowledge industries, there is a major prospect of diversifying the Gold Coast's economic activities into those fields.

References

ABS (2011a) *Gold Coast City: Industry Sector of Employment.* Australian Bureau of Statistics, Melbourne. http://goo.gl/2FtwGZ.

ABS (2011b) *Tourism Industry.* Australian Bureau of Statistics/Gold Coast City Council, Gold Coast. http://goo.gl/pw4Kcw.

ABS (2013) *2011 Census Community Profiles: Gold Coast (C).* Australian Bureau of Statistics, Canberra. http://goo.gl/1zpf5E.

Davies A, Lodge T (2011) *Gold Coast Rapid Transit: Corridor Study August 2011.* Gold Coast City Council, Gold Coast. http://goo.gl/yq2db1.

GCCC (undated a) *The Gold Coast.* Gold Coast City Council, Gold Coast. http://goo.gl/ICz2jY.

GCCC (undated b) *Safety Camera Network.* Gold Coast City Council, Gold Coast. http://goo.gl/6tQseJ.

GCCC (2013a) *Gold Coast City Transport Strategy 2031.* Gold Coast City Council, Gold Coast. http://goo.gl/PNaTbR.

GCCC (2013b) *New Active and Healthy Program Out Now.* Gold Coast City Council, Gold Coast. http://goo.gl/7qrYx8.

GCCC (2013c) *Gold Coast City Transport Strategy 2013: Technical Report.* Gold Coast City Council, Gold Coast. http://goo.gl/1KBzKY.

GCCC (2013d) *Draft Economic Development Strategy 2013–2023.* Gold Coast City Council, Gold Coast. http://goo.gl/dO18Em.

Griffin G (1998) The good, the bad and the peculiar: cultures and policies of urban planning and development on the Gold Coast. *Urban Policy and Research* **16**(4) 285–292. doi:10.1080/08111149808727776.

Griffith University (undated) *Gold Coast Health and Knowledge Precinct.* Griffith University, Gold Coast. http://goo.gl/rjLTv8.

Mullins P (1991) Tourism urbanisation. *International Journal of Urban and Regional Research* **15**(3) 326–342. doi:10.1111/j.1468-2427.1991.tb00642.x.

Queensland Government (2009) *South East Queensland Regional Plan.* Office of Urban Management, Brisbane.

Queensland Government (2011) *Next Generation Planning.* Council of Mayors, Brisbane.

Queensland Government (2013) *Broadwater Marine Project.* Queensland Government, Brisbane. http://goo.gl/0CQJho.

Stephens K (2013) *Gold Coast 2015 City Plan Makes Sky the Limit.* Fairfax Media, Sydney. http://goo.gl/gwqiX2.

Tourism and Events Qld (2013) *Gold Coast, Famous for Fun.* Tourism and Events Queensland. http://goo.gl/TEui9j.

Chapter 16

State of the environment

T. Hundloe

What have we done? What have we learned?

In this chapter we turn our attention to the people of the Gold Coast and their environmental impacts, as experienced in the 21st century. The past is gone. The damage is done. Dramatic change in landforms and ecological relationships are inevitable in building cities. From this we can only learn and do things better in the future. This is why there will never be another Gold Coast like the one we describe in this book.

Having built this city, how are we treating its environment today? In several earlier chapters we presented evidence that shows there is a variety of wildlife, most native to the Gold Coast, in the urban and farm environments that we have created. This is a result of our propensity to plant trees and bushes attractive to native birds, and to maintain aquatic environments suitable for frogs, turtles and fish. Noting this, we remind readers that experts have determined that much more of the city's remaining near-natural environment requires protection. This task will become ever more difficult if the city's population growth is encouraged. If there has to be population growth, much depends on where it occurs and how it is managed.

Fortunately we have maintained some small areas of World Heritage Rainforests within the city boundaries. Small parcels of reasonable-quality land are slowly being purchased by the Gold Coast City Council to configure wildlife corridors. A public tram system (light rail) has been built along the busiest part of the tourist strip with the aim of reducing traffic congestion. Finally, changes in business attitudes, in particular the adoption of corporate social responsibility programs, are indicative of positive environmental care initiatives. Positives are not too difficult to identify.

As we have seen, quite dramatic impacts occurred in building the city. The construction stage is only the beginning of the environmental impact of city building. A city 'up and running' has its own impacts. These are called 'operational impacts' in formal environmental impact assessment terms. This is the focus of this chapter. While we delve into this it is important to keep in mind the following question: what environmental, social and economic impacts are likely to result if the city's population is allowed to increase substantially? Keep in mind there are only half a million plus residents living in the city of the Gold Coast. You will note in the quotes below from Gold Coast City Council spokespeople and council publications that population growth has been identified as a major factor to be managed. It troubles the city's planners and engineers as much as it poses very profound questions for those of us who ponder and research the sustainability of the city.

Before discussing the issues referred to, it is necessary to provide a range of socio-economic and geographic data. Where people live, the distance they travel to work and their style of housing influence the state of the local environment. Environmental impacts are correlated with population densities. There are both benefits and costs of high numbers of people concentrated in discrete parts of a city. And it is not simply numbers that count. Where in the city population densities are high does matter. The closer to the CBD, the better, all other things being equal. Lifestyles are also paramount in determining environmental impacts. Taking pleasure in the surf and local coffee shops, eating locally produced foods and 'holidaying at home' results in a greatly reduced ecological footprint compared to making the opposite choices.

The questions

Where does most of the present population live? We know most are urban dwellers not farmers or hobby-farmers. The choices in terms of style of housing (apartments, conventional detached houses) and location (beachfront, canal estate, inland suburb, rural residential) are varied. How many residents are there in these different housing types? What type of work do they do and where? How far do they travel to take children to school and to shop?

Then there are the temporary visitors, the tourists who make the Gold Coast the unique city it is. How many of them? What form of accommodation do they use? What demands do they make on the natural resources of the city? These are the types of questions we pursue to the extent that the available data will permit.

Our focus will be the state of the urban, suburban and near-natural environments today, and this means we will consider the conventional forms of urban pollution (e.g. air and water pollution) as well as other traditional measures, such as traffic congestion. Because the World Heritage area, the national parks and some other areas are protected by strict laws we will leave their environmental state out of our assessment.

We are dealing with a relatively large city in Australian terms, even in global terms. Would we not expect some level of pollution? Before we can answer that we need some background data, particularly on the matters raised above: on the size of the permanent population and their style of housing; on the extent of tourist visitation and where they stay if not day-trippers; on the preferred forms of transport; on waste disposal methods and other factors that influence the residential, commercial and industrial environments.

Visions of civil leaders

As we engage in our task, it will pay us to be mindful of the vision that the Gold Coast politicians and managers set for their city in 1996. It was a far-sighted vision, and an ambitious one: 'the City of the Gold Coast ... is (to be) ... recognised for its world's-best-standard sustainable environment, and its facilities and services' (quoted in Thomas 1997, p. 1). In 2010, the Gold Coast City Council advertised its city vision in the following terms:

> *Defined by spectacular beaches, hinterland ranges, forests and waterways, the Gold Coast is an outstanding city which celebrates nature and connects distinct communities with the common goal of sustainability, choice and wellbeing for all.*

As we write, the recently elected Gold Coast City Council is preparing a revised 'vision statement' and a new Town Plan is awaiting approval. We cannot rule out the possibility that the present council will rescind the commitment to sustainability made by its predecessor. That, though, would be an extraordinary decision for a city administration that calls upon the world to recognise it according to the standards of the 21st century.

Some necessary data

Let us consider the data that help to answer some of the questions above. The permanent population of the Gold Coast was 526 173 in 2012. Just under half had lived in the city for less than 10 years. This is one indicator that suggests that the Gold Coast is different from other Australian cities. Its population has grown fast, due to migration from elsewhere in Australia. The population increase is not due to natural birth rates exceeding mortality rates. Only continued migration will see the city's population increase. If housing costs increase relative to average wages, we can expect a significant slow-down in migration. However, the price we pay for a residence or for rent is a function of demand – and demand is driven by more people wanting to reside on the Gold Coast. Immigrants seeking work will push housing prices up, as will immigrating retirees. This is just one of the many issues we face in any attempt to predict the future of the Gold Coast.

Most of the Gold Coast's residents live in the linear conurbation stretching from Paradise Point north of Southport, to Coolangatta on the border of New South Wales. In the past 20 or so years the width of this linear city has increased significantly as urbanisation has pushed westwards, first to where the Pacific Motorway divides the mainly urban area from the rural and semi-rural area, more recently north-west of the Pacific Motorway into the new suburbs closer to Beenleigh and then north-east into the lower Coomera River area. We can and should ask how the city was able to expand in recent years. Much of the expansion was onto previous farming land, alluvial plains laid down over millions of years by the silt deposited by the water eroding the rock faces of the hinterland mountains. Good-quality farming land is an increasingly scarce resource, but we are yet to recognise this or see it reflected in the market.

Prior to the establishment of the expanded city boundaries, there was a large area of land in the Albert Shire (west of the coastal strip that was known as the Gold Coast) zoned for urban development. Another book is required to explain why this was the case. Some farmers will fight tooth and nail to protect arable land. Yet other farmers will be enticed to sell by developers who work to change the zoning so that the farmland can be subdivided and sold as urban land. We can but point to this as a basic issue.

Many of the farms that became urban land were small dairy farms. While strong dairy-producer co-operatives existed and milk and cream prices reflected local costs of production, the farms remained viable. But the deregulation of the dairy industry changed the economics of farming. It was no longer viable except for a few larger farms; speculating land-developers bought farmland and lobbied to have it rezoned for residential and tourist purposes. In this they were successful. It is a moot question whether or not the farmers who sold were better off. On the other hand, the speculators were as likely to face bankruptcy as bounty.

Between 1970 and 1993 there were 3375 ha of land in Albert Shire approved for urban development, about two-thirds (2209 ha) approved in 1989. It was in these rural locations that new suburbs have formed, in particular in the north-west. Coomera is the prime example. There was also a residential push westwards of the M1 in the Nerang region. Notwithstanding the demand for housing land that a rapid population growth has required, there remains considerable rural land in Numinbah Valley, in the upper reaches of the Tallebudgera and Currumbin Valleys, in the north-east sugarcane fields and in the north-west of the city. Population densities, as we will see, tell the story. Before we get to these metrics that illustrate what happened, we can note the following, based on the 1997 Gold Coast City Council's State of the Environment (SoE) Report (Thomas 1997).

Approximately 41 per cent of the city was zoned rural, about two-thirds of it rural-residential and one-third used for farming of one sort or the other (grazing, dairying, sugarcane growing, small-scale horticulture). In an analysis by Ryan *et al.* of the Queensland Herbarium (2003) it was reported that the same percentage of the city (56 158 ha) was vegetated in natural and near-natural conditions, not completely natural as it was before European settlement but still not denuded or degraded. That estimate was made some years ago and the city's population has grown since then. However, on the positive side the upper catchments of the big rivers and creeks have, so far, remained in the state they were some decades ago.

People and land use

The 1997 Council SoE (Thomas 1997) noted that about 9 per cent of the land was under Protected Area management (including the World Heritage property, national parks, conservation parks, state forests and designated water catchments), 7 per cent comprised waterways (excluding beaches, the Broadwater and waters of southern Moreton Bay), commercial/resort/industrial land accounted for ~10 per cent, roads about 7 per cent and public open space (urban parkland and the like) about 9 per cent, leaving ~17 per cent for existing urban residential use and 4 per cent available for future development. There has been a significant increase in urban development in the city since then; however, the percentages above are generally indicative of the land uses of the city today. Much of the population increase has occurred in the new suburbs. Readers can turn to Plate 4 to refresh their knowledge of present land use.

Residential densities

The Australian Bureau of Statistics has calculated densities for all Gold Coast statistical areas. The highest density is in Mermaid Beach–Broadbeach area at 3748.6 persons per km^2, and the lowest at Guanaba–Springbrook at 13.9 persons per km^2. Table 16.1 lists the top 10 and Table 16.2 the bottom 10 in terms of density. We should note that, all other things being equal, the folk living in the less-dense, more distant suburbs are likely to be contributing more to global warming (due to travel to work, school and for leisure) than their closely settled inner-city cousins. There are convincing arguments against beachfront high-rise apartments: the long shadows cast over beaches designed for sunbaking; the complete disregard to the views once enjoyed by neighbours; the scramble for parking space where it is not provided by the apartment owners. Yet, once we put greenhouse gas emissions from daily travel into the cost–benefit analysis, an accountant working in the Surfers Paradise CBD and living in a high-rise adds far less to the planet's global warming bill than someone who commutes from, say, the hills of Tallai.

The areas with the highest growth rates over the five years 2007–12 were Pimpama, nearly doubling its population; Coomera, also nearly doubling its population; Upper Coomera–Willow Vale, increasing by ~50 per cent; Hope Island increasing at 40 per cent; and at equal fifth Ormeau–Yatala and Pacific Pines–Gaven, at a little over one-third

Table 16.1. Highest population densities

Suburb	Persons per km^2
Mermaid Beach–Broadbeach	3748.6
Surfers paradise	3657.3
Labrador	3519.0
Coolangatta	2963.6
Varsity lakes	2567.1
Palm beach	2311.7
Miami	2242.6
Burleigh waters	2180.8
Biggera waters	2115.6
Southport	2113.5

Source: ABS 2011 *Census* (ABS 2011).

Table 16.2. Lowest population densities

Suburb	Persons per km^2
Guanaba–Springbrook	13.9
Jacobs Well Alberton	22.6
Tamborine–Canungra	26.2
Currumbin Valley–Tallebudgera	62.1
Hope Island	167.7
Upper Coomera–Willow Lake	208.5
Ormeau–Yatala	236.1
Mudgeeraba–Bonogin	272.6
Worongary–Tallai	300.1
Nerang–Mount Nathan	322.9

Source: ABS 2011 *Census* (ABS 2011).

increase. It is obvious that the growth area is to the north-west of the coastal strip that we commonly think of as the Gold Coast.

At present there remains in the order of 8500 ha of native vegetation in the urbanised area. As discussed in Chapter 5, most of the good-quality native vegetation is in the protected estates in the hinterland and on the southern Moreton Bay islands. The fact that there is a considerable amount of native vegetation in the suburbs allows a variety of wildlife to make urban areas home. Of course, if the city is allowed – or encouraged – to grow and this takes place in the near-natural areas, native flora and fauna would be the losers. Being aware of this and not allowing growth would be a profound environmental decision.

The city supports 202 893 full-time equivalent jobs, most in retail (a very broad classification).[1] These people work in 60 015 registered businesses, most of which are micro-businesses and small to medium enterprises (SMEs). These tend to be spread along the coastal strip, and in the Nerang and Yatala–Beenleigh area. There are places where the Pacific Highway verge comprises small retail businesses for kilometres on end, for example,

Mermaid Beach and Palm Beach. At the high end of employment the large retail stores, the casino, the hospitals and the universities are obvious sources of jobs.

The availability of employment on the Gold Coast is an interesting matter, particularly if the residential population is allowed to expand significantly. At the time of writing the so-called 'self-sufficiency' of the city is well below 100 per cent, sitting between 80 per cent and 90 per cent. Obviously, a significant number of workers have to travel outside the city for work; most go to Brisbane. If the proposed population growth is to occur in the far-north suburbs, we would expect workers to seek jobs in Brisbane. This would indicate a stronger community of interest with Brisbane than with the city in which they live.

Household demographics from the ABS show that over half the city's population comprises couples, roughly equally split between those without children and those with. One-person households comprise approximately one-fifth of the population. In comparison to Brisbane, there are considerably more couples with families living in Gold Coast households (32 per cent versus 27.5 per cent). Home ownership on the Gold Coast mirrors that of Brisbane except that there is a higher percentage of people renting on the Gold Coast.

Those who do not live in the suburban areas live on hobby farms or rural retreats, or engage in commercial farming. Where farming was the mainstay of the Gold Coast economy in its early days, with the exception of sugarcane cultivation, it has shrunk in importance. Only a handful of farmers remain in Numinbah Valley and some horticulturists in the other valleys.

The ABS five-yearly Agricultural Census (the most recent 2010/11) shows the extent and changing levels of production of various farm products. Measured in value of production terms, in 2010/11 milk returned a minute 3.3 per cent of the Gold Coast's agriculture production. Today, milk production is at zero. Meat production was a small 6.9 per cent. Both these agricultural pursuits declined in value over the previous five years. On the other hand, the Gold Coast catchments now support a significant number of nurseries and cut-flower producers. Roughly half the dollar earnings from Gold Coast farming comes from these two enterprises. Sugarcane produces just under one-third the total farm income.

Returning our attention to the suburbs, there are other major enterprises and users of land to consider. First are the relatively small light industrial areas at Nerang and the Yatala–Beenleigh area, with other much smaller light industrial locations throughout the city. For example, there are marine industries at Broadwater and some further north. There is a boutique brewery at Burleigh.

There are the commercial and administrative centres. This has been Southport's role from the time it outgrew Nerang early in the 20th century. Today, most of the larger suburbs are home to bank branches, post offices and professional services such as medical clinics. Some have small manufacturing enterprises. Next there are various hospital precincts and university campuses. Then there are the theme parks, which are a key component of the Gold Coast's tourism industry. That leaves tourism, in particular tourist accommodation. While it could be argued that much of the hospitality industry – the restaurants, coffee shops, clubs and pubs – are a component of the tourism industry, it is just as valid to view them as one of the service industries supplying permanent residents as well as tourists. Clearly, they serve both groups. The same can be asserted about the golf courses.

The visitors

The Gold Coast receives nearly 80 000 visitors per day on average. There are, not unexpectedly, major peaks in visitation – holiday periods and events such as local AFL matches and to a lesser extent the other football codes. Over a 12-month period, there are 7.4 million day visitors, 3 664 000 domestic overnight visitors and 778 000 international visitors. The domestic overnight visitors spend 14 million–15 million nights on the Gold Coast, while the foreign ones spend 7 486 000 nights on the Gold Coast. The tourism industry generates nearly $4 billion annually. In terms of accommodation, there are about 150 hotels, motels, guesthouses and serviced apartments.

What are the environmental impacts?

How does the Gold Coast's environment fare with its present level of permanent population and such a large number of visitors? The most recent comprehensive data are relatively old, being for 2007. More recently, in 2010 the Australian Conservation Foundation ranked 20 Australian cities on sustainability terms. The Gold Coast was included. The city's overall rank was eighth (the Sunshine Coast came top). The Gold Coast had the lowest place for public participation, was ranked 18th for air quality and had the reasonable rank of seven for its green buildings (ACF 2010).[2]

An official State of the Environment report was published in 1997, the only formal such report for the city. This itself is a matter of some interest. We would expect regular updates, say, every five years? Findings of the 1997 report are summarised in Table 16.3. Following this, we report the major findings of the 2007 assessment.

The 1997 assessments reported in Table 16.3 suggest that air and water quality (two of the fundamental indicators) were of high to good standard. Water quality did vary a little. But, as shown in the 2007 report, matters have changed.

The 2007 sustainability assessment

In January 2007, the Gold Coast City Council published *Our Living City: A Sustainability Report*. This was what we could call a State of the Environment Report by another name. The 1997 report was the first of its kind for the Gold Coast and, as we go to print, the 2007 report could be the last of its kind for some time. The Mayor of the Gold Coast in 2007 was Ron Clarke, a much-respected Australian athlete and the name behind the eco-tourism/athletics resort on South Stradbroke Island, called Couran Cove. This resort failed

Table 16.3. Gold Coast State of the Environment Report, 1997

Air quality	Indicators	Pressures	Assessed
	Particulates, NOx, SOx, lead in atmosphere	Licensed emissions from industrial sources, traffic volume and flow	High standard (mains electricity comes from elsewhere)
Water quality			
	E. coli, pathogens, pH, salinity, nutrients, chemicals, suspended solids, temperature, rubbish and weeds in canals/lakes/streams	Recreational use of waterways, volume of water extracted, dams, disruption of stream, flow/stormwater, detention/channelling due to urbanisation	Drinking water consistently meets all health standards, surface waters meet national guidelines most of the time, Currumbin Rock pools can exceed acceptable pollution standards at high-use times

Source: Thomas (1997).

financially and we are yet to see how its new owners position it in the tourism market. We ask the question, is eco-tourism not viable on the coastal part of the Gold Coast? It is viable in the hinterland.

In the preface of the 2007 report, Ron Clarke informed readers that: 'Council is not required to undertake environment or sustainability reporting. It is something we have chosen to do, willingly.' As Mayor Clarke retired in 2012, there is considerable uncertainty as to when we will next learn of the environmental, economic and social status of the Gold Coast. We are forced to utilise this somewhat dated analysis to present an overview of the state of the Gold Coast environment.

We believe we should note the vision that Ron Clarke's Council had for the Gold Coast Council. Council promotional documents from 2007 stated that the Council wanted the Gold Coast to be 'naturally the world's best place to be'. The Council saw the city as a 'model for maintaining important environmental values and quality of life while managing growth and development'. Quite what the model is, or was, is not clear. It certainly is not clear what limits might be put on resident and visitor numbers. Population growth was identified as a major concern throughout the Council documents, yet no solutions were suggested. We will see below that the Gold Coast City Council does not call the shots on this matter.

As shown in the 2007 report, air quality remained relatively high; however, during summer, levels of ozone at the Helensvale monitoring station 'occasionally exceed ... Guidelines' (GCCC 2007, p. 13). Of some concern is the statement that 'more data and analysis is required to identify the potential link of ozone air pollution and the implications of increased traffic volumes for the city' (GCCC 2007, p. 13).

Water quality was assessed to be 'reasonably high ... poorer water quality is ... (e)xperienced in wetter years and urbanised catchments indicating that much of the pollution is being generated from urban landscapes' (GCCC 2007, p. 14). Population growth was identified as the driver of urbanisation and all the other pressures on the environment.

The extent of the city's impervious surfaces on which sit houses, high-rise apartments, shopping centres, hospitals, universities and roads is significant; they are concentrated in the coastal strip, from the beach to the Motorway (M1). Water picks up pollutants and carries them to receiving environments. Groundwater runoff is not treated and a large variety of potential pollutants are swept into the rivers, canals and finally the Pacific Ocean. While it is possible to clean floating materials from the canals and rivers (something that is done), the herbicides, pesticides, fertilisers, vehicle lubricants and road-surface deposits escape human intervention. These build up over time. A future Rachel Carson is likely to document the impacts on local wildlife and, inevitably, humans.

The 2007 report also discussed the state of the city's biodiversity. It said that the amount of remnant bushland[3] was just under 50 per cent, presumably based on the 41 per cent remnant vegetation of good quality plus the 5.4 per cent (7417 ha) classified as disturbed (Ryan *et al.* 2003). The area of protected habitat had increased marginally through the purchase of small lots of bushland for restoration. As pointed out previously, the figure of nearly 50 per cent is completely misleading if we consider the city of the Gold Coast as confined to the urban area. There is virtually no native vegetation left in the built-up areas between Paradise Point in the north and Coolangatta in the south.

The 2007 report dealt with waste generation and disposal, noting that 'increasing population and visitation will continue to place pressure on our waste management system' (GCCC 2007, p. 18). Under the heading 'economic sustainability', the report focused on the city's use of two primary natural resources, energy and water. The assessment was that on a per capita basis more energy was being consumed in 2007 than in 1997, due primarily to the increased uses of (household) appliances and motor vehicles. The consequence was an increase in greenhouse gas emissions. The drivers were population growth and economic growth (as conventionally defined).

The Nature Conservation Strategy

In 2009, the Gold Coast City Council published its Nature Conservation Strategy 2009–2019. Among other things it promised to increase native vegetation coverage to 55 per cent of the city's land by 2040. While this is encouraging, the document includes the following fact: 'Given land use commitments … 4400 ha of native vegetation could be cleared over coming decades for urban, industrial and infrastructure requirements. This will have significant impacts on the … extent and diversity of natural habitats.' This use of natural land is not necessarily the Council's doing, as the following statement in the Strategy (p. 8) makes clear: 'The SEQ Regional Plan requires that Council's land use planning make provision for 137 500 new dwellings by 2031'. The Queensland government is requiring the Gold Coast City Council to drastically expand its urban footprint. Where is the analysis (environmental, economic and social) that shows that this is a wise decision, that its benefits outweigh the costs?

Housing density determines the area of land needed to accommodate this number of houses. Add in the land needed for schools, local shops, roads and other infrastructure and the total land required is likely to be 14 000–20 000 ha. This is three to four times the amount of land the Council stated could be cleared. Where would it come from?

Population growth as the key driver

In the 2007 report the Gold Coast City Council put more emphasis on population growth as a driver of negative changes than was done in any similar assessment prepared in Australia. This comes as a surprise as the conventional call to action on the Gold Coast is 'more': more tourists, more high-rise buildings, another casino, a cruise-ship terminal and a cable car. The latter two tourist projects have a long but unsuccessful history on the Gold Coast. None of the attempts have been able to get off the ground yet.

Let us note what the 2007 report said about population growth:

- increasing population is decreasing participation rates in community organisations, resulting in a decline in social capital;
- pressure is being placed on the city's heritage sites and buildings as a consequence of urban expansion;
- the number of people exposed to potential hazards is increasing;
- housing is becoming less affordable;
- there is increased risk of mosquito-borne diseases as more residential development occurs adjacent to waterways;
- there is increased traffic congestion.

Other minor population-related impacts are also noted. Yet the Queensland government regional plan requires the population of the Gold Coast to grow to the extent that 137 500 new dwellings will have to be built in the next 16 years.

We estimated that 14 000–20 000 ha of land would be required to allow this residential growth. One way of conceptualising this amount of land is in terms of lost koala habitat (not that we imply that the urban development, if it occurs, will be fully or partially in koala habitat). We would expect that the development would be distributed to areas where koalas were not threatened. Mindful of that, on average, one koala in the Gold Coast region requires ~10 ha of land (Biolink Ecological Consultants 2007). There would be 1400–2000 fewer koalas if all the new residences were built on koala habitat land. The present koala population of the Gold Coast is estimated to be 4300–5100. The worst case would be a loss of nearly half, and the best case would be a loss of 27 per cent. While we don't expect that new residential development will be permitted to cause that extent of damage, we need to ask where the residential development will occur. There is no room for it on the coastal strip where the beaches and sea breeze remind you that you are on the Gold Coast. Are the remaining agricultural areas to remain in the hands of farmers?

On 8 February 2010, at the 549th Gold Coast Council Meeting, councillors were presented with a report by consulting firm SGS; it included population, business and employment projections to 2026. Of most interest is where residential population growth is expected. From 2011 to 2026, the city's total residential population is expected to increase by 40%. A very significant increase is predicted for the Pimpama–Coomera area, to three times its current population. At Hope Island the residential population is set to double, Robina and Varsity Lakes are to grow by 50% and a one-third increase is suggested for Biggera Waters–Labrador, Helensvale, Kingsholm–Upper Coomera, Nerang, Palm Beach and Southport. Surfers Paradise will experience a 25% increase.

In 2007, the then Gold Coast Mayor and its Chief Executive Officer were promoting the city as 'naturally the world's best place to be' and to achieve that 'the city must strive to be ecologically sustainable', recognising that this would be possible only if population numbers were managed, pollution reduced and natural habitat preserved (GCCC 2007, p. 6). They noted that sustainability must pay particular attention to 'the way (the) population lives and consumes'. These are positive statements in recognition of the pressure that increased population, consumption and waste generation place on a city. The city was envisaged as one that would be presented as sustainable in all senses of the concept.

Let us contemplate what that city could be. Cicero wrote: 'If you have a garden and a library, you have everything you need'.[4] In a Gold Coast garden you would expect a wide range of visitors, from small lizards to song birds and the occasional large snake. Socrates is reported to have said that he 'found all the wisdom he needed within the walls of Athens'. The Gold Coast is a vastly different city from ancient Athens. Quite where in the Gold Coast we would find a modern Greek 'agora' (market/meeting place) I cannot answer. Still, the citizens of the Gold Coast are proud of the city's natural and educational attributes, the large number of high schools, three university campuses, art centre and good coffee shops where scholarly discussion just might occur.

One of the defining characteristics of the urban parts of the Gold Coast is that they are contiguous with rural land. In this respect the Gold Coast has what the 18th century's largest city, Paris, had in an earlier era – a half-hour walk from the inner city of Paris into the quiet countryside. While it could take a little longer on the Gold Coast (much depends where in the linear urbanised area you commenced the walk) it would be nowhere as long as the six hours you need to walk in modern Paris to escape suburbia. The Gold Coast has at present the premier place as Australia's tourist city. There is little that can be done to improve on that. Much can be done to spoil it.

Notes

1. The usual classifications used for the Gold Coast are tourism, construction, retail and the service industry.
2. Air quality was measured by the level of particulate matter.
3. Remnant vegetation includes 'vegetation that has at least 70% of the height and 50% of the cover of the dominant stratum relative to the undisturbed height and cover of that stratum and which is dominated by species characteristics of the vegetation's undisturbed canopy.' This definition includes vegetation that has not been cleared or has been lightly thinned of trees, or vegetation that has been cleared or heavily thinned but substantially regrown (Wilson *et al.* quoted in Ryan *et al.* 2003, p. 14).
4. Quoted in Skidelsky and Skidelsky (2013, p. 140).

References

ABS (2011) *Census 2011.* Cat. No. 2001.0 Australian Bureau of Statistics, Canberra.

ACF (2010) *Sustainable Cities Index: Ranking Australia's 20 Largest.* Australian Conservation Foundation, Melbourne. http://acfonline.org.au/sites/default/files/resources/2010_ACF_sci_index_report.pdf.

Biolink Ecological Consultants (2007) *Koala Habitat and Population Assessment for Gold Coast City LGA.* Uki, NSW.

GCCC (2007) *Our Living City Report: A Sustainability Update.* Gold Coast City Council, Gold Coast.

Ryan TS, Bean AR, Hoskins BB, Wilson BA, McDonald WJF (2003) *Gold Coast City Council 1998 Nature Conservation Mapping Review Stage 1.* Queensland Herbarium for the Gold Coast City Council.

Skidelsky R, Skidelsky E (2013) *How Much is Enough?* Penguin Books, Melbourne.

Thomas E (1997) *State of the Environment Reporting: A Review of the Concept and its History, and its Application to the City of the Gold Coast.* Gold Coast City Council, Gold Coast.

Chapter 17

In conclusion, something to chew on: native plant foods of the Gold Coast

S. Grigalius and D. McPhee

Introduction

Ask most people what Gold Coast food is and you may hear answers like the ubiquitous prawn cocktail with avocado, a burger with 'fresh' pineapple available at the local surf club, or fish and chips (eaten on the beach to give it the seaside connection), with the fish often imported from New Zealand or Vietnam. None of this is the true food of the Gold Coast.

The true food of the Gold Coast is being rediscovered as concepts such as food providence, a focus on Australian native food and food products, and a general consumer focus on more healthy and sustainable food choices has formed and fairly rapidly increased in popularity. For all the 'Yin' (action on the Gold Coast coastal strip), the 'Yang' (the hinterland side of the Gold Coast) may be a place of recuperation with an abundance of edible plants and plants with medicinal qualities (Setzer *et al.* 2001; Miller and Brewer 1992).

In the pre-industrialised age, human settlements occurred where food grew. Now, due to technology, engineering and advances in preservation techniques and transport, food more often than not follows the people. Other changes are much more recent. Or so we think, until we read a little history on the matter.

The Australian native edible plant industry has expanded rapidly (Ahmed and Johnson 2000). Not only does this provide culinary benefits but environmental ones. The recognition that a considerable number of native Australian plants are edible and are suitable (or proven candidates) for various forms of horticulture can assist in the conservation of native bushland which may otherwise be seen as valueless or of low value. It also represents a potential source of sustainable income for remote indigenous communities, particularly in arid regions of Australia (Walsh and Douglas 2011).

On the Gold Coast, there are native foods in the area reaching from the hinterland to the ocean foredunes. Some, like the macadamia (*Macadamia tetraphylla*) are well known and have a strong commercial presence; some like the smooth-leaf Davidson plum (*Davidsonia johnsonii*) are relatively unknown but may be the next superfood. In this chapter, key native plant food species from rainforests, open woodlands and coastal areas of the Gold Coast are described with the aim of identifying the local native varieties that can be incorporated into an interesting and enjoyable diet. Elements of the natural history of the plants are described, as is knowledge of indigenous uses of the plant and the scope for planting in backyard gardens and commercial production. While this chapter focuses on plant food, it also recognises that bushfoods include various animals, aquatic and terrestrial.

Before extensive land clearing in the early 19th century, the Gold Coast had widespread areas of rainforests of various types. Many of these rainforests types now exist locally as remnants only, although more extensive stands of vegetation persevere in the hinterland World Heritage area. An abundance of plant species can be found in the Gold Coast rainforests and although many of the plants look tempting to eat only a few are safe for human consumption (McKenzie 1997). The toxic compounds that many rainforest plants possess to deter herbivores can pose risks to human health or at the very least, be not an enjoyable dining experience. Over thousands of years Australia's Aborigines have worked out the best way to prepare these often toxic plants. Methods range from simple preparation such as peeling and drying in the sun, to advanced methods such as peeling, pounding, running in fresh water, grinding or baking (Isaacs 1987). Knowledge of edible native plants is at risk of being lost as the main method of passing on this knowledge has been oral, through generations of indigenous Australians. The interest in passing on the knowledge can be lost, particularly if the foods are not commonly used (Packer *et al.* 2012).

Smooth Davidson plum *Davidsonia johnsonii*

The smooth Davidson plum (*Davidsonia johnsonii*) is one of three species in the genus *Davidsonia*, which is endemic to Australia (Harden and Williams 2000). The Davidson plum (*Davidsonia pruriens*) which occurs in north Queensland is one of the best-known native fruits in Australia. The rainforests of the Gold Coast that extend into north-eastern New South Wales are home to a unique variety, the smooth-leaf or smooth Davidson plum (*Davidsonia johnsonii*). The smooth Davidson plum is a nationally listed endangered species, as is the Mullumbimby plum (*Davidsonia jerseyana*) which occurs in New South Wales.

The smooth Davidson plum is a species that occurs in lowland subtropical rainforest and wet eucalypt forest at low altitudes. Unlike its north Queensland counterpart *Davidsonia pruriens* and the New South Wales variety Mullimbimby plum *Davidsonia jerseyana*, the smooth-leaf Davidson plum has a hairless fruit and minimal hair on the leaves. Purple fruit develops from dark pink to red flowers on panicles on the main stem of the plant, and for this reason harvesting must be done by hand. The fruit grows from green pea size into smooth, purple-skinned plums when ripe, similar in appearance to a traditional purple plum. The inside flesh surrounds two seeds and when ripe has the same texture as a traditional plum, but an extremely tart taste. Due to its low sugar content and high acidity it is unappealing to eat as a fresh fruit. However, the Davidson plum is one of the most common native varieties seen in shops as it can be made into a range of different chutneys, jams, sauces and marinades.

A common bushfood that has been a staple of Aboriginal diets, the Davidson plum has substantial antioxidant and anti-inflammatory properties. The Blackmore Institute has commissioned Southern Cross University to study this native species (SCU 2013). Studies may find this plant to be the next superfood, and it's in the Gold Coast's backyard. Even now the Davidson plum is considered an iconic element in many sweets, savouries and even cocktail sauces.

Australian finger lime *Citrus australasica*

Australia has six species of true native species of citrus (Family Rutaceae) including the Australian finger lime (*Citrus australasica*) which ranges from the Mt Tamborine area of the Gold Coast to Woodburn in northern New South Wales (Cooper 2013). The group of species as a whole has attracted significant research and commercial interest. Commercial use of the Australian finger lime commenced in the mid 1990s with most fruit harvested from the wild; commercial orchard production has now commenced and may eventually replace wild-harvested fruit. Commercially, plants are propagated by grafting or budding onto other *Citrus* rootstocks, easily sourced by the home gardener. The native Australian limes are generally better known in the international culinary community than locally, as over 50 per cent of all product is exported (Clarke 2012).

Early settlers recognised the value of the Australian finger lime. They retained the trees when clearing for agriculture, and consumed the fruit. Colonial botanists suggested that the lime should be cultivated (Low 1991). As the name suggests, the Australian finger lime is a slender, finger-shaped fruit 3–12 cm long, ranging in skin colour from green to purple to a reddish brown. Many different colours are observed in the flesh of the species. The plants grow from low shrubs to trees of 10 m and have thorns or spines to 25 mm long which make harvesting difficult and sometimes painful (Cooper 2013).

The outside skin is similar in texture to a lime with very small pores and very thin skin. Inside the flesh are hundreds of small caviar-style beads or spheres which hold a lime-like citric liquid. Unlike a traditional lemon or lime, which have interconnecting segments that exude juice when cut, the finger lime emits juice only once the individual spheres are burst. This unique characteristic enables these 'citrus caviar' to have various food applications from a novel garnish on sashimi to its use in pastry where it can be undetected in a sauce or paste until chewed. The beads can also be used in icecreams, sauces, jams and syrups as well as some beauty products. As the fruit does not ripen once picked, care needs to be given to the ripened fruit before processing. Fortunately the fruit has an ability to keep a high quality of shape and flavour when frozen, meaning it can demand a premium dollar in kitchens around the world. Ripe finger limes require only a gentle squeeze to split the skin and have the citrus spheres ooze out. The variety of colours of the fruit can add visual appeal to a dish when mixed together, while maintaining consistency of texture and flavour.

Small-leaved tamarind *Diploglottis campbellii*

The genus *Diploglottis* is in the Family Sapindaceae (soapberries). There are 10 species in the genus *Diploglottis* with eight of them, including the small-leaved tamarind (*Diploglottis campbellii)* endemic to Australia (see Plate 10). The small-leaved tamarind is a nationally endangered species, the decline of which can be attributed primarily to loss of and disturbance to habitat (DEC 2004). The number of plants remaining in the wild is very small, but its ease of cultivation as a general garden plant has resulted in a large amount of available stock and use of the plant commercially; growers are not reliant on the limited wild stock.

Unique to the area from Springbrook to Tintenbar, as the name suggests the small-leaved tamarind resembles the introduced tamarind in flavour, suggesting a unique fruity flavour with a tart taste. Although there are similar types of plants in other regions in Australia, this plant is unique in the size of its fruit. The plant has a husky-type outer shell which holds one to three seeds of 18–20 mm. The tree can grow up to 20 m tall (Cooper 2013). There are two types of this plant, which hold either red or yellow fruit in their outer shell. As the fruit has a lychee-style sourness it can be used in many ways. It is most popular in Asian-style sauces that require pungency of flavour. Various species of tamarind are widely used in Asian dishes, with curries utilising the unique flavour for piquancy.

Lemon myrtle *Backhousia citriodora*

Lemon myrtle is a native Queensland tree originating in coastal rainforests with rainfall higher than 800 mm (Clarke 2012). The tree grows from 3–20 m and produces leaves that have an intense lemon flavour. The fresh leaves are mainly used to make oil although the majority of uses in cookery involve the dried leaves, of which over 90 per cent are exported (Clarke 2012). Once the leaves are dried they are ground to the size needed. Applications for dried leaves include seasoning fish and flavouring icecreams, sauces, baked goods and curries. The oil from the fresh leaves is extracted by steam distillation and can be used for flavouring; due to its high antioxidant, antimicrobial and antifungal properties its use in personal care products is increasing as well as its use against food-related bacteria (Dupont *et al.* 2006; Konczak *et al.* 2010). Due to the potency of the dried ingredient, its use in milk-based sauces and creams is widely regarded as it does not curdle or turn the processed food as lemon juice can.

Although large doses of lemon myrtle have proven to be toxic to humans (Hayes and Markovic 2002), other research suggests that the oil can be used to cure viral infections and some skin disorders (Burke *et al.* 2004).

Native raspberry *Rubus parvifolius*

There are 10 known native species of raspberry in Australia, and although the most common is the *R. parvifolius* there are six other species found in the Gold Coast area from the rainforests down to the tall eucalypt forest. They are generally categorised as the native raspberry or bush raspberry and include the *R. moorei*, *R. rosifolius*, *R. x novus*, *R. moluccanus* var. *moluccanus*, *R. moluccanus* var. *trilobus* and the *R. nubulosus* (Barker and Barker 2005). The plants feature prickly stems and in some cases prickly leaves with small pink to white flowers bearing fruit. Depending on the variety, the plants can be freestanding shrubs up to 3 m (*R. moluccanus*) or the climbing vine variety which can reach tree canopy height in the rainforests (*R. moorei* and *R. nebulosus*) (Bean 1999). The fruits are small and red when ripe (apart from the *R. moorei* which ripen black), with a soft and segmented feel and a sweet and succulent taste, not unlike a European raspberry.

Unlike many other native fruits that display a sour taste, the raspberry may be one of the few native Australian fruits that has a sweet flavour, which may support its claim for commercial success. It can be used in a variety of dishes, predominantly desserts, but due to its soft body when ripe it requires care when transporting. As well as the small fruits eaten for energy and sustenance, there is evidence to suggest a tea made from the young leaves can treat 'bad belly' as a native herbal medicine remedy (Isaacs 1987).

Pandanus palm *Pandanus tectorius*

The *Pandanus* palm, or simply the pandanus, grows mainly in coastal areas from northern New South Wales up to the top of Australia and throughout south-east Asia. A visit to any Gold Coast beach will find these trees along dune areas. The Burleigh Head National Park headland is characterised by the unique silhouette the palms give the skyline. The trees can grow to a height of 20 m although the typical height on the Gold Coast region is 3–4 m. They have long dark green leaves with shiny, sharp-toothed edges. The leaves grow in clumps upwards with newer leaves originating from the centre and older leaves forced to the outside of the clump, sometimes giving the appearance of a grass skirt surrounding the newer leaves. Not only were these plants an important food source for the aboriginal people, they were used for many other purposes. The wood was used for didgeridoos and the leaves were woven into carrying implements, as well as used for treating various ailments (Pickering 2012).

The fruit grow to the size of footballs and have tightly packed individual nuts. The fruit ripens from green to yellow then to a reddish brown and is traditionally collected once it drops from the tree at this stage of ripening. Cutting the base away from the ripened fruit will expose several nuts that have a flavour likened to that of a peanut-flavoured coconut (Pickering 2012), with a high fat content of 74% (Brand-Miller and Holt 1998). Indigenous Australians collected the unripe, hard woody fruit and gained access to the nuts by roasting the fruit, suggesting its reputation as a luxury food (Isaacs 1987). Today the pandanus is widely used in south-east Asia to flavour rices and curries. On the Gold Coast it remains relatively untouched as a food source.

Warragul greens *Tetragonia tetragonioides*

Also known as Botany Bay spinach, New Zealand spinach and Cook's cabbage, this herbaceous plant is part of the assemblage on dune areas and the foreshore. It is native to Australia but not endemic, as it also occurs naturally in Japan, Chile, Argentina and New Zealand. The leaves look like a rounded speartip and have fine hairs almost resembling fur which glisten like dew in the early sun, and its flowers are small and yellow, branching from the main stem. Important as groundcover, the plant assists in stabilising the sandy base in which it grows. Due to high levels of oxalates in the plant, the leaves must be blanched in boiling water and chilled in fresh water before preparing for consumption, although it is believed the young leaves can be eaten fresh (Isaacs 1987). The flavour is similar to that of spinach although the leaves are more fibrous in texture. The plant has been identified as having an anti-ulcerogenic function that has been traced to two cerebrosides, and an anti-inflammatory function that has been traced to novel water-soluble polysaccharides (Cambie and Ferguson 2003). The plant can be found on coastal dunes including those of the Gold Coast beaches and some parts of the Broadwater foreshore. It may be used as a substitute for European-style spinach either served as a side dish or tossed through pasta or a quiche.

Pigface *Carpobrotus glaucescens*

Pigface is a common groundcover plant found among shallow, rocky or deep sandy soils close to the sea, and in saltmarsh areas from Queensland to Victoria (Jacobs and Highet 1999). The plant is a pioneer species, meaning it stabilises the soil and facilitates the growth of other plants. The green leaves look similar to small finger-length smooth cactus and have three sides, giving a triangular shape in cross-section. The foliage can give great cover to unstable sand areas with plants trailing stems up to 2 m long (van Eeten 2005). The plants can survive high salt and low water and can even survive being covered in sand, by growing upwards (van Eeten 2005). The fruit, which are red with two 'horns', are the edible part. The taste has been likened to a slightly salty kiwi fruit (Leiper 2013). It is well known as a garden plant, but its edible nature is less known. Indigenous Australians used sap from freshly broken leaves to treat stings from bluebottles and insects (Stephens and Sharp 2009). It was also used by early European explorers to ward off scurvy (van Eeten 2005).

Macadamia nut *Macadamia tetraphylla*

Of all of the plants discussed in this chapter, the macadamia is the most widely known. Also known as the bush nut or Queensland nut, the plant is native to the area between Ballina in far north New South Wales and Maryborough in Queensland. The tree can grow to a height of 18 m and has shiny slender green leaves with a rounded end and a slight serrated edge. The flowers are yellow to pink to purple and grow in wattle-like clusters of 200 or more (Quinlan and Wilk 2005), giving way to a hard round husk containing the nut. Successfully planted in Hawaii in 1892 from a bag of nuts a US naval officer took home from Pimpama, the macadamia is now an important export crop for Hawaii and Mexico as well as Australia and is one of the most commercially valuable nuts in the world (Hohenhaus 2011).

The nut can have a variety of applications: it is roasted with salt, coated in dark chocolate or finely chopped and used as a crust for fresh fish in praline icecream. Due to its high fat content (around 75%) the macadamia has flavours of rich butter, enhanced as a toasted flavour when the nut is roasted (Birch *et al.* 2010) making it ideal as a coating on local fish when ground into crumbs. Common in the Gold Coast area and other south-east Queensland rainforest areas, the nut is often left to drop to the ground.

Sour currant bush *Leptomeria acida*

Also known as acid drops plant, the sour currant bush is still found on parts of the Gold Coast near the Coolangatta Airport and at Pine Ridge. It has been reported as far south as Port Stephens in New South Wales. The sour currant bush is a hemi-parasitic plant, meaning it parasitises a host plant by robbing it of water and nutrients. The plant can grow to 3 m with branch-like shoots accounting for the fruit. The bush is reported to flower throughout the year, but chiefly in spring (Stephens and Sharp 2009). When a plant flowers in early spring the fruit ripens in early summer, with masses of 1 cm round fruits containing sour juice (Leiper 2013). It is suggested that they are best eaten fresh off the plant and are a high source of vitamin C (Leiper 2013), or cooked with sugar to make a jam (Stephens and Sharp 2009).

Moreton Bay chestnut *Castanospermum australe*

Also known as black bean, this tree is native to patches of coastal rainforests from Lismore in New South Wales to Cape York in Queensland (Boland *et al.* 2006). The tree can reach a height of 40 m when mature and the bright red/orange flowers attract many birds, bats and butterflies. Like many native plants, the plant is highly toxic. However, safe preparation techniques handed down through generations of Aborigines enabled the species to become an important part of some indigenous diets. The Ngadjonji people from the southern end of the Atherton Tablelands in far north Queensland prepared the seed for consumption using the following method (Hartly and Ngadjonji Elders 2004):

- cooking – the seeds were first cooked by steaming in an earth oven or roasted in the ash of a fire;
- grating – the cooked seeds were then roughly ground using stones, or finely sliced using the shell of a forest snail;
- leaching – the resulting meal was placed in a finely woven mesh bag and left in a running stream for one to four days, depending on the species;
- consumption – the meal was then made into loaves or cakes and baked on the hot stones of a fire, or simply eaten wet as a porridge-type food.

This method of preparation was also used by the Ngadjonji people for other potentially poisonous rainforest seeds. The extent of its use of the Gold Coast is unknown.

Bracken fern *Pteridium esculentum*

Bracken fern, or bracken as it is more commonly called, is plentiful to such an extent that it is considered a troublesome weed. However, the small new-growth fronds can be eaten raw and the starchy roots can be roasted or ground into a paste before eating (ANBG 2012a).

Native rosella *Hibiscus heterophyllus*

The native rosella, or simply rosella, is related to the *Hibiscus* genus of which 35 species are native to Australia (ANBG 2012b). The young leaves and shoots can be eaten raw and the petals can be used for a garnish or in salads. These plants tend to grow in many soil environments, allowing urban residents to use them as a source of food for themselves or for native bird and insect species.

Selected native flowers of Grevillea, Bottlebrush, Banksia

Not only a rich food source for many species of birds, insects and mammals (HSC 2013), the nectar and pollen of many types of these species have been used as a source of refreshment and sweetness by indigenous people. In the early morning, men and women carried containers of water and went from flower to flower dipping them up and down until the water became a sweet drink (Isaacs 1987).

Conclusion

In the massive transformation of the Gold Coast in the last 100 years, much of the coastal area's natural vegetation has been cleared. The remaining land with native vegetation will continue to be under threat from a variety of direct and indirect human influences, including climate change and urban development.

The edible nature of numerous native plants, and the health benefits that many bring, result in community pressure to retain the small amount of natural vegetation that remains. A focus on food providence and the search for novel tasty additions to menus and home cooking reinforce the importance of native Australian plants as a food source.

Maybe the real Gold Coast food could be macadamia-crumbed bream on warragul greens with small-leaved tamarind curry and finger lime. Or a grey gum-smoked mullet on a wild yam hash with macadamia butter and Davidson plum jam.

Future visitors to the Gold Coast could be presented with a menu consisting of fresh, native foods.

> ***Entrée:*** *Freshwater yabbies served with a salsa made from pandanus nuts, rosella leaves, avocado and finger lime.*
> ***Main:*** *Whole bream stuffed with pigface, cooked in paperbark, with Moreton Bay chestnut cakes with sour currant chutney.*
> ***Dessert:*** *Native raspberry pannacotta, jellied Davidson plum and macadamia brittle.*

These are the native ingredients that help tell the story of the Gold Coast. We should share in them.

References

Ahmed AK, Johnson KA (2000) Horticultural development of Australian native edible plants. *Australian Journal of Botany* **48**(4), 417–426. doi:10.1071/BT99042.

ANBG (2012a) *Growing Native Plants*. Australian National Botanic Garden, Canberra. http://www.anbg.gov.au/apu/plants/pterescu.html.

ANBG (2012b) *Growing Native Plants: Hibiscus heterophyllus*. Australian National Botanic Garden, Canberra. http://www.anbg.gov.au/gnp/interns-2002/hibiscus-heterophyllus.html.

Barker R, Barker B (2005) *Blackberry: An Identification Tool to Introduced and Native Rubus in Australia*. CD-Rom. State Herbarium of South Australia, Adelaide. www.cbit.uq.edu.au/software/blackberry/.

Bean T (1999) *Queensland Raspberries*. Australian Plants Online. http://asgap.org.au/APOL22/jun01-1.html.

Birch J, Kim Y, Silcock P (2010) Compositional analysis and roasting behaviour of gevuina and macadamia nuts. *International Journal of Food Science and Technology* **45**(1), 81–86. doi:10.1111/j.1365-2621.2009.02106.x.

Boland DJ, Brooker MIH, Chippendale GM, Hall N, Hyland BPM, Johnston RD, Kleinig DA, Turner JD (2006) *Forest Trees of Australia*. 5th edn, CSIRO Publishing, Melbourne.

Brand-Miller JC, Holt SHA (1998) Australian Aboriginal plant foods: a consideration of their nutritional composition and health implications. *Nutrition Research Reviews* **11**, 5–23. doi:10.1079/NRR19980003.

Burke BE, Baillie J, Olson RD (2004) Essential oil of Australian lemon myrtle (*Backhousia citriodora*) in the treatment of molluscum contagiosum in children. *Biomedicine and Pharmacotherapy* **58**(4), 245–247. doi:10.1016/j.biopha.2003.11.006.

Cambie RC, Ferguson LR (2003) Potential functional foods in the traditional Maori diet. *Mutation Research/Fundamental and Molecular Mechanisms of Mutagenesis* **523–524**, 109–177.

Clarke M (2012) *The Australian Native Food Industry Stocktake*. RIRDC Publication No. 12/066. Rural Industries Research and Development Corporation, Canberra.

Cooper W (2013) *Australian Rainforest Fruits: A Field Guide*. CSIRO Publishing, Melbourne.

DEC (2004) Approved NSW and National Recovery Plan, *Diploglottis campbellii* (Small-leaved Tamarind). Department of Environment and Conservation, Sydney. http://www.environment.nsw.gov.au/resources/nature/recoveryplanTamarindDec04.pdf.

Dupont S, Caffin N, Bhandari B, Dykes GA (2006) Lemon myrtle, in vitro antibacterial activity of Australian native herb extracts against food-related bacteria. *Food Control* **17**(11), 929–932. doi:10.1016/j.foodcont.2005.06.005.

Harden GJ, Williams JB (2000) A revision of *Davidsonia* (Cunoniaceae). *Telopea* **8**(4), 413–428.

Hartly J, Ngadjonji Elders (2004) *Forest Resources, Food and Other Ngadjonji Uses of Rainforest Plants and Animals*. http://www.ngadjonji.bigpondhosting.com/Food/food0.html.

Hayes AJ, Markovic B (2002) Lemon myrtle: toxicity of Australian essential oil *Backhousia citriodora* (Lemon myrtle). Part 1. Antimicrobial activity and in vitro cytotoxicity. *Food and Chemical Toxicology* **40**(4), 535–543. doi:10.1016/S0278-6915(01)00103-X.

Hohenhaus R (2011) *Geneticists Seek the Mother of All Macadamias on the Gold Coast*. Queensland Alliance for Agriculture and Food Innovation. http://www.qaafi.uq.edu.au/geneticists-seek-the-mother-of-all-macadamias-on-the-gold-coast.

HSC (2013) *Nectar Food Trees and Fleshy-fruited Trees in the Hornsby Shire.* Hornsby Shire Council, Sydney. http://www.hornsby.nsw.gov.au/media/documents/environment-and-waste/bushland-and-biodiversity/gardens-for-wildlife/Nectar-Food-Trees-Information-Sheet.pdf.

Isaacs J (1987) *Bush Food: Aboriginal Food and Herbal Medicine.* 2nd edn. New Holland Publishers, Sydney.

Jacobs SWL, Highet J (1999) PigFace, *Carpobrotus glaucescens.* Plantnet. Royal Botanical Garden, Sydney. http://plantnet.rbgsyd.nsw.gov.au/cgi-bin/NSWfl.pl?page=nswfl&lvl=sp&name=Carpobrotus~glaucescens.

Konczak I, Zabaras D, Dunstan M, Aguas P (2010) Antioxidant capacity and phenolic compounds in commercially grown native Australian herbs and spices. *Food Chemistry* **122**(1), 260–266.

Leiper G (2013) Sour currant bush. Extract from correspondence 13 September 2013 by coauthor, *Mangrove to Mountains: Field Guide to the Native Plants of South-east Queensland.* Logan River Branch, Society for Growing Australian Plants, Browns Plains, Qld (2008).

Low T (1991) *Wild Food Plants of Australia.* Harper Collins, Sydney.

McKenzie R (1997) *Australian Native Poisonous Plants.* Australian Plants Online. http://anpsa.org.au/apol7/sep97-4.html.

Miller JS, Brewer SJ (1992) The discovery of medicines and forest conservation. In *Conservation of Plant Genes: DNA Banking and In Vitro Biotechnology.* (Eds RP Adams and JE Adams) pp. 119–134. Academic Press, San Diego.

Packer J, Brouwer N, Harrington D, Gaikwad J, Heron R, Yaegl Community Elders, Ranganathan S, Vemulpad S, Jamie J (2012) An ethnobotanical study of medicinal plants used by the Yaegl Aboriginal community in northern New South Wales, Australia. *Journal of Ethnopharmacology* **139**(1), 244–255. doi:10.1016/j.jep.2011.11.008.

Pickering A (2012) *Pandanus spiralis.* Department of Parks and Wildlife, Northern Territory. http://parksandwildlife.nt.gov.au/_data/assets/pdf_file/0018/15705/pandanus.pdf.

Quinlan K, Wilk P (2005) *Macadamia Culture in NSW.* Primefact 5. Department of Primary Industries NSW. http://www.dpi.nsw.gov.au/_data/assets/pdf_file/0005/75740/Macadamia-culture-in-NSW-Primefact-5—final.pdf.

SCU (2013) Quote from Professor Stephen Myers, Director NatMed Research Unit, Southern Cross University. http://www.scu.edu.au/news/media.php?item_id=6881&action=show_item&type=M.

Setzer M, Setzer W, Jackes B, Gentry G, Moriarty DM (2001) The medicinal value of tropical rainforest plants from Paluma, North Queensland, Australia. *Pharmaceutical Biology* **39**(1), 67–78. doi:10.1076/phbi.39.1.67.5944.

Stephens KM, Sharp D (2009) *The Flora of North Stradbroke Island.* Queensland Herbarium, Brisbane.

van Eeten P (2005) *Growing Native Plants: Pig Face Carpobrotus glaucescens.* Australian National Botanic Gardens. http://www.anbg.gov.au/gnp/interns-2005/carpobrotus-glaucescens.html.

Walsh F, Douglas J (2011) No bush foods without people: the essential human dimension to the sustainability of trade in native plant products from desert Australia. *Rangeland Journal* **33**(4), 395–416. doi:10.1071/RJ11028.

Appendices

Appendix 1. Queensland Heritage Register: places listed in the Gold Coast City Council area

Currumbin Wildlife Sanctuary, 26 Tomewin Street, Currumbin & Currumbin Creek Road, Currumbin Valley; 0001, p27	Schmidt Farmhouse & Outbuildings (Former), 8 Worongary Road, Worongary; 0011, p111
David Fleay Wildlife Park, 244 West Burleigh Road, Burleigh Heads; 0004, p29	Southport Bathing Pavilion, Marine Parade, Southport; 0012, p119
Dux Hut, Dux Anchorage, South Stradbroke Island; 0005, p33	Southport Cable Hut (Former), Cable Park, Main Beach; 0013, p121
H2 Hinde on Colliston (Macadamia Tree), 926 Gilston Road, Gilston; 0020, p51	Southport Drill Hall, Owen Park, Southport; 0014, p123
Humphreys Boat Shed and Slipway Remnants, 26A Sea World Drive, Main Beach; 0068, p57	Southport Town Hall (Former), 47 Nerang Street, Southport; 0015, p127
Kinkabool, 32 Hanlan Street, Surfers Paradise; 0019, p61	Springbrook Road and Associated Infrastructure, Road reserve from intersection with Austinville Road to intersection with Old School Road, Springbrook; 0016, p131
Laurel Hill Farmhouse, Ruffles Road, Willow Vale; 0007, p67	Springbrook State School (Former), Old School Road, Springbrook; 0006, p133
Main Beach Pavilion & Southport Surf Life Saving Club, Sea World Drive, Main Beach; 0008, p71	Tallebudgera Post Office (Former), 17 Trees Road, Tallebudgera; 0017, p135
Numinbah Valley School of Arts, 2136 Nerang Murwillumbah Road, Numinbah Valley; 0009, p89	West Burleigh Store, 33 Tallebudgera Creek Road, West Burleigh; 0018, p149
Pimpama & Ormeau War Memorial, 246 Creek Street, Pimpama; 0010, p95	

Updated from the 2013 Gold Coast City Council Local Heritage Register (GCCC 2013), which listed 19 state heritage places within the council area. Reference and page number are to the Gold Coast City Council Register.

Appendix 2. Register of the National Estate

St George's Anglican Church, Beenleigh	Border Ranges Region
Lutheran Church, Bethania	Warrie National Park
Southern and Eastern Moreton Bay	Gwongorella National Park
The Knoll Environmental Park	Wunburra National Park
Burleigh Head National Park	Palm Grove National Park
Lamington National Park	Cedar Creek National Park
Canungra Land Warfare Training Centre Area (part)	Natural Bridge National Park

Appendix 3. National Trust of Queensland: Registered Places – City of Gold Coast, October 2013

Present name	Former/other name	Address	NTQ file no.	Trust status
Alex Griffiths' Cottage		66 Teemangum Street, Currumbin	GCC 1/2	Registered on 06.07.1999
Antiques and Collectables	Jazzland	31 McLean Street, Coolangatta	GCC 1/40	Registered on 04.10.2002
Broadbeach Seal Sculpture	The Lennon's Seal & Pup Sculpture, Water Inlet Sculpture at the Pool	2684 Gold Coast Highway, Broadbeach	GCC 1/37	Registered on 02.06.1997
Burleigh Head National Park	NP41	Julia Street, Burleigh Heads	GCC 1/24	Registered on 15.11.1982
Cedar Creek National Park	Tamborine Mountain National Park (part)	Mt Tamborine	GCC 2/1	Registered on 15.11.1982
Currumbin Wildlife Sanctuary	Currumbin Bird Sanctuary	Cnr Tomewin Street & Teemangum Street, Currumbin	GCC 1/0	Registered on 23.02.1981
Gwongorella National Park	NP 465	Mudgeeraba	GCC 2/8	Registered on 15.11.1982
Infant Saviour Church	Relocated to Mt Tamborine – now Heritage Winery	43 Connor Street, Burleigh Heads	GCC 1/38	Registered on 30.06.1997
Kinkabool		32 Hanlan Street, Surfers Paradise	GCC 1/34	Registered on 31.01.1994
Kirra Hill Community and Cultural Centre	Coolangatta State School (former); Coolangatta Special School (former)	1 Garrick Parade, Coolangatta	GCC 1/41	Registered on 30.10.2008
Kleinschmidt's Arrowroot Mill		Otmoor Road, Upper Coomera	GCC 2/11	Registered on 05.06.1997
Lamington National Park	NP 469	Canungra	GCC 2/9	Registered on 15.11.1982
Laurel Hill Farmhouse		Ruffles Road, Willow Vale	GCC 2/14	Registered on 04.12.1997
Main Beach Bathing Pavilion		Macarthur Parade, Main Beach	GCC 1/32	Registered in 1998
Mt Cougal National Park	NP 694	Mudgeeraba	GCC 2/7	Registered on 15.11.1982
Mudgeeraba Post Office (former)	Nerang Shire Council Chambers	57 Railway Street, Mudgeeraba	GCC 2/30	Registered on 30.03.1998
Natural Bridge National Park	NP 752	Natural Bridge Road, Natural Bridge	GCC 2/6	Registered on 15.11.1982
Nerang Uniting Church	Nerang Wesleyan Methodist Church, Nerang Presbyterian Church	9–11 Price Street, Nerang	GCC 2/39	Registered on 22.09.1986

Appendix 3. (*Continued*)

Present name	Former/other name	Address	NTQ file no.	Trust status
Nicholl's Scrub		Tomewin Currumbin Creek Road, Currumbin	GCC 2/10	Registered on 27.02.1984
Pacific Cable Station (former)		Dixon Drive, Southport	GCC 1/23	Registered on 28.07.1980
Palm Grove National Park	NP 601; Tamborine Mountain National Park (part)	Mt Tamborine	GCC 2/2	Registered on 15.11.1982
Pimpama and Ormeau War Memorial		246 Creek Street, Pimpama	GCC 2/12	Registered on 25.08.1986
Southport Bathing Pavilion		Marine Parade, Southport	GCC 1/31	Registered in 1998
Southport Council Chambers (former)	Southport Town Hall	47 Nerang Street, Southport	GCC 1/29	Registered on 30.01.1995
Southport Drill Hall	Lawson Street Barracks	Veivers Way, Southport	GCC 1/30	Registered in 1991
Southport Surf Lifesaving Club		Marine Parade, Main Beach	GCC 1/33	Registered in 1998
Tomewin Environmental Park	EP 1207	Tallebudgera	GCC 2/5	Registered on 15.11.1982
Warrie National Park	NP 465	Mudgeeraba	GCC 2/4	Registered on 15.11.1982
Wunburra National Park	NP 1083	Mudgeeraba	GCC 2/3	Registered on 15.11.1982

Reference

GCCC (2013) *Gold Coast Local Heritage Register – Introduction.* Gold Coast City Council, Gold Coast. http://heritage.goldcoast.qld.gov.au/uploads/heritage-register-pdf/GOLD%20COAST%20LOCAL%20HERITAGE%20REGISTER%20INTRODUCTION%20AND%20INDEX_NEW_.pdf.

Index

www.ingramcontent.com/pod-product-compliance
Lightning Source LLC
LaVergne TN
LVHW061221100826
845148LV00004B/823

* 9 7 8 1 4 8 6 3 0 3 2 9 8 *